··

NO MEDALS FOR TRYING

··

Also by Jerry Izenberg

THE JERRY IZENBERG COLLECTION

THE GREATEST GAME EVER PLAYED

HOW MANY MILES TO CAMELOT?

THE RIVALS

AT LARGE WITH JERRY IZENBERG

THE PROUD PEOPLE

CHAMPIONSHIP: THE NFL TITLE STORY

NO MEDALS FOR TRYING

A Week in the Life of a Pro Football Team

JERRY IZENBERG

Macmillan Publishing Company * New York

Collier Macmillan Canada * Toronto

Maxwell Macmillan International
New York * Oxford * Singapore * Sydney

Macmillan Publishing Company
866 Third Avenue, New York, NY 10022

Collier Macmillan Canada, Inc.
1200 Eglinton Avenue East, Suite 200
Don Mills, Ontario M3C 3N1

Library of Congress Cataloging-in-Publication Data
Izenberg, Jerry.
    No medals for trying: a week in the life of a pro football team/
Jerry Izenberg.
        p. cm.
    ISBN 0-02-558215-1
    1. New York Giants (Football team)   I. Title.
GV956.N4I98   1990   90-35716   CIP
796.332'64'0974921—dc20

10 9 8 7 6 5 4 3

Printed in the United States of America

For my wife, Aileen,
who made the coffee, kept her patience,
and forever holds my heart.

CONTENTS

ACKNOWLEDGMENTS

This book would not have been possible without the time, patience, and participation of a great many people. First and foremost, my deepest thanks to Bill Parcells, who took the time during the most difficult moments of his season to serve as guide and focal point through a complex maze of seven days and nights of men at work under tremendous emotional and physical strain. His candor about himself, his business, and the people around him was monumental.

Special thanks is offered to a coaching staff which did its best to assist a football moron in search of truth and understanding—defensive and offensive coordinators Bill Belichick and Ron Erhardt and their assistants Tom Coughlin, Romeo Crennel, Al Groh, Ray Handley, Fred Hoaglin, Lamar Leachman, Johnny Parker, Mike Pope, and Mike Sweatman.

Thanks also for the invaluable insights of George Young, Tim and Wellington Mara, and Ronnie Barnes along with Mike Ryan, Ed Croke, Tom Power, Jim Gleason, Harry Hulmes, Tom Boisture, Ray Walsh, Ed Wagner, Jr., and all the Giants beat writers with particular thanks to Mike Eisen and Vinnie Di Trani.

Deepest appreciation to the dedication and the belief in the project by my agent, Jay Acton, and a gifted editor at Macmillan named Rick Wolff, whose guidance was invaluable, along with the long-distance hot-line aid of Bob Izenberg, who kept the computer operable when it was in the hands of a mechanical idiot.

Finally, there are the Giants players—every one of them, with particular thanks to Phil Simms, whose kind of honesty is a rare quality, Erik Howard, Jeff Hostetler, Myron Guyton, Renya Thompson, Bart Oates, Joe Morris, and William Roberts; also Buddy Ryan and his Philadelphia Eagles, who provided the necessary Darth Vaders for this journey through a 100-yard Star Wars.

Jerry Izenberg
February 5, 1990

PROLOGUE

There are twenty-eight teams and 1,230 active players in the National Football League. Barring ties, every weekend only half of them will win. Bones will break and muscles tear. Someone's career will end and someone else's will begin. On an average weekend, 840,000 people will pay their way in all kinds of weather into all kinds of stadiums, from that frozen food locker disguised as a ballpark which is Cleveland's Municipal Stadium to the thermostatically controlled warmth of the Hubert H. Humphrey Metrodome in Minneapolis. Another 70 million will watch on television.

All across America's 100-yard face, they will bear witness to an unbroken chain of moments of truth. Someone will catch the ball and someone will drop it. Someone will claw his way through a wall of flesh and drill the quarterback to his knees before he can throw it and some other quarterback will turn that same kind of impending disaster into the impossible forward pass, the impossible catch, and the impossible 6 on the scoreboard.

Behind those moments—away from the crowds, away from the drama, and away from the cheers—are six days (and, for the coaches, six nights) in which the video ghosts of confrontations past dance across meeting-room screens and a lonely charade of repetition is played out on the floors of closed-door stadiums against the backdrop of empty seats . . . six days during which team trainers will try to make warriors out of their walking wounded . . . six days during which veteran Pro Bowlers and special teams rookies are all brothers under the skin, each asking himself questions he knows must be answered at the end of that week.

This is the story of one of those teams during one of those weeks.

··

NO MEDALS FOR TRYING

··

1. *MONDAY AND TUESDAY, NOVEMBER 27 AND 28, 1989*

Monday, 11:30 P.M. P.S.T., San Francisco International Airport

SAN FRANCISCO 34, NEW YORK GIANTS 24

It wasn't a football game. It was their worst nightmare come to life and nobody had to ask who won it. You could see it in their faces and hear it in their silence. As they limped wearily down the boarding ramp to United Charter Flight 5306, none of them had the strength to even begin sorting out the pieces—not yet. For most of them, that would come later when they were alone with their private pain through three time zones in the mercifully darkened cabin of the DC-8. Now they were passing out the premeal snack, or what Phil Simms likes to call "them sorry cheeseburgers." Most declined. Even fewer would have any appetite when the regular meal service was offered.

There were simply too many bruises on their bodies and too many demons in their minds.

Simms, their thirty-three-year-old quarterback, had reinjured his ankle. Once he settled into his seat, Ronnie Barnes, the head trainer, would remove the pressure pack of ice and wrap a new one in its place while the quarterback drank two small bottles of fruit juice. Dr. Russ Warren, one of three team physicians, would administer Endocin, an anti-inflammatory medication, and then both would tactfully leave him alone with his thoughts.

Further down the aisle, Erik Howard could feel the familiar spasms spreading through his lower back. Howard plays with a chronic disc problem and when the Giants win, the discomfort is a kind of barometer that seems to tell the big nose tackle, "I'm just reminding you that you played well, old friend, and you won." But tonight it's simply pain, each spasm a kind of a cappella accompaniment to the dull ache from a fresh knee injury.

Lionel Manuel, a wide receiver, has bruised a thumb and twisted his knee. John Elliot, a six-foot-seven-inch, three-hundred-pound offensive tackle, has a badly swollen ankle. Five other players, thirty-two-year-old running back Ottis Anderson among them, are still exhausted. Each of them had been treated for leg cramps during the game. And David Meggett is still shaking the cobwebs from his head.

Meggett is the hot rookie on this team, a punt returner and a "situation" halfback out of Towson State. He has added a new dimension to its attack. At five feet seven inches and 180 pounds, he has worked hard to build his upper torso. For weeks, he has strutted through the locker room telling all who would listen, "Look at these muscles. Come on, now, tell the truth, don't you wish you had them?" And for weeks, through the laughter, the veterans had been telling him, "You wait until you get your first official NFL hit. Then you come back and tell us how much those muscles are worth."

"Mr. Barnes," Meggett asks the trainer one day, "what's an official NFL hit?"

"I can't tell you that, David."

"Well, how will I know when I get one?"

"You'll know, David, because you will be looking out of your ear hole."

It is now five hours since David Meggett took his first official NFL hit.

He stood under a punt, looked up into the lights at Candlestick Park, made the catch, and started to run. It's all he remembers about the play.

"He knew he was in San Francisco," Barnes says. "He knew his social security number. He knew we were playing the 49ers. But he couldn't recall a single play in the playbook. We treated him with ice and ammonia and cold towels. I sat Jeff Rutledge (the third-string quarterback) next to him and said, 'Tell me when he's OK.' Each time I walked back, Jeff would roll his eyes up in his head and say 'he's still goofy.' It took almost a whole quarter."

They lost to the San Francisco 49ers, 34–24, after spotting them a 24–7 lead, rallying to tie the score, and then giving it back. They did everything wrong and Joe Montana did everything right for San Francisco but still they were alive at 24–24 with 4:16 to play when Mike Cofer missed a 50-yard field goal for the 49ers. The Giants' field-goal-blocking team was firing clenched fists at the sky and the offense had started in from the sidelines and then suddenly the kaleidoscope of motion froze dead in its tracks as they heard the thunder of the crowd echoing down from the upper deck. The noise cut through the celebration like an emotional spear. Nobody had to tell them what it meant. The yellow penalty flag on the ground spoke volumes.

Reyna Thompson, the most dependable player on the unit, had lined up offside on the play and Cofer got another shot from 45 to make it 27–24. Then, with 4:16 left, Simms threw the interception that tore it apart for the Giants and dropped them back to a tenuous one-game lead in their battle with Philadelphia for the division title.

Clearly, all the pain on this flight is not physical.

And then there is Lawrence.

In 1981, Lawrence Taylor joined the Giants fresh off the University of North Carolina and put together a rookie year so spectacular that it immediately placed him a cut above anything anyone had ever seen before. He became and remained the guts of this defense. He is six feet three inches tall and weighs 243 pounds, and at age thirty he can still run 40 yards (the pro football measuring stick) in 4.6 seconds. Once, against the Eagles, he had cut across the field in the final seconds to make a game-saving tackle although he had actually torn his hamstring in the middle of the pursuit. Only a Hollywood script or Lawrence Taylor could get away with that.

He became LT or simply The Linebacker. You could take your choice because it didn't matter. Under either name everyone knew exactly who you were talking about.

In the mind's eye of all the Giants he had long since emerged as the resident catalyst of defensive miracles: Lawrence the sacker of quarterbacks . . . Lawrence the intercepter of passes . . . Lawrence, able to leap blockers with a single bound, dominate a game like Gulliver on a field of Lilliputians, and wake the stadium echoes with chants of "de-fense . . . de-fense."

But moments earlier, as they filed slowly toward the boarding gate, his teammates saw a different Lawrence Taylor. He wore his same trademark black shirt, black slacks, black loafers without socks, and black leather coat. But he moved slowly and with great pain, supported by crutches, whose image hung over this team and its future like a set of accusing question marks. And no matter how casual they tried to be about it, each of them sneaked a look and wondered.

In the second quarter that evening, with the Giants trailing, 17–7, the 'Niners took over on the Giants' 35 following an interception. On the next play, they predictably ran away from Taylor, sending Roger Craig on a sweep to the right side. As the play developed across the field, Wesley Walls, the tight end, came in low to block LT. They tumbled to the ground together and the impact of the fall appeared to roll Walls against Taylor's leg, which bent the wrong way.

And then the nearest Giants to the play heard something they had never heard before and something they will never forget. Lawrence Taylor screamed.

The first one to reach him was his cornerback, Mark Collins, who knelt beside him. Even before Collins arrived, Ronnie Barnes and his assistant, Mike Ryan, were sprinting toward them from the Giants sideline.

"He's pretty emotional," Barnes said, "but I have never seen him like this. His actual words were 'I blew out my knee . . . it's over . . . it's over,' and he was wailing—actually wailing—it was unbelievable with what you know about Lawrence to see him like that. But you have to understand that he's never had an injury to a joint and that's every player's nightmare.

"Essentially what happened is that we were wearing long cleats because the sod is so loose and the field is so bad there. We're always in a panic about what kind of shoes to wear and what kind of cleats to wear when we play at Candlestick. The guys were all rushing around changing shoes and cleats before the game. Apparently Lawrence got hit around the knee, his foot was caught in the sod, and he felt his knee collapse.

"It's not the knee," Barnes said. "It's the ankle. We X-rayed him at halftime and it appeared to be a very severe sprain."

They ice it down as the plane sits on the runway and give him the same anti-inflammatory as Simms. Then Taylor turns off his overhead light and withdraws into his private thoughts.

The pilot, Captain Jim Wright, announces a four and a half hour flight plan. He is a veteran of twenty-five years. Things being what they are at this moment with his passengers, and since he would like to live to make it twenty-six, he does not offer to narrate the points of interest en route.

Reyna Thompson tries to forget as much as he can as the plane leaves the runway, banks, and turns toward the east. He knew that later in the week, as they prepared for the Eagles and a game that could have meant far less had they won tonight, he would sit in a darkened meeting room with the rest of the special teams players and gaze at his own image on the screen.

And no matter what Romeo Crennel, the special teams coach, would be saying, the only thing he would see would be his own right arm just beyond the legal scrimmage zone. And no matter how many times they replayed it and how many times Mike Cofer missed the kick, the zebras would see the right arm and throw the flag and Mike Cofer would get to kick again.

"Funny," Thompson thought, "when you win, you look ahead. When you lose, you can't help but look back."

Until that evening, the season had been glorious for Renya Thompson. He had been signed by the Giants as a free agent after the Miami Dolphins had failed to place him on their protected list. He caught Bill Parcells's attention because he had been in the league for three full seasons, had played as the nickel back in Miami's special pass defense, and had been a regular on special teams.

When he was invited to preseason minicamp before preseason training, Parcells had asked him to drop by the office to talk. "Tell me about yourself," the coach had said.

"Well, I played special teams and—"

"No," Parcells interrupted, "I mean tell me about yourself. I know about your football."

"Well, I'm from Dallas and I went to Baylor. I've been working on my master's degree in business and I . . ."

Parcells didn't need any more than that. The discipline required for a full-time professional football player to go back to school and get a graduate degree meant a lot to him. Primarily, it meant maturity, something he felt he needed more of on special teams.

Years ago, the whole concept of special teams emerged as professional football moved into a world of specialization so defined that some defensive players would enter the game only in passing situations. There were only three kinds of players who ran down under punts or threw their bodies at the protective wedge of blockers on a kickoff or fought through a wall of flesh at just the right angle to block a kick: the rookies trying to stick with a team at any price, the veterans who will do anything to hang on in hope that the opportunity eventually arises to prove the coach wrong, and the crazies.

Reyna Thompson is none of these. But had he played back then he would still probably be doing exactly what he does now. He is a professional who treats the job professionally. He studies videotapes intensely. The number of one-on-one tackles he has made against kick returners is impressive. He is clearly the stand-out on his units. But with the game tied earlier this night, he made a crucial mistake. He lined up offside and a lot of what would follow in this season would be that much tougher because of that mistake.

As they flew through the night nobody sought him out directly, but Reyna Thompson's teammates did a very important and deliberate thing. Each one who walked down the aisle toward the rest room or to visit quietly with another player reached over as they passed him and silently patted his shoulder or rubbed his head.

It helped—but not a lot.

Further down the aisle, Bart Oates, the center, is trying to sleep. It does not come easily. He is thinking about Wednesday morning. Next month, he will be thirty-two years old and he knows that as bad as today will be, tomorrow will be even worse. "It's always worse on the second morning," he says. "I guess it has something to do with anatomy. I can't explain it. All I know is that it hurts.''

Part of the evening had been spent in close contact with an old friend named Jim Burt. In January of 1987, when the world was colored Giant blue and Super Bowl gold for both of them, Oates and Burt had been teammates and best friends. When Burt failed the Giants' preseason physical this year, he turned his frustration on both Parcells and George Young, the general manager, but the two players and their wives remained close friends. Ultimately, Burt caught on with the 49ers. This very week, as the two players prepared for what at times would be a head-to-head confrontation, Burt's wife, Colleen, has given birth to a second child. In the absence of her husband, her natural childbirth coach was Michelle Oates.

Earlier this evening the positioning of the 49ers' defense had placed Burt directly across from Oates. Three thousand miles away in Bergen County, New Jersey, the two wives had watched the game together on television, each holding something back as they rooted for different teams.

But that's history now. In the darkened cabin his thoughts tripped forward through a mental checklist. Its focal point was six feet, five inches tall and 285 pounds wide. Its name was Reggie White, the Eagles' magnificent pass rusher. Whatever else he would do this week, Bart Oates knew that the last thing he would see when he closed his eyes each night from here to Sunday was Reggie White.

Tuesday, 12:45 A.M. P.S.T., somewhere over Nevada

As always on these trips, Bill Parcells sits alone. He has already met with Dr. Warren. Now he talks briefly with Barnes about Simms and Taylor. They go over the injury list and decide on a treatment schedule, which they will announce shortly before the plane lands in Newark. Taylor, Simms, and Manuel will go directly to the stadium for treatment. Since he has given the team the day off, the rest of the wounded can report to Barnes and Ryan at 3:00 P.M.

During the four and a half hours in flight, Parcells will be the only passenger who doesn't sleep at all. He never does on planes. Now he was heading home for the Eagles, the team the Giants must beat for the NFC East title, coming into the Meadowlands on Sunday and a short work week in which to get ready because of the Monday night game against the 49ers.

Despite the prevailing theories about 100-yard geniuses, nobody is born to coach. Parcells, who has been at it on one level or another for close to three decades, would be the first to laugh if you even suggested it. But it is not farfetched to wonder if the people around you in your formative years just might have cultivated the qualities you most need for survival in this business.

He won the Super Bowl and most of the men coaching in the National Football League will never even get there. But he remembers his father once telling him, "Success is never final— but failure can be." His team had played with incredible courage in Candlestick just hours before but Parcells recalls his father telling him, "You don't get any medals for trying. You're *supposed* to do that." And now, limping back home to play the Eagles in a game which should have been far less important to the future of this team, he remembers something else. "It's always darkest," his father had told him with wry Irish humor, "before it goes pitch-black."

On this night, there is more than enough darkness to haunt his thoughts.

There are decisions to be made. Do you plan with Taylor or without Taylor or do you draw up alternate plans? He discards the last option because such a task would place a Herculean burden on defensive coordinator Bill Belichick and his staff. He discards the first because deep within him the feeling grows that this one might be too much, even for LT.

What will he tell them on Wednesday morning? How will he approach this week when the division lead (and, logically, the division title) is on the line? What possible approach can wipe away the wake of the disaster this team suffered just hours ago? On the other hand, how much do you really need to tell them? After all, this will be the Eagles.

He knows that coaching a professional football team is always a tomorrow kind of thing. What has already happened has happened. You can replay it in your mind for hours. But if you won, then you won, and if you lost, then you lost. Nothing is going to change.

But still it eats away at him. Without Taylor, with Simms limping, with Montana coming at them at his very best and with a gift field goal because of the penalty on Thompson, they still were only three down with 4:16 to play. They still were a team which time and time again has put together long, clock-swallowing drives. They could go the 80 yards, squeeze the clock down to its final ticks and win it.

And then Simms threw the interception.

In his mind's eye, Parcells sees it happening again and again and again. He should have run, Parcells is thinking. It was a bad pass. If . . . if . . . if . . . He tries to think about the Eagles and for much of the trip he is successful. But every once in a while as they cross from time zone to time zone the thought returns: he could have . . . we should have . . . if . . . if . . . if . . .

Tuesday, 4:00 A.M. C.S.T., over Goodland, Kansas

The passenger light has been on all night. On the tray table before him sits a large looseleaf notebook and a pile of index cards. Bill Belichick is only thirty-seven years old but this is his eleventh season on the Giants' coaching staff. For thirty-four years his father was an assistant coach at the U.S. Naval Academy. Football for him was not a career decision. It was a genetic inevitability. As assistant special teams coach with the Lions at age twenty-four, he was the youngest coach in professional football. Since 1983, he has been the Giants' defensive coordinator. All weekend on the Coast, he and his staff held early morning meetings about the Eagles in an effort to compensate for the short workweek.

He saw Lawrence Taylor go down. He saw the concern in Parcells's face when he huddled with Ronnie Barnes and Dr. Russ Warren. He knows that when the plane lands, he and his troops will fight fatigue and lack of sleep and the disappointment over what happened in Candlestick Park that will not die. He knows the coaching staff is a long way from the end of this day.

Now he sits with his cards and his tendency charts and plays mind games with a linebacking corps that may well have to go without Taylor. On into the night he works and reworks the cards. He finally sleeps briefly in self-defense.

Tuesday, 6:00 A.M. E.S.T., somewhere between Erie, Pennsylvania, and Cleveland, Ohio

There is no rosy-fingered dawn here. The sky has turned a slate gray in the early half-light before sunrise. Phil Simms comes awake with his ankle throbbing. He has slept fitfully all though the flight. He had removed the ice hours earlier and they had given him some painkillers and sleep was as much an enemy as staying awake.

Phil Simms dreamed. By his own reckoning he felt as though he had awakened every ten minutes. The sleeping was as painful as reality. Each time the dream was the same. He was standing tall in the middle of a wall of flesh so real you hear the pop of shoulder pad against shoulder pad. And then the protection was beaten down and now he was trying to step up toward the line to buy some time when a hand grabbed him around the ankle. As he went down, the ankle twisted. Each time he awakened the gap between the pain in his dream and the pain in his body was an anatomical replay. This season had not been kind to him.

On Monday night, October 30, the Giants had played the Vikings in the Meadowlands. The Vikings are a no-nonsense, basic muscle defensive team. Like a New York cabdriver, they will hit you and then back up and make sure they got you. On the sixth play of the game, the Giants dropped Simms back in the shotgun, a maneuver designed to buy more time for the quarterback in an obvious passing situation. A big lineman named Al Noga had ripped through the offensive line like a runaway freight. Simms never had a chance. Noga slammed him to the artificial turf with the preordained violence of a lumberjack felling a California redwood. As soon as he was hit, the Giants quarterback felt the pain in his ankle and knew this was one he wasn't going to be able to walk off.

He missed the rest of the game. A week later, he did not play at Phoenix. The following week, against the Rams, he had been tentative on a day when the rest of the Giants played their worst game of the season. And just a week ago, the offense had been ordinary at best in beating Seattle.

He had come to this game against the 49ers with his sore ankle heavily taped and his frustration level high. The 49ers jumped on him early.

When he went down, Barnes said, "He was as white as a sheet. He didn't say anything. At first, I couldn't help him because I didn't know what he had done. He just sat there with his head slumped down and finally I said, 'Roll over, Phil, and sit down and let us see what's going on,' and it was his ankle. We took a lot of time because I wanted to know then whether he could go back for the next series.''

In the half-light over Cleveland, depression remained a formidable adversary. Phil Simms thought of old injuries and the lonely battles fought and won to defeat them. He was angry at himself and angry at his body.

Then he began to think about the Eagles—and it didn't get any better.

Tuesday, 8:30 A.M. E.S.T., Giants Stadium, East Rutherford, New Jersey

They had straggled through Newark Airport's Terminal A like an army of candidates in search of a casting call for *Return to Zombie Island*. Half of them had wandered off to wait for transportation to the long-term parking lots. The rest proceeded out the front door, wincing at the sunlight as they boarded charter buses for the return to the stadium where they had parked their cars. Parcells spoke to nobody as the buses nosed out of the airport and onto the New Jersey Turnpike. Needless to say, nobody said anything to him.

It was cold and they were miserable. As the buses neared Exit 16 W, the twin towers of the World Trade Center and the concrete spires of Manhattan dominated the view to their right. The stadium loomed on the skyline to their left. It is not much of a skyline. If truth be told, the stadium *is* the skyline. In a strange way it symbolizes what was the major transition period in one of professional football's oldest and most prestigious franchises.

Once, not so long ago, the Jersey Meadowlands, on which Giant Stadium was built, was a refuge for ecologically protected swamp rats and the rusting shells of long-abandoned automobiles. It was also the desolate place where "scientists" in expensive imported suits, with large bulges under their jackets, once carried on serious midnight experiments to determine how far a man from the wrong "family" could sink with an old juke box tied to his ankles. There are still people today who insist that the stadium was built on the bridge of Jimmy Hoffa's nose.

In an earlier incarnation, the people of New Jersey had voted down an attempt to build a racetrack here. But when the politicians linked such a track to financing a stadium for the Giants, it was as close to an offer the electorate couldn't refuse as any they had ever had. Ironically, the negotiations that brought the football team over to the Jersey side of the river were conducted by David "Sonny" Werblin and Wellington Mara.

Back when pro football ownership was trying to stone itself to death with its own wallets, Sonny (who paid the unheard-of number of $427,000 for a quarterback named Joe Willie Namath as president of the upstart AFL Jets) and Mara (president of the old-guard NFL Giants) were mortal enemies. But now with Werblin heading the New Jersey Sports and Exposition Authority and Mara heading a stadiumless, losing football team, the marriage raised no eyebrows.

Revenue for the project was assured by profits from the racetrack, which would be built as part of the package. The stadium itself, imaginatively named Giants Stadium, is a magnificent state-of-the-art home for bread and circuses with luxury boxes, unlimited parking, the largest stadium sound system in the world, and 76,891 seats. The team that came here in 1976 had won only nine games in the previous three years and would go five more without a winning season.

The season ticket–holders bitched, whined, burned tickets in a parking lot ceremony, and hired a plane to fly overhead, schlepping a banner which denigrated the team, the franchise, and the owners. But you couldn't have kept them away with a gun, a whip, and a chair—a not-inappropriate method based on the alcohol consumed in the pregame parking lots. Watching the transition in the team's fortunes (it won the Super Bowl in January of 1987), social critics appear to be divided as to whether the constituency is more volatile as bad losers or sore winners.

Certainly, the way the season was going on this gray morning, both ends of the spectrum were alive and well.

Inside, where the team lives, the trainer's room would do honor to a small county hospital. It was there that Barnes and Ryan immediately went to begin the reclamation work on Taylor, Simms, and Manuel. Bart Oates headed in the same direction. His destination was the immediately adjacent weight room, where he would go through his own personal routine under the supervision of the Giants' strength coach, Johnny Parker. Oates, with a degree in accounting from Brigham Young, is a part-time law student at Seton Hall University. He will graduate the following spring.

Meanwhile, the coaching staff staggers into its floor of offices. While they begin to draw up the game plan for the Eagles, Parcells closes the door to his office, collapses on the small couch, and tries to silence the tug-o'-war which has been going on in his mind between the Ghosts of the 49er Game Past and the Eagles Game Yet to Come. He will sleep for exactly ninety minutes.

Tuesday, 8:45 A.M., coaches' wing, Giants Stadium

Ron Erhardt, the offensive coordinator, stares at the automatic coffee machine on the corner counter in the big utility room through eyelids that seem to be sinking in an ocean of concrete. He is not to be confused with Al Groh, the linebacker coach, who is clutching his Styrofoam cup as though it weighed forty pounds and contained pure nitroglycerin. In tandem, their eyes look like the bottoms of separate but equal bloody Mary glasses. Both, like the rest of the staff, are now in the twenty-sixth hour of what will become a thirty-nine-hour, three-time-zone day.

Just down the hall in parallel meeting rooms, the rest of the defensive and offensive staffs have already gathered to begin the rudimentary breakdown on their game plans. In a small office at the extreme corner of the wing, Romeo Crennel, the special teams coach, and his assistant, Mike Sweatman, have their own puzzles to solve.

As Erhardt walks back to join his staff, he still cannot be sure which quarterback, Simms or his backup, Jeff Hostetler, will be asked to lead the troops. But the Eagles are still the Eagles and on balance they will come at Erhardt's people as they always have, with few gimmicks, much muscle, and pure joy in putting strength on strength and letting weakness go to hell. His game plan will not vary all that much no matter who plays quarterback.

The problem next door is more complicated. Bill Belichick, the defensive coordinator, still cannot say with certainty whether Lawrence Taylor will be available and if he is, then for how long and in what ways.

Already the grease pencil has turned the wall-length white board into a smear of trial and error diamonds and zeroes. You do not point to someone and simply say "Lawrence can't play, you're it." His duties are so diverse that a number of people are going to be asked to do a number of different things.

Because this is a short workweek, some of the Eagles planning took place when the team was on the Coast. Still, there are offensive plays and defensive calls to be selected, rejected, and then selected again. But before the defense can get down to the task of constructing a new composite Lawrence Taylor, there remains some painful old business of which to dispose.

The 49ers, through the technological wonder of videotape, are pouring fresh salt into recent wounds. The room is dark and the voices come from all sides of the table.

"That's awful," Belichick says, and shakes his head almost as though the result could have been different on videotape. "We haven't done one damned thing right. Look at that missed tackle on 'slant 19.' How could he blow that? I could feel it coming as soon as the guy cut inside."

"Can I see that again?" Groh asks. "It's terrible. Everyone knew the play."

"What's Kinard doing out there?" Belichick says. "He hasn't hit anybody yet! He missed the guy in 'slant 19,' he missed (Jerry) Rice, and look at Reasons. They have a no-hitter. They haven't hit anyone yet. We're gonna talk about this in the meeting. Sheldon (White) is 12 yards deep. He ought to make this play at the line of scrimmage."

"Hold it," Groh interrupts. "Here it is—roughing the passer."

Joe Montana takes a tremendous hit. "Hell," Belichick says, "it's getting so that now you can't even touch the quarterback."

"Well, I'll tell you one thing," Groh offers in consolation, "those 'Niner championship years will be over whenever that guy hangs his crown up."

The sequences roll by and Groh continues, "I think the problem here is—"

"The problem here," Belichick shoots back with some intensity, "is that they got eleven guys and we're playing like we got eight out there. Damn, look at Banks play his ass off. Next time we play these sons of bitches, we've got to build up some hate. Look at that! Look at that guy spear! Did you see it? These are the worst cheap-shot, career-ending bastards in the league. Just look at that."

The exercise has become pointless now and someone hits the lights. Belichick sighs and opens the large loose-leaf notebook in front of him. It is time for the Eagles.

Empty coffee cups litter the table—all except for one which Lamar Leachman, the defensive line coach, holds in his hand. He is chewing tobacco, and through the tape session there were long periods of silence, punctuated only by the soft ping of Lamar spitting the excess juice into his cup. "I'm gonna talk with my people," he says. "I don't wanna hear about backups. Backups are expected to come in and play. If they can't, then you gotta get them off your team."

"If we win, we win the division," Groh says, "so when we talk to 'em, that's gotta be the target. We got to tell 'em that we better have our stingers out because we're playing a team that will rub your nose in it. I'm not telling you what to say, but we ought to let them know we're pissed off."

"Individually," Belichick says, "we got to get on these guys. At least Howard, Washington, Leonard (Marshall), and Banks competed. They move the ball and Leonard comes off and tells me, 'I played shitty on that drive. I'll get 'em next time.' That's honest. I can live with that. I'll take that."

Ping . . . ping, goes the sound of Leachman's cup and then he looks over at Belichick and says in a voice still heavily laced with the flavor of his native Cartersville, Georgia:

"We got people hurt. We got people playin' out of position. And that's just the way it is. What we got to do is push them."

"I'm assuming Taylor is out," Belichick says, "so let's put some people up on the board and see what we got to work with."

Suddenly, the Eagles are very real.

Tuesday 11:00 A.M., Bill Parcells's office

The head coach is sitting behind his desk. In front of him is a Styrofoam cup of coffee and a pack of Marlboros. In light of the stature of this franchise, the room is surprisingly cramped. Junior partners in accounting firms who sit in the stadium seats on Sundays have larger offices. The desk and chair, the small couch on which he slept briefly this morning, a large easy chair, and a television set comprise all its furniture.

He has already seen the films, met briefly with his coaches to discuss the injuries, and worked on the rest of the week's schedule. Had they won, he would have given the players an extra day off. Now he'll bring them in on Wednesday, but they'll work the rest of the week without pads. "I'm not going to give them any excuse to be tired," he tells the coaching staff.

There is no mystery about the task this week, but later in the day, Parcells will sit alone and watch the Eagles again on the video screen in his office. Coaches are by their very nature prospectors and the fact that they are working a creek bed which they have already thoroughly mined is of no consequence to them. They still look for the nugget that got away.

They rarely find it and, in truth, Parcells is carrying out an exercise more in form than substance. He knows this team—in some ways as well as his own. "I've seen them so often and know their personnel so well," he says, "I could probably coach them."

And who are these people who have beaten him three in a row, who beat him down there this year during a game in which the Giants seemed to run up and down the field going just about wherever they wanted to go—except into the end zone when it counted?

"They're very aggressive," he says. "They're the most talented defensive team on our schedule. And, of course, they have that improvisational ability, which is a big factor."

Big?

Hell, it's the biggest.

Even as Parcells speaks, its architect's is the name with which the defensive coaching staff now conjures. Randall Cunningham is six feet four inches tall, weighs 203 pounds, and is clearly the most physically gifted quarterback in the league.

"You have to be able to control his scrambling ability to where it doesn't beat you in a game. Most of the time when they've beaten us [and the Eagles have now won three in a row over Parcells], it's come down to where he's made a few running plays that have continued drives and allowed them to score."

What he is is a lineman's migraine, a cornerback's nightmare, and a linebacker's embarrassment. Now you have him, now you don't. Now you see him, now he's gone. Now you chase him and shut down the running lanes and suddenly the ball is in the air for 60 yards and they get six on the board while all you get is egg on your face.

When all about him appears to be breaking down, he's got you right where he wants you.

"What pisses me off," Parcells says, "is that they talk about Cunningham being a great athlete and that seems to supersede the development of him as a quarterback. In other words, I think he's paid his dues. He's learned. He didn't have monumental success when he first came up. He's learned what to do, he's become functional within the system, and he's using the ability that he has. I think he's developed into a good quarterback not because he's a great athlete but because he also did the other things to develop into a good quarterback.

"But I don't think you can term anybody great until he puts pelts on his pony and right now he don't have any. When he does that I think you can put him into a different category. But I respect him because I've seen him develop.

"The formula for beating him and them is not complex but the practice takes a lot of discipline. But let me tell you something. Their real strength," says Parcells, the old defensive coordinator within him surfacing, "is not that. It's their defense. It creates turnovers, pressures the quarterback and makes turnovers. They're not a high-powered offensive team. They have some pretty good weapons but they're not complex. Now on defense they have a couple of great players. Reggie White is a great player.''

But at that very moment, across the hall where the defensive coaches live, the enemy they refer to as "that damned number 12" fills the room and is the wellspring from which every move on the crisis board develops.

Tuesday, 11:30 A.M., the equipment room

A mountain of laundry spins wildly in the huge washing machines and hammers against the walls of the dryers. This is the place the Tide commercials forgot. If you want your whites whiter, your soft things fluffier, you have come to the wrong address. The name of the game here is volume. It's wash day for the equipment manager, Ed Wagner, Jr., and the Giants. It's also repair the helmets day, fix the shoulder pads day, find the missing hip pads day, and every other kind of day it will take to get this football team through the next week.

Ever since United Charter 5306 touched down at Newark Airport, the keeper of the Giants' stuff has been on a nonstop treadmill. He and his father, Ed Wagner, Sr., who has been the locker-room manager since the Giants moved here in 1976, rode the charter buses back to the stadium and went directly to the ramp outside the locker room to wait for the equipment truck. The stone-cold corridor has all the charm of an unmade bed. The Meadowlands Wind, that natural dagger that on December Sundays cuts directly at the heart and soul of visiting football teams, was slamming around the inside of the concrete oval. Occasionally, they could hear the frostbitten grunts of the grounds crew as the wind drove the echoes through the field tunnel. The crew was out there on its hands and knees, zipping out the carpeted end zone that read "Jets" (New York's other "home team" had played at the Meadowlands on Sunday) and replacing it with the one that said "Giants."

Once the equipment had been secured, Ed Wagner, Jr., eyes at half-mast in the aftermath of the desultory all-night plane ride, stood at the foot of a mountain of dirty clothes. Just like Monday morning wash day at Grandma's (only it was Tuesday), he was separating his whites. As he and his helpers worked, they made a separate pile of game clothes for the dry cleaner. He has been awake since 4:30 A.M. the previous day. He may or may not begin equipment repairs before he finally leaves at 2:00 P.M.

When he does go, John Washington's jersey will leave with him. It had been ripped off Washington by an ungentle 49er the night before. During the game he used string to repair it. Now he will drop it off at his mother's house. Gertrude Wagner is the emergency couturier of the New York Giants. A retired seamstress, before the day is over she will sit down at her sewing machine and put Washington's jersey back together again.

At 6:00 A.M. on Wednesday, he will be back at the office, schlepping the field equipment out of its storage bins.

Tuesday, 12:00 noon, offensive coaches' conference room

They are watching the first Eagles-Giants game of 1989. This is not to be confused with the two 1988 games, which they screened on the Coast. The confusion is legitimate. The Giants lost all three. As the Eagles' defensive unit throws itself at the Giants, they are basically operating out of two formations—the 43, which they use most often, and the 46. Long before he was a head coach, the Eagles' Buddy Ryan, like Parcells, was a defensive coordinator. These, with subtle variations, have always been his bread and butter.

The ubiquitous coffee cups litter the table. The group of offensive coaches is larger than the defensive brain trust next door. Ask an offensive lineman why and he will tell you that you have to be smarter to play offense. Ask a defensive player why and he will tell you that offensive players are dumber and, thus, require more help. It is an argument that has been raging ever since two-platoon football jumped off the drawing board. An offensive lineman out of Stanford named John Wilbur, who once played for the Washington Redskins, claimed to have settled this debate when he won the team's preseason training camp chess tournament. His defensive counterparts on the 'Skins said the argument was totally invalid, since the head coach, George Allen, had told them he had never bothered to learn to play chess at all because checkers was a far better game.

In any event, the assemblage this afternoon includes Ron Erhardt, the coordinator; Tommy Coughlin, the receivers' coach, who is handling the blackboard chores; Fred Hoaglin, the offensive line coach, a former Pro Bowler who played center for the Browns, the Colts, the Oilers, and the Seahawks; Mike Pope, who coaches the tight ends; and Ray Handley, in his sixth year as running back coach.

As the taped sequences skip by, Erhardt is calling out possible plays which Coughlin posts. The staff then suggests additions, modifications, or deletions. Each time a play or a formation goes up, vigorous discussion follows.

This is the chess match portion of coaching. Here they are watching the videotaped history of their own play calls and how the Eagles handled those plays in the first game. The list of plays which will ultimately comprise the game plan continues to grow.

"We got eleven sub coverages against us, eleven where they're not blitzing and here the weak backer blitzes. Looks like they only gave us one-zone defense here," Erhardt says.

"But wait, look at this one," says Handley. "The whole thing here is that they changed during the course of the game because of what Meggett did to 'em. They hadn't seen him before. They came in concentrating on one thing and they changed because they couldn't handle it and they went to a different theory. Now we hadn't used Meggett very much in the backfield in the first four games, and—''

"Well," Pope interrupts, "if they can't do it without blitzing that's why I'd like to go with some sort of a scat pattern and slide the protection to the weak side and pick up what they did to us last time."

"Give him a chance to buy some time," says Hoaglin, "and operate on that guy. You know they're playing to . . . what about 74 scat Y [tight end] delay?"

In simple English, half right 74 scat Y delay, a play they believe can work, looks like this against the 43 defense:

There are four wide receivers, evenly divided on either side. The blocking scheme is 74. Against the 43 defense, they will slide the protection, passing off certain rushers to other blockers after the initial contact. The Y delay is a pattern for the tight end. The scat is Meggett, whom they dearly would love to isolate one on one against anybody because of his speed and hair-trigger moves. But the Eagles will surely have someone to try to keep Meggett from breaking free. Bart Oates, the center, will have to engage that man and spring the Giants' scatback.

"Oh, yeah," Erhardt says, "go ahead, Tommy, and draw 74 scat. Let's go half-right 74 scat. There is where we might want to make a change."

"Split these people out and he's a long way away. He's a long way from the numbers," Coughlin says. "Let's put him on the inside."

"Can't do that . . . can't do that," Erhardt says. "Half-right 74 scat. Put the Y over there."

"Motion?" asks Coughlin, who is diagramming the play.

"OK, but remember we want to keep the two receiver side over there where we can go comeback post. Isn't that the idea?"

"Damned right," somebody says.

"All right," Erhardt continues, "now gimme five down [referring to another Eagles defense with five down linemen] with the backer on Meggett's side. They're gonna put a guy on Meggett. Now gimme the other look. Same formation and gimme the other look. The end is on Meggett's side. Has this got any merit? You got the top look on the board there. You block it just like you block the regular 74. That's how we got to block it. One of the two guys is gonna take Meggett. We don't know which it is. Odessa [Turner] got the DB [defensive back], right? We block across the front. Jumbo [Elliott, offensive tackle] got nobody unless somebody comes [blitzes]."

"Now wait a minute, 74 and the left tackle is scanning [waiting to pick up an unblocked player]?" Handley asks.

"Well, it's the only way we can do it, right? If that backer comes, who's gonna take him?"

"We gotta scan," says Hoaglin. "It's the only way we can do it."

"Other than that," says Erhardt, "how you gonna get the scat out?"

"Last time we didn't want to do that," Hoaglin says. "We wanted to slide our line."

"Well, last time we gambled," Erhardt replies. "Now hear me out here. If they give us that look," he says, pointing to the board, "then you'd like to be able to say you're gonna run the tackle scan. The tackle's gonna take one of those guys. Now if they give us the bottom look, you'd like to slide the blockers and Odessa will take either one of the two guys. Now forget about the pattern. The pass pattern is not the problem. It's the protection."

"OK," says Handley, "I'm gonna tell Meggett if that backer's coming and he sees that safety coming to square up on him and go either way on him. In other words try to make [Wes] Hopkins [the Eagles' free safety] change directions.''

"If he could go outside," Pope offers, "he [the defender] could probably break both his legs trying to stay with him.''

"But I can't let him go too far," Handley says. "I can't let him run all the way up to the guy. He's probably got to make it in five yards.''

"Put up Counter 62," Erhardt says.

"We're tryin' for the home run on both these plays," says Pope.

And the mind games go on. On the blackboard, every play always works.

Tuesday, 2:00 P.M., Ronnie Barnes's office

Ronnie Barnes is thirty-seven years old. Twice the four-thousand-member National Athletic Trainers Association of America has named him trainer of the year. He holds a B.A. degree from East Carolina University and a master's from Michigan State. The first time he knew he wanted to be a trainer was back in junior high school in North Carolina. "I was really small," he'll tell you. "I weighed only one hundred pounds when I graduated from high school. In junior high I went out for the basketball team. The coach took one look at me and said I could be the trainer. I didn't know what that was so he told me that you put on Band-Aids and you're the first aider. I wanted to know if I had to wash towels and he said no. He got me a little box with a white cross on it and taught me to wrap ankles.''

Today the ankles are bigger. So is the pay.

Barnes is waiting for the main assault force of the walking wounded to hit his private beachhead. These are the bumps and lumps and limps who have been scheduled to report in at 3:00 P.M., but already he and Ryan have put in a full day that morning with Taylor and Simms. Each has had his wounded ankle treated in the cold boot, a compression device that fills up with cold water and pressure, designed to force the swelling out of the ankle and up the leg. Each received electric stimulation, a combination pain inhibitor and swelling reducer, massage, and another compression bandage. Each will continue to take Endocin.

Based on the immediate evidence, Taylor's condition is the more serious. "He can't walk right now," Barnes says. "If he can't walk, he can't run, and if he can't run, he can't play. We sent him back for another X ray. The Tuesday report is that I don't think he can play. I have to do that because he's the kind of guy you build a game plan around. I'll do my best to get him ready but I have to be sure Parcells understands he may not play. So I told Bill just as soon as Lawrence left. Now he'll be on my ass every thirty minutes, calling and asking, 'Is he better? Is he better? Can he walk now?'

"And if he can't call me, he'll find me. It's impossible to hide from him. He'll show up anywhere in the building any time. He sees everything. If a piece of equipment has been moved, he'll know it. Sometimes at practice, I'll sort of hang out on the other side of the field. Maybe we have a lot of guys hurt and I just don't want to go over the whole list. So I'll sort of try to blend in with the scenery but he'll come over to me or else he'll yell across the field, 'What's the matter, Barnes? You hiding from me?'

"He's superstitious, you know. He wants nobody to change anything when we're winning. Last year we were going great and I have this sweatshirt I hadn't worn all year but it was one of those awful cold days so I put it on to go out to practice and he yells over at me, 'Take that damned thing off. Go back inside and put on what you're supposed to wear.'

"And I was mumbling to myself, Do you really think Tom

Landry is telling the Dallas trainer to go back and put on his
official Cowboy trainer's uniform this afternoon?''
    And did he tell Parcells that?
    ''Are you kidding?''

Tuesday, 3:00 P.M., Bill Parcells's office
    The cigarette pack rests on the desk next to the half-empty
coffee cup. He is wearing a blue sweater with the single block
letter legend ''Giants'' across the front in white. During the
off-season he took off thirty-eight pounds. The players say it has
changed his attitude for the better. He says he has a lot more
energy. But at this moment, after the all-night plane ride, the
trauma of Taylor's injury, the uncertainty of how his defensive
coaches will plan without LT, and the clear pressure of a ''must''
game at the end of a short week closing in on everyone in the
joint, he is visibly tired.
    In an hour, he will walk across the hall and meet with both
offensive and defensive staffs to share information, to critique
what they have begun to prepare for him, and to tell them about
tomorrow's practice plans.
    But now he is thinking about ''that other guy.''
    Other than the fact that each built his football reputation as a
defensive coordinator, there are few similarities between Bill
Parcells and Buddy Ryan, the man who coaches the Eagles and
who now has beaten him three straight times.
    ''Buddy Ryan,'' he says, ''is a very dangerous opponent be-
cause he has no regard for anything but trying to put the best team
he can on the field. He doesn't care about anything except what
he deems to be his job.''
    On the surface, that statement could mean a lot of things,
particularly in view of the fact that just this past week, Luis
Zendejas, the Dallas placekicker, who was injured in the

Cowboys-Eagles Thanksgiving Day game, has charged Ryan with placing a two-hundred-dollar bounty on him in connection with that injury and another one on the Dallas quarterback.

But Parcells is speaking about a different kind of danger. He is talking about the menace generated by a single-minded counterpart who, in the view of the Giants' head coach, is unencumbered by the rules of the game that highly visible pro coaches must play with the public, the press, and their own bosses.

"He's very dangerous because he's not afraid of consequences. He doesn't care what anyone else thinks, including his coaches, his personnel people, and even his owners. He has no sense of public relations or anything beyond what he deems his job. That makes him a very dangerous adversary because he's going to do whatever he thinks he has to do to win—and if you don't like it, that's too bad.

"Personally, I like him. He's caustic and unpretentious. I wouldn't say we're close friends but, yes, I like him."

It is almost as though he envies the route Ryan has taken. Almost.

Later, in an oblique remark, he will hint at the consequences facing Ryan and a handful like him if they don't succeed. Coaches, like aging ballerinas, are hardly blessed with job security. In a real sense, that knowledge is something he thinks about—both from the obvious standpoint and from some not so obvious ones.

"My father worked for U.S. Rubber for twenty-eight years. And right at the end of his career—and he was pretty well up in the company, I'm talking about, say, the top fifteen people in the corporation—and just when he could have made it to the top two or three, a new president came in the company. As with those corporate structure changes, someone else was chosen to do things that would have put my father into a very big bonus and profit-sharing group.

"He was bitter. So he retired when he was fifty-five instead of staying with it."

The coach is hardly naive, but there is something in that story he surely finds hard to square with the concepts with which he was raised and, in fact, which all coaches in all sports tell their players: Work hard and good things will happen.

"My father had very good values as a person—better than mine, unfortunately. It's funny, he always used the word "wrong." You know, he'd say things like, 'Well, you don't do that because it's wrong.' He was always involved with right and wrong. Certain things were wrong. You didn't do them and that's all the explanation you needed—or were going to get.

"That's why I sometimes think about what we're doing here and how hard some people work at it and then when it isn't happening, some player will say to me, 'I'm sorry, coach, but I'm trying,' and I'll tell him exactly what my father told me: you don't get any medals for trying."

Doing what he believes to be the right thing and not looking for a gray-area hedge is very much a part of the coach. Parcells has, for example, a standing rule against injecting players with pain killers. "He told me that when he became head coach," Barnes said earlier in the day. "It's something we do not do here under any circumstances. It's not that way everywhere—believe me."

Another thing passed down from his father is the attempt to keep things in perspective. His father was an all-American football player at Georgetown in the early 1930s, but he didn't intrude on his son's athletic career.

Still, he managed to make his point.

"I didn't know it at the time," Parcells says, "but he was in cahoots with Mickey Cochrane, my high school basketball coach. You'll see Mickey on Thursday. He's sixty-nine now but he always makes the Thursday practices. Anyway, I really didn't know when my father was even at the games. Mickey used to sneak him through the field-house door and my father never used to say much about my games one way or the other.

"So now I'm playing for River Dell High School and I'm leading the state of New Jersey in scoring and one night at dinner he says to me, 'Are you getting to play very much down there?' Now that's a humbling experience."

Off and on during the day, Parcells has been giving thought to what he will tell the players when he meets them tomorrow morning. The idea is to set a tone in perhaps just three minutes. Then everything he tells them during the week—both individually and collectively—will flow from that, right down to the final words he gives them in the dressing room before they go out and play the game.

In individual conversation, he is, as Simms says, the master at using a casual sentence or two to praise (sometimes with just enough sarcasm to hold a little back) or to rip. Sometimes there will be no sentences at all. That, too, is no accident.

"The worst thing that can happen to a player," Parcells says, "is for him not to know what the coach is really thinking about him. I know. I used to play football, too. Sometimes, I use that. There are guys who need that once in a while."

What about the last speech, the one they hear just before they go out?

"Well, I'll give you two examples. One was the opening Monday night football game down in Washington two years ago when Taylor had just been suspended [for drug abuse]. I told 'em about Vietnam. I said I don't know if many of you guys are old enough to remember Vietnam and the degradation and the way this conflict was being fought and the poor guys we had going over there in the face of not only the enemy but very adverse reaction at home.

"I told them—and now this is right after Taylor had been suspended—about a unit that I knew about that had gone over there with about one hundred guys and the first day they lost eighteen guys in battle. My brother [a West Point graduate and former Army football player] told me this story. And the next day they had to go back out there. The point I was trying to make to them was that right now Bavaro and Banks ain't ready to play and, of course, they're sitting there right in the locker room. You lost your punter. Marshall can't play, he's a Pro Bowl guy. Benson retired, he's a Pro Bowl guy, and Taylor just got suspended, so really that's six Pro Bowl guys who aren't functional—and four of 'em can't be in the game and two of 'em ain't ready to go.

"Now we're not talking about losing any lives here. Some of those guys will be back, but now even the press is feeling sorry for you because they don't know what you're gonna do. You're playing the defending Super Bowl champions and nobody thinks you can win. Nobody thinks you have a chance. And they're feeling sorry for you and they're talking about Taylor's suspension. They're doin' all those things but on Tuesday morning, they're only gonna want to know one thing—who won the game. That's all—who won the game. And then I sent them out.

"And when they came in after winnin' the game, that's all they were shouting, 'Who won the game? Who won the game?' So I knew I had gotten to 'em.

"The other thing is I always try to tell the team that the only way you're judged in this business is by who's standing at the end. It's not a weekly judgment. It may appear that way to you because of the publicity you get—the Giants were dogs . . . the Giants were this—but in the end, you're just like the pioneers. They got to the Rockies and they started the last part of the journey. Some of them were killed by Indians. Some of them drowned in the rivers. Some were killed by rock slides. Some of them even turned back. But some of those sons of bitches got through. And the only way you're judged is whether you got through or not.''

On a different level, just two weeks earlier, Meggett had played his best game of the season. As he stood in front of his locker, Parcells leaned across a reporter and said: "It's about fuckin' time." And then he smiled.

And when he walked away you could almost see an aura taking shape over his little running back's head.

"Yeah," Parcells says when reminded, "well, it's the only way I know. I'll tell you where I learned that. Mickey Cochrane was the master. Once he got me with just one sentence after a basketball game. Now understand, I'm the high scorer, and he walks over and says to me, 'Parcells, you weren't worth the two points you cost us on that technical foul you drew and if you ever get another one, you ain't gonna play another minute here.'

"See, I was fifteen years old and we were up by seventeen and he took me out of the game because I got a technical foul and we got beat by one. But you see, if he put me back in I would've had him—forever. He knew that. I thought he'd put me back in at the time but he didn't. I learned something that day.

"I'll tell you another great thing he did. I took him to the Chicago playoff game in 1985. He must've been about sixty-five then. We got beat. They had a good team. I mean we could have beaten them maybe two out of ten that year. That day was one of the days we could have beat 'em had things gone just a little differently. It was 7–0 at the half. We dropped a touchdown pass that would have tied it. I think—since they weren't a great offensive team—if we could have gotten the game into the fourth quarter something might have happened for us.

"But after the game I'm pissed and there's this magazine writer at the press conference who asks me, 'Shouldn't you have used more three-step drops?' And I say, 'You wouldn't know a three-step drop if it grew teeth, jumped up, and bit you in the ass.' Then I kind of blew the Chicago press off and I went to the coaches' dressing room and I didn't say a word to anyone. I didn't say a word to the coaches. I didn't say a word to Mickey. I didn't say a word to the owners. I didn't say a word to nobody.

"So we pack the bus and it was freezing and I get on the bus and I didn't say a word to anyone and now it's two hours after the game. So now we're flying and we get over Pittsburgh and Mickey was sitting next to me and I still hadn't said a word to him. He tapped me on the shoulder. Now we just finished the season and we had won eleven games and lost seven and he knew how I felt. He didn't say, 'Nice goin'.' He didn't say, 'Good season.' He didn't say, 'Your franchise is makin' progress.' All he did was tap me on the shoulder and say, 'You gotta figure out a way to beat those fuckin' guys.'

"Perspective.

"I think that one sentence is what got me going for the next season—and we won it all."

He had been fooling with a single sheet of yellow notepaper as he spoke. "Well, I made some notes about what I want to tell them tomorrow but when I go down to the locker room, I'll leave it up here like I always do and probably say something different. See, the problem is, we've got the worst-possible-case scenario. We've got a lot of guys beat up. We've got a devastating loss. We've got some psychological problems. We've got some physical problems and we've got a very strong opponent. So I've gotta collectively get everyone focused immediately, if not sooner."

Some of the focusing begins soon after, directly across the hall.

Tuesday, 4:00 P.M., coaches' conference room

They are all there, even the special teams coaches. The cross talk as they wait is broken in half. The defensive people are talking about what happens if Taylor can't play. They have moved Johnie Cooks, a well-traveled linebacker in his eighth season, to outside linebacker. He will assume some of Taylor's responsibilities. Added duties now fall to Pepper Johnson, a part-time player. Adrian White, a backup cornerback, will now assume the role of "mirror," the special shadow assigned to track Cunningham and keep his scrambling from becoming a long gainer on the ground. In the shifting of personnel to create what is called the "sub" portion of any spot defense, Mark Collins now becomes the sub—often a designated extra blitzer. The loss of Taylor, should it be definite, will require a lot of people to do things they did not expect to be doing.

At the other end of the table, the offensive people are talking about a matchup between Mark Ingram, the Giants' slick receiver, and Sammy Lilly, an ex-Giant who plays in the Eagles' nickel or passing-down defense. They are discussing the opportunities when the Giants' offensive formation and the Eagles' reactions to it might open up the middle of the field. "Hell," says Erhardt, whose voice carries above the cross talk, "Odessa is the best we've got. Let's just throw it up there and let him go up and wrestle it away from Frizzell (another Eagles' nickel back).

Then Parcells walks in and you can almost feel the faces of the defensive coaches sag in unison with his first statement.

"Taylor is out. That's what I told the press and that's what I'm going to tell the team tomorrow morning. If he comes back and plays, that's fine. But right now he's out and I want our people to know it. I don't want them tip-toeing in on Sunday and peeking into his locker to see if he can save them.

"Odessa and [Steve] De Ossie [a linebacker] will probably play. Manuel's thumb still hurts. He can't catch in practice but he'll probably play. Simms is still limited."

"Meaning what?" Erhardt asks.

"Meaning, he'll practice but so will Hostetler. Let 'em divide the snaps tomorrow. We may have to juggle some on the offensive line. Jumbo is still limping. What about Moore? Can he block Pitts?"

The opinions—which are many—are lost in the crosscurrent and Parcells looks at his offensive coordinator. "It's up to you. Put Moore out there and Williams at tackle if we have to. All right. I'm going to talk ten minutes tomorrow morning. I'm gonna point out that the team that wins this wins the division." The Giants had a one-game lead over Philly with four to play at that point. "If they need any more motivation than that, we're all in trouble."

"I want them on the field without pads. I'm not going to give them any excuse to say they're tired on Sunday."

Then he runs down the minute-by-minute practice schedule.

"Is Matt Darwin [the Eagles' offensive tackle] hurt?" Parcells asks. "The guy who goes in for him stinks."

"They give him help," Belichick explains.

"He needs it," Parcells replies.

Now Parcells voices what all of them are hoping deep down inside. "I'm not counting Taylor out. Something could happen. We've seen him do too much to jump. I'm listing him with the league office right now as questionable. Bill," he asks Belichick, "what about Adrian as the mirror? He ain't the best reader."

"It's the best route to go," Belichick replies, shuddering at the myriad combinations and possibilities with which his staff had wrestled much of the day. "We'll do what we have to do. But if 56 [Taylor] returns, well, then . . ."

Nobody said amen. But they sure as hell thought it.

The last lights in the coaches' wing went out at 9:00 P.M. For some of them, the workday—which had begun with a defensive meeting about the Eagles at 7:00 A.M. on Monday morning in San

Francisco and ended a continent away in East Rutherford, New
Jersey—had lasted thirty-nine hours.

Tuesday evening, various places

WOOD RIDGE, N.J.—Reyna Thompson is running through the
twilight. Bundled against the wind, sweatshirt hood pulled tightly
against his skull, he has come to a kind of aerobic truce with
himself as he swallows the cold air in large gulps. He tries to run
every evening and tonight he'll do almost six miles. For him,
the running is more than just conditioning. He runs to sort
things out. As he says, "I'm really into it," and as he pounds
through the early evening chill, he is very much alone with
himself.

No blaring Walkman breaks the private sound of his own
thoughts. Less than twenty-four hours ago, he put his knuckles
down on the wrong side of the line of scrimmage and it cost his
team three heart-breaking points. Now, as he runs, he is thinking,
"It's time to put this thing away. It's time to think about the
Eagles."

But he knows that it will take a few more days before the
frustration fades. When he returns to his apartment, he changes
clothes and heads out to Sheldon White's place. The two of them,
along with teammate Adrian White, will watch some television
and shoot some pool.

NEWARK, N.J. —There are no rookies in this 7:00 P.M. class.
Most of them have come directly from work. His job description
may be a little different, but Bart Oates is no exception. After a
morning at workout in the weight room, he finally went home and
slept briefly. Now he is sitting in a classroom at the Seton Hall
University Law School and the professor is passing out the blue
books which are the symbol of just about every test ever held on

any college campus. The course is called legal writing. He will not get back home until 10:00 P.M.

And when he finally closes his eyes, sleep will not come easily. In his mind's eye, he will see Reggie White—all three of him. Reggie White, the power rusher; Reggie White, preceded by the vicious slap and the move inside; and Reggie White, driving his right forearm into the body and taking an outside move. Oates will play and replay his countermoves. He will refight each battle here. But he will drift off to sleep, reminding himself that he did not win many the last time they met in Philadelphia.

HOBOKEN, N.J.—It is Reggae Night at the Down Under Bar in Hoboken and Erik Howard and Jumbo Elliot are sitting at a table listening to the Caribbean sounds of Johnny and the Black Sheep. The band is very good this night. It better be. Howard and Elliot own the joint.

As the West Indian sounds fill the room, Howard finally begins to relax. All day, he has paid a heavy price for those sins of commission of the 49ers' offensive line that he couldn't prevent. At 3:00 P.M. that afternoon, he was in the ice-cold hands of Barnes and Ryan. They were treating a thigh bruise, a swollen left hand, a sore back, and an aching knee with that miracle cure-all of locker rooms—ice.

They strapped it on his thigh. They wrapped it on his knee. They shoved his hand into an ice-cold bucket. By the time he left, he didn't know whether he'd played a football game the night before or tried to swim Lake Erie in December.

FRANKLIN LAKES, N.J.—They sat up late, each trying to reassure the other. "It's not good," Phil Simms told his wife, Diana. "We lost, my ankle hurts, and I don't know whether I'll ever get rid of this stupid pain."

"It'll be all right," Diana Simms says. "We've been through this before. This week is the one you have to win and you will. We've been through a lot worse."

It is 12:30 before he turns out the lights. He thinks back to where he was weeks ago when he first limped off the field with the injury against Minnesota. There is no point going backwards. He has been in this thing too long for that. So he thinks ahead.

Ahead are the Eagles.

He sleeps very little.

The ankle throbs all night.

2. WEDNESDAY, NOVEMBER 29, 1989

5:15 A.M., Upper Saddle River, New Jersey

Judy Parcells is asleep. The routine has been chiseled in stone for so long that the muted sounds of her husband getting ready to leave for work at a time when the world belongs to milkmen, turnpike toll collectors, and longshoremen makes no impact on her rest. If you marry a coach, it is simply one of the things that comes with the territory.

He is up and gone in twenty minutes.

Everyone in Upper Saddle River knows where the coach lives. They do not intrude beyond an occasional "good luck on Sunday" when they see either of the Parcells at the dry cleaners or one of the local stores. But there are some itches that simply have to be scratched. More than a few times he has found folded notes in his mailbox which begin with some variation of the following:

Dear Coach,
  Phil Simms has been sacked a lot lately. I think I've found a way to avoid that. If you would adjust the spacing in the offensive line so that Jumbo Elliott could . . .

That also comes with the territory.

"The house is too big for us now," Parcells says. "We rattle around in it. My oldest daughter is married and lives in Philadelphia. The middle one works for Sony and is out on her own. My youngest is away at Gettysburg College.''

There are four bedrooms in the large brickfront Colonial, which sits on a quiet street in this affluent residential community. But then all the streets are quiet, all the houses large, and most of the residents affluent. It is light years from Hastings, Nebraska.

They were kids fresh out of Wichita State University where they had met and married and had their first child back when Bill Parcells was playing linebacker for the Shockers and every Saturday was New Year's Eve. In one game against Tulsa, he had twenty solo tackles and six quarterback sacks. He made the Missouri Valley Conference All-League Team two years in a row. He played in the Sun Bowl, the Blue-Gray Game, and the Senior Bowl.

And then the cheering stopped and reality came knocking. He didn't want to play professional football (he had been drafted in the seventh round by the Detroit Lions). He didn't want the nine-to-five world of his father. What he wanted to do was coach.

Nobody was killed in the stampede to hire him.

Hastings College had eight hundred students and a budget to match. It offered him three months' work as an assistant coach at a salary of one thousand dollars. With one baby in the carriage and another on the way, Bill and Judy Parcells marched off to Hastings in search of fame, fortune, and the chance to coach against such football powerhouses as Doane College and Kearney State.

''We lived in a basement apartment underneath a dentist's office,'' Judy Parcells would later recall. ''There was a small closet and no windows. We didn't have anything and a thousand dollars seemed like a lot of money. I think we paid something like fifty dollars a month for it. We managed. I don't know how.

Obviously, we didn't eat steak and shrimp. At the end of the season we went back to Wichita State so Bill could work on his master's, but there was a coaching change there and Alex Karras, who'd been an assistant when Bill played there, got the head coaching job and hired him."

Since then their odyssey across the face of a series of squares on a 100-yard checkerboard has taken them to West Point, New York, Tallahassee, Florida, Nashville, Tennessee, Lubbock, Texas, Colorado Springs, Colorado (where for a year he was finally a head coach at the Air Force Academy), Foxboro, Massachusetts, and East Rutherford, New Jersey.

"Until the children started to really grow up, it was fun," Judy Parcells says. "I was caught up in all the beauty and patriotism at West Point. And I'm from Wichita, so I liked all the flat country around Lubbock. During those years there was always something exciting and I couldn't wait for the next move. I always assumed there'd be one in a year or two. But now we were in Colorado and the idea of moving back East really hit the two oldest kids. They had friends and school and it was kind of devastating for them.

"So that was the only year since I'd known him that Bill gave up football. He worked for a land-development company and he helped coordinate one of their recreation centers. But what he really wanted to do was get back into football.

"Bill was all right in the spring and he made it through the summer, but as soon as autumn came I knew he was going to coach again. He was lost. He didn't know what to do with himself on the weekends. We went to a couple of Air Force games and then we went down to Denver to see the Broncos play and then we both knew he ought to be coaching. But it was a scary thing because once you're out of it, you never know if you're going to be able to get back in."

But the chance was there. Ron Erhardt took him on in New

England—ironically, Erhardt runs the Giants' offense today—and a year later, Ray Perkins, the Giants' head coach, offered him the spot of defensive coordinator.

"Looking back," Judy Parcells says, "all the moving was a kind of a cultural shock for me and when Bill was offered a job as defensive coordinator here, I was really upset. We'd only been in New England a year, even bought a house. He's from New Jersey and I'd been back with him for a couple of visits and I didn't like it at all. I thought the people were rude. I couldn't deal with it. I thought, I don't want to raise my kids in this. I'd go shopping and I'd come home and I'd be in tears. You know, people would yell at you and I'm from the Midwest and it was like I was in cultural shock.

"But now I love it. Maybe now I yell like they do. Whatever it is, it's great."

Parcells has backed the bronze Lincoln down the driveway now. The predawn is spectacularly gloomy. As the wind slams against the windshield, he reaches down and fiddles with the car radio until he finds the big-band sound of the 1940s he likes so much. On the half hour, the weather report confirms his fondest hopes. The week will be frigid. The winds will hammer away. "Let it be worse by Sunday," he says to himself. "Let it be much worse." Later in the day, when he meets with the press, he will ask, "What do you hear about the weather? I want it cold and blustery and snowing on Sunday."

Next to his playbook, the wind that rips across his stadium is the football Giants' best friend—and the home field won-lost record documents that fact.

The Lincoln is out of the driveway now, left, left again, then right on Lake Street, and out to the next traffic light, where he pulls off the road and parks in front of Elmer's Country Store. This is his morning pit stop. The joint has been there for about fifty years although very few of its customers know it. Here he picks up his first container of coffee. Before he meets with the players at noon, he will have had five.

The trip to Giants Stadium takes about twenty minutes this time of day. If truth be told, he could have made it sooner. What New Jersey State Trooper worthy of the uniform is going to give the coach a ticket when the Eagles are about to come to town?

The first streaks of light are beginning to stretch across the Meadowlands when he pulls into the parking lot. He is not the first to arrive. Already the offensive and defensive coaches have begun the daily search for something new in the history of an opponent so familiar they could diagram what's coming at them next Sunday in their sleep. But this morning remains more complex than usual. The injuries to Taylor and Simms are on everyone's minds.

As Parcells noses the car down the ramp to his parking space beneath the stadium, a violent burst of wind hammers against the tunnel. He looks toward the sky as if to say, "Hang in there, pal. Don't use it all up now. We're gonna need you on Sunday."

6:45 A.M., defensive coaches' conference room

More coffee, more red eyes, and Lamar Leachman's ubiquitous tobacco-juice cup. The Eagles are moving the ball on the big screen. This is a tape of the last time they met down in Philadelphia and nobody has to tell anyone in the room who won that one. The only time the Giants put the ball in the end zone came off a fake field goal. They went after touchdowns and settled for field goals. Raul Allegre (who will not play Sunday because of an injured groin muscle) kicked four, but Cunningham turned that math around in the final two minutes and beat the Giants.

Getting into the end zone is somebody else's job, but the failure to do so made it that much tougher on the defense. Still, every defensive maneuver is always successful on the blackboard. Losing, for any reason, is therefore inexcusable. In the final minutes in Philadelphia, Cunningham took the Eagles 81 yards in ten plays to wipe out a week's worth of the staff's Xs and Os. Now the defensive coaches are juggling new ones in their place. And none of them stands for Lawrence Taylor.

They are concentrating on what they call the Red Zone—the last 20 yards between the offense and goal line. It was here in the fourth quarter that first Cunningham and later a running back named Anthony Toney scored from the two and the one.

It is the memory of Cunningham's score that particularly stings them because it capped a drive where everything had gone wrong. First, the special teams broke down on the kickoff. Allegre boomed it down to the five but a rookie named Heath Sherman saw daylight and the Giants' specials let the blocking wall form and he ran it back 45 yards. Down the hall at this very moment, Romeo Crennel, the special teams coach, and his assistant, Mike Sweatman, are wrestling with their own private heartache over that one.

Then Toney got away and turned the corner to his right, which is about as far away as you can run a play from Lawrence Taylor's office, and that was good for 44 more to the Giants' 6. That run put them in the red zone. If the red zone has a crimson spot, the remaining six yards were it. Twice, Leachman's people down front drove the Eagles back off the line of scrimmage and Banks slammed up the middle from his inside linebacker's spot to drill first Toney and then Cunningham. So now it was third down on the three and Cunningham tried to hit Cris Carter in the corner of the end zone for one of those precisely timed leaping kangaroo catches. It didn't connect but a yellow flag hit the ground.

It was a pass interference call against Reyna Thompson and the Eagles got to start all over again from the one. Two shots from the backfield at the center of Giants' defense got nothing. Then on third down Cunningham rolled out and sprinted for the corner of the end zone with Giants all around him. When the force came up to meet him, he launched himself and dove straight over the top.

The tapes show he didn't get in. But the referee and the instant replay officials thought he did and they're the ones who count. The score brought the Eagles within two points and changed the ebb and flow of what was left of the final quarter.

Working from a videotape of all the game's red zone situations, the defensive staff has turned its attention back to that shrinking slice of geography.

"Now this is our adjustment," Belichick is saying. "If we change the call down in there tight, [Keith] Byars [the Eagles running back who catches so many passes swinging out of the backfield] comes out there in the flat, Perry [Williams] jumps him and [Mark] Collins goes over the top. Then we make the decision when they get down in there tighter to go red two mirror. Once we put the mirror on Cunningham and Johnie [Cooks] has got the back in the flat along with Banks, the corners can go ahead and cushion back there and give the safeties some help on the outside of the field."

"So if we put it in tomorrow," says Groh, looking up from his notebook, "let 'em walk through it in practice, give 'em some more on Friday plus we assign Banks to make the call so that now when they hear it, it'll alert everybody. OK, here we go—and remember, it's a little different now."

"Yeah," Belichick says, still considering the possibilities. "If Cunningham scrambles, we still got the mirror on, so all he should get is a couple of yards, which is all right if it keeps him out of the end zone. But, hell," he slaps his open palm down on the tabletop, "what are we gonna do with [tight end Keith] Jackson? If they bring Jackson inside, we're still running Cooks into the flat and both safeties are trying to cover deep. I mean, Jackson's gonna have the whole field to work inside. He could kill us. We're gonna have to be careful on that.

"So I don't know about this. If they come in on third down with that spread look, maybe we either gotta blitz it or just play a man coverage and maybe double Jackson. We're still gonna have the same problem with Cunningham with the rush we have on. We're just not gonna get there."

"Hell, seems to me that inside the five, even with the mirror," Leachman says, "he [Cunningham] is gonna hurt us. Let's make him work for it. Let's rush six instead of four and make him throw the damned ball 'cause if that sucker breaks out and runs from down in there, you know he's flat out gonna beat us."

With quarterbacks, the defensive theory is to flush them out of the pocket and make them run. But because Cunningham is the best in football at the broken-play scramble, the theory is to make him throw, viewing his strong arm as the lesser of two evils.

"And if we make him throw it," Leachman drawls, pausing like a man who is about to reveal a great truth, leaning forward in his chair and *ping-ping*ing another small stream of tobacco juice into the cup in his hand, "we got a chance to catch it, too."

Then the lights go back on. Belichick stares at the big loose-leaf notebook on the table in front of him for a moment, sits back in his chair, shakes his head, and explains:

"What we have to do with Cunningham is to play him as though he were a sixth receiver because, when you think about it, if he's spread the field and he's got all that room, he's gonna move like one in the open field. That's why assigning a guy to mirror him is so important. And that's a major reason why we miss Lawrence so much.

"What happens is we got too many guys who just almost get to him. When he decides to take off they don't have a chance to go with him, and then, 'almost getting there' winds up being more dangerous to you than not getting there at all. All you've done is to set things up for him.

"And when that happens without Taylor . . ."

The unfinished sentence hangs there like an accusing finger.

Wednesday, 9:00 A.M., trainer's office

Ronnie Barnes is waiting for his star patients to drag their throbbing ankles and their aching psyches into his workshop. The affected anatomy is the same but the reactions are worlds apart. "Phil has been through so much," Barnes explains, "that you can understand why he just naturally wonders what can happen next. I've worked with him and rehabbed him through all those injuries and it's amazing that look he gets in his eyes when he's got something wrong. You know, he comes to me like, 'Uh-oh, here we go again and you gotta fix me.' It's getting really tough every time now. You keep wondering, Is this it? Is this it?— every time you run out on the field you wonder if this is the one. And, of course, the same thing is going through his mind and sometimes he'll verbalize it.

"You know, he lost almost two of his first three seasons to freak injuries. Somebody else probably couldn't have made it back—especially at quarterback. But he's always been a self-starter, a hard worker with a great focus. He loves the game, loves to play, loves to be in shape. He has this incredible concern for his body. He spends an enormous amount of time with Johnny Parker, the strength coach, and I think that's really helped him.

"He comes and stays all day. He comes in the morning—let's say treatment begins at 8:30—he'll come at 7:30 and he'll be waiting for me and the first thing he'll say is, 'Where were you?'

"The players will be off the field at 4:00 and at 7:30 he'll walk out the door, not in any hurry, just interested in getting his treatment. And while this ankle's bothering him he'll still be going in the weight room. You can bet he'll be coming to me and saying, 'Is it OK if I squat? Will it hurt my ankle?' He'll go through his entire upper body weight program even though he's injured. We have a lot of people on this club who would use an ankle sprain as an excuse to miss everything.

"Taylor, of course," Barnes says, breaking into a grin, "will be the opposite. What he'll say is, 'I'm gonna play,' and he really thinks that's the final word because he's Superman—and for so long he was. For years he'd get an injury I honestly didn't think he could play with and he'd just tell me to tape him up and he'd go. Even with a hamstring, he played the following week. Even with a bad shoulder, he played. He's missed only one game since he's been here.

"In the opener at Washington, this year, he was dehydrated. That's not new for him. He plays himself into shape. He doesn't spend time running. Simms runs the road, I mean you might find him out running on a Saturday. He bikes, he lifts. He works in the weight room to get himself into football shape.

"Not Lawrence. He works on the field to stay in shape and that doesn't give him enough aerobic activity. He's getting older. His metabolism is changing and he can't control his weight. He's been known to take a diuretic, diet pills, even a laxative. He'll stay for hours in a sauna. In short, everything you're not supposed to do.

"He worked out all preseason in a scuba-diving suit. Can you believe that? We preach the detriments of that in sports medicine. Do not wear a rubber suit, we tell them. It will kill you in the heat of the day, we tell them. So what does Superman do?

"Anyway, essentially, he had dehydrated himself in Washington and it got him in trouble there and the same thing happened in Atlanta a year ago. We had to give him an IV each time and then it was like watching a flower come to life, he snapped back so quickly. He's still in alcohol and drug rehab so unfortunately everyone who sees him in that state thinks that's what it is. But believe me, it's not anything like that at all.

"We'll know more about both of them today.

"I give the coach a report at the end of each day, but you know this one's different. Bill will be ringing my phone all week: 'Is Taylor in yet? Is Simms there? Can they walk? What does it look like? Are we doing enough?'

"He (Parcells) believes nobody can be continually successful without getting heat and pressure on him. That's why sometimes he'll walk in here and suddenly say to me, 'You don't want to win, Barnes. How come other people are playing on other teams? Why don't I have all my people back?' But he doesn't want me to cut corners. In a way, it's like he's trying to motivate me, too. One day, after Phil hurt the ankle against the Vikings, he yelled at me, 'What are you doing for Simms?' I told him, 'Treating him with ice like everyone else,' and he said, 'Yeah? Well, is it our coldest ice?' And I thought about saying, 'No, I'm using the warm stuff.'

"But I didn't.' "

10:30 A.M., offensive coaches' conference room

Ron Erhardt is fifty-seven years old and he still speaks in the slow, flat tones of his native North Dakota. Except for three years in the military, he cannot remember an autumn without football dictating his daily routine. The wrinkles around his eyes conjure up the image of a man who knows the feel of the wind slamming a North Dakota cold front across the playing fields of the cultural crossroads of Williston and Minot and Fargo, where he coached on just about every level the state had to offer.

He did not come to the pros until he was forty-one years old when Red Miller brought him out to the Patriots from North Dakota State, where for seven years he had been the X and O king of small-college football. Six years later, he was the head coach.

Since 1981, he has been the Giants' offensive coordinator, working for a man who used to work for him. It has been said (and not without logic) of the Sunday Faithful who regularly pack Giants Stadium, that they would boo Mother Teresa if she called the plays and didn't have Phil Simms throwing at least one 50-yarder each sequence. If a little knowledge is a dangerous thing, these people are positively hazardous to their own blood pressure.

Most of them are not aware that when Bill Parcells walks the sidelines all bundled up and wearing his headset, he can tap into the plays both his offensive and defensive people are calling from the coaches' booth. Nor are they aware that the head coach's participation in moments like that often goes far beyond the stereotypical "Do we go for it on fourth and one?"

So in the New York area Erhardt takes more heat than many of his counterparts elsewhere. He can handle it because he and Parcells share a lot of common philosophy. The game plan he puts together during the week generally holds no surprises for the boss.

In about an hour, he will join the other coaches in the locker room in preparation for the basic explanation of this week's assault on the Eagles. Right now he is explaining some of the nuances of what his staff has fashioned and why they have done it this way.

"The big thing we looked at and studied are spots where we can get some physical mismatches in our favor and that doesn't include just the glamour part of the game—throwing and catching. What we need to decide is where we can get some protection, which most people in the stands don't understand. They feel like, well, it's Simms's job to get the ball off, and if he can't, they'll just run a shorter route or something like that.

"We have to look and see places where we can control Reggie White or Brown and Simmons, the guys who are their big sack people. What do we do to offset them? Well, for one thing, when we're not involved with a guy like Meggett in some phase of going out to receive a pass, we'd like for him to be involved in the blocking. A lot of people might overlook that, saying, 'Well, he's not big enough to help.' But we'll have him peel off and bump a guy just to give the linemen some help.

"Then we go ahead and look at the best possible matchup we can get. Are they gonna line up and take their best defender and put him on what we think is our best receiver? Sometimes you plan all week that they'll play what we've seen off the tapes but when the game starts, that's not how they're playing. You have to make the adjustments right there in the booth where I have my receiver coach [Mike Pope] and my line coach [Fred Hoaglin] sitting next to me.

"Sure, we know that might happen but during the week, we're figuring what's going to work off what we know. Bill likes to control the ball and that's a factor, because in our situation he's very active in controlling what we do.

"Now this Sunday we'd like to be able to line up, take the ball, and sort of nip at them with 3- and 4-yard running plays and not get greedy. That will put us into third down situations where we have the upper hand. We won't have all those third and 10s where they know we have to throw and they're pinning their ears back and coming right at Phil.

"I think against Minnesota I counted twelve situations like that or even worse. Well, now the poor guy is throwing from China. All he's doin' is pumping and nobody is there for him.

"It's a cat-and-mouse game when you play a team like this for the second time in a season. We want to bait them into doing what they think they want to do . . . like, say, they think they're holding our receiver in and we let 'em because instead we're coming with a counterplay.

"Last time they had a backer blitzing Meggett, so this time we'll let them and we'll counter with our two wide receivers and let Meggett be the bait. Now if they don't take the bait, we still have to have created a spot for Phil to go with the football—so Meggett's back in it then.

"Looking elsewhere we think [Lionel] Manuel is solid on shorter patterns. And if we see it right and do it right, we'll draw Eric Allen on him and we think Lionel can handle him.

"They're good up front, but the guy we'd like to attack is Simmons. We felt like he's the softest of the four but he's still a decent player, although a year ago down there we made some big plays over Reggie for big yardage. A lot has to do with the linebacker on Simmons's side. I don't think they'll change much this Sunday. They do what they do well and they'll play the intimidation factor as hard as they can push it."

In a strange way the attempt has already been set in motion.

11:00 A.M., press room

Buddy Ryan is on the speakerphone from Philadelphia and the regular Giants beat writers are clustered around it. Because of the tremendously physical defensive style which his team plays and his calculated public persona, which runs the gamut from belligerent to tactless, he is alternately viewed by the press as Buddy the Barbarian, Buddy the Crude, and Buddy the Ruthless. Parcells says that with Buddy, what you see is what you get, but that's not necessarily so.

He picks his spots like a veteran sapper laying out a mine field. Every public "feud" has its calculated roots and all roots lead to Sunday's game. He has no problem at all creating and then dropping a charade as long as it is related to a goal. And he's shrewd enough to inflate it when it comes along by accident, to keep it going for the particular football purpose it serves, and to act like it never happened when it becomes yesterday's tool. It is often helpful in coaching his type of team.

A week ago, on Thanksgiving Day, one fell in his lap which ultimately ranked as the biggest turkey issue of the 1989 season. Luis Zendejas, the Dallas kicker, who used to play for Buddy and Philadelphia, was flattened by the Eagles' Jessie Small during a kickoff. Zendejas started toward Ryan at the sidelines. Afterward, he claimed that four or five players and one coach had warned him before the game that Ryan had put up a two-hundred-dollar bounty for the man who could knock him out of the contest and five hundred dollars for anyone who could do the same to Dallas quarterback Troy Aikman.

What actually happened was that Zendejas made a kicker's effort to block Small, which is to say it was not very effective. In so doing, he lowered the upper part of his body, leaned into Small, and took the blow on his helmet. Once the ball is kicked, the rule book says that kickers become players—although most of them don't much perform like they are. Small's hit set large bells to ringing inside Zendejas's skull.

All hell broke loose.

Zendejas called a press conference and threatened to sue. Buddy wondered rhetorically why he would put a bounty on a kicker he had cut simply because he didn't kick accurately enough, inferring that, the way Zendejas had kicked for him, the last thing he wanted was to get him out of the game. Jimmy Johnson, the rookie coach whose Cowboys were on their way to finishing this season with the most losses in the franchise's history, was more than happy to find something other than that to talk about. Then Ryan verbally went to work on him, too. The league office launched an investigation. The writers were now asking Buddy to expand on the incident.

"I don't have any comment on it," Ryan said. "You hear that macho stuff everywhere. When somebody makes a big deal out of nothin', the league has to check it out, but when all the marbles are in there won't be no question about who was the clown. We play the game the way it's supposed to be played.

"I told you I want to talk about the Giants. You don't wanna talk about the Giants. I'm sick of that bounty stuff. Let me tell you something, what's important this week is if you want to beat the Giants, you gotta block Lawrence Taylor. If you want to beat the Eagles, you gotta block Reggie White."

"Well," somebody asked, "would it help you if Lawrence didn't play?"

"I don't know. I think he'll play. They say he pulled a hamstring against us last year, but then he turned around and played pretty good the next week against New Orleans."

It winds up being not much of an interview. The writers want to hear more about bounties. Buddy says a lot of things and sometimes he even contradicts himself, but despite the volatile appearance of what he says, the truth is that he never says anything without a reason. He helped keep the battle of the bounties alive for a couple of days but now it no longer serves its purpose—publicly.

From the standpoint of the Giants' players, it never did in the first place. Myron Guyton, the talented rookie safety who forced Parcells to break his own commandment ("thou shalt not start a rookie"), was Jessie Small's teammate at Eastern Kentucky. But the relationship goes much further back. He is Guyton's oldest friend. They were teammates as far back as junior high school in Thomasville, Georgia. Hot prospects on a hot high school team, they stuck together and went to Eastern Kentucky as a package.

"I saw the play on the tube," Guyton had said. "I know Jessie a long time. We were roommates and we still keep in touch by phone. I dropped by his home to visit the night before we played the Eagles down there. We had a quality coach and a quality program at Eastern and nothing like that ever happened. I'm quite sure it didn't happen here either."

In their heart of hearts the media aren't going to knock Buddy for this one. He filled a lot of otherwise white space in their newspapers for them through an otherwise slow-news holiday weekend.

12:00 noon, Giants' locker room

Bill Parcells is addressing the troops. He wears a blue wind-breaker and gray sweats. They had been told to report by 11:30 and, with the exception of Simms and Taylor who had arrived early for treatment (Taylor has left for new X rays), most of them had milked the last seconds of free time, arriving as close to the deadline as possible. Reyna Thompson uses the free time to get his car fixed. Clearly, life goes on.

But just to make sure, the coach is on a search-and-destroy mission. If they are to have any success at all this Sunday, he has to eradicate any more talk and any more thoughts about what happened in San Francisco on Monday night. After giving them the minute-by-minute practice schedule, he goes after the task at hand.

He tells them pretty much what they expected to hear. The Eagles are the team they must beat. The winner will surely take the division title. Lawrence Taylor is out (that one raised a few eyebrows, although Al Groh has already spoken at length with Johnie Cooks, telling him that he is going to have to move to outside linebacker), and that Simms is a probable. Finally he gets to his bottom-line purpose.

"You made a valiant try against San Francisco. That's what you're supposed to do. You don't get any medals for trying. You get paid to win in this league and you lost."

Then the quarterbacks prepare to meet with Erhardt while the rest of the group has a special teams meeting. In the training room, Ronnie Barnes is on the phone checking out the problems in ordering a special brace for Taylor, who has unusually small bones in his foot. Parcells wheels and starts to walk down the corridor beneath the stands and down to the press room for a chore he doesn't normally mind as long as he can challenge them now and then. But his mind, at this instant, is filled with only one thought: Is Lawrence going to be able to do it?

As he walks out the door, the sign over the doorway reads Individuals Win Games but Teams Win Titles.

Across the room on the wall next to the training area is another sign which reads Blame Nobody. Expect Nothing. Do Something.

The coach knows that if Superman has to put away his cape on Sunday and emerge from the phone booth as plain old Mr. Taylor, those mottoes will get their strongest test.

12:30 P.M., press room

The joint is packed. Because it's the Eagles with first place at stake, television and radio have suddenly discovered pro football in the City. There are enough crews to film the original *Exodus*. Writers up from Philadelphia, still photographers, and the regular beat men form a human U with the coach sitting in a chair at its foot. Jonas Salk never drew a crowd like this for a progress report on his week at the office. There are roughly a dozen daily newspapers with a man assigned to the ball club. Their ranks are swelled by the columnists, who do not attend regularly. On Sunday, Parcells will get all of the above, more television, more radio, and as many as two additional reporters from each of the local papers, as well as the visiting press.

But he sees the locals on a daily basis from the time the team reports to its preseason training camp. He knows their names,

their writing styles, and the approach to news each of their pub-
lications takes. They don't know it, but the difference in newspaper styles fascinates him. He ties that directly to his relationship
with his father.

"When I was a kid," Parcells will tell you, "we had a lot
more papers in New York City and my father would explain to
me that a story that appeared in the *Journal-American* wasn't
handled in the same way as the same story appearing in, say, the
Herald-Tribune. He explained to me that you had to understand
that if you wanted to get to the truth."

Another thing they don't know about him is the fact that despite his passionate involvement in a world of Xs and Os, the
written word intrigues him. "I was an assistant coach up at West
Point and each summer, there was a group, some of our coaches
and writers like Red Smith of the *Herald-Tribune* and Tim Cohane from *Look* magazine, and Willard Mullin, the old cartoon-
ist, which took over the commandant's bungalow at Bull Pond
for a two-week vacation.

"So one day I see Cohane out on the raft, and I swim out to
him and I haul myself up and I say, 'I want you to do me a favor.'

"He's reading this book and he's kind of a sarcastic guy anyway, so he looks at me and just grunts. Then I tell I want him to
teach me to write.

"Now he grunts again, but I'm persistent, so he says, 'All
right, go swim back and go in the house and write me something
about Bull Pond.'

"So now I'm really into it. I'm back there with a pad and a
couple of pencils and I mean I'm really into heavy thought. I'm
writing about the woods and the sunrise and the mist on the lake
in the morning and all that stuff. Now I'm really excited. I go
back out to the raft and he starts to read it. And every few
paragraphs he gives that same grunt or he says, 'My God,' or he
just shakes his head and I'm crushed.

"Now he says to me, 'Why do you come here?' And I tell him

that I have a good time and I like the people. So he rolls over and says, 'Go away and don't come back until you write about that.'

"So I did, but the best I could get out of him was a 'Well, that's a little better.'

"Now years go by and I'm the head coach at Air Force and I'm going to Boston to play B.C. He's putting out a New England sports magazine so he calls me up and wants me to tell him about my team and I tell him I have to go to practice but I'll write him a letter. 'Well, make sure you get everything in,' he grunts.

"So I write him—and this is great for me—I write a letter which says,

> Dear Tim:
>   My team is slow and very friendly.
>   Signed, your friend,
>   Bill Parcells.''

The coach knows a lot more about who writes what and the style in which they write than most of the regulars think. Now he sits down and looks at the faces around him before he speaks. The strangers do not matter. It is the regulars and talk of Taylor which he has to be careful about.

"What about Taylor?" is the first question.

"He's out."

"Out of the game?"

"No, out of town. Of course, he's out of the game. I talked to him today and he didn't think he could make it. His ankle is swollen and he can't walk. You want an honest appraisal, I'd have to say he's out of the game."

"Same ankle for Simms?"

"Yeah. Now I'm not saying Simms is out of the game."

"Coach, about this bounty thing," which inevitably comes up, "how would you feel if they put a bounty on your punter (Sean Landeta)?"

"I'd be real happy."

The room breaks into tremendous laughter because the regulars know the relationship between the two has been caustic. Then Parcells stops laughing along with them and says, "Now, come on, we're just jokin' here. That's not for publication."

Another bounty question and Parcells counters with "Now, come on, fellas, you tried to get me into this thing twice and I told you I'm not gonna do it. This is an aggressive game. People hit each other. Sometimes guys get hurt. That's just the way the game is. We wouldn't even be talking about it if all these accusations hadn't come up."

Someone wants to know about Simms and the key interception in San Francisco. "Look, he was completely healthy going into the game the other night. He still ran out of the pocket after he got hurt. He could have run that one out of there, too."

He tells them that Cooks will play outside and Pepper Johnson will pick up Cooks's inside duties. When they press him about whether or not Johnson will pick up some of Taylor's duties, he steers the subject in another direction.

"This is the division championship game. The players will play. You know it's not like there's a dance after the game that we're waiting for, and if there is, I don't have anybody to take. Maybe I'll call Kathleen Turner."

After the laughter, someone else asked, "Are you still mad at Meggett?" Two weeks earlier, after a strong game against Seattle, the punt returner had gone into great detail about what he had done, as had another rookie, tight end Howard Cross. Parcells was irritated because rookies rarely play major roles on his teams and when they do, he's still of the school that first-year players should concentrate more on being seen on the field than heard in the locker room.

"I never said I was mad at Meggett. You said that. I just said he's not the team spokesman and he's not."

"Are you talking to him this week?"

"No, I'm not talking to him."

"Are you talking to Kathleen Turner?"

"Hey, listen, guys," he says over the laughter. "I just used her as an example. I don't want to get any letters from Kathleen Turner. Gimme a break. I just used her as someone I'd like to take to a dance. I take Mrs. Parcells out, you know."

"I can see it now," a guy interjects, "*USA Today* lists Parcells's top five dance dates."

Laughter fills the room again.

They talk about whether the backup quarterback, Jeff Hostetler, could replace Simms if needed. They talk about the weather ("I wouldn't mind if it's cold, blustery, and snowing. Why? Because I like it when it's cold, blustery, and snowing"). They talk about the Eagles' defense. They talk about the practice schedule. But nobody mentions Taylor's ankle again.

12:30 P.M., locker room

The squad has begun to break down into specialized meetings and Ron Erhardt is talking with Simms, Hostetler, and Jeff Rutledge, the third-string quarterback. Later, they will go over detailed specifics of the game plan, making modifications each day as a result of what the coaches learn from watching daily practice tapes and from the input of the three quarterbacks themselves.

Player by player and position by position, Erhardt goes through the Eagles' defense. He reminds the three of the coverages they will have to throw into and the various defensive fronts Philly will show them. Then, using the game plan, he lays out the first- and third-down situations the Giants hope to employ.

"Reggie White," he reminds them, "is the big-timer up front but I don't have to tell you that they have other people who can hurt us there and all of them like to bring a lot of heat to the quarterback. And just remember that all four of them can bring it. Now we might think there's a hole somewhere in their secondary but we have to remember one thing. As long as those four guys down front are coming, they make whatever else is behind them that much better.''

At the same time, Romeo Crennel is meeting with the troops to review the kickoff and kickoff return duties for special teams they will develop against the Eagles' style. Reyna Thompson has evolved his own technique for dealing with such meetings. He does not focus on the player he will have to confront; that will come later this evening when he takes the tapes home. Instead, he tries to put his finger on the other team's general ebb and flow.

"I sit there and pretty much listen to what he's saying about them," Thompson says. "I try to be like a dummy and let my eyes go to the spot he's discussing. That way, I get the whole feel of what they're trying to throw at us. The Eagles have a lot of guys on short drops and attacks. Basically, they use an I'm-tougher-than-you kind of approach. No finesse. I mean, they won't drop back and look you off and then another guy nails you. What they say is I'm better than you so here I come and I'm gonna whip you. I like it better that way. I'm just gonna go for the guy who hooks me first, whip him before he can whip me, and fight through to the ball carrier.''

Meanwhile, back in the trainer's room, Ronnie Barnes has just received a call from the hospital, where Taylor has gone to have a more sophisticated form of X ray done, an MRI, short for magnetic resonance imaging. The patient is placed on what amounts to a conveyor belt that carries his body into a cylinder where the pictures are taken.

"What's wrong with the guy you sent us?'' the technician asks.

"What do you mean?''

"He's so nervous, we're having a hell of a time getting him into the cylinder."

"Be gentle with him."

"Why?"

"Because he's Lawrence Taylor."

"Oh."

1:00 P.M., press box hospitality lounge

When Timothy J. Mara, a legal bookmaker, sportsman, and entrepreneur, paid five hundred dollars for the right to establish a National Football League franchise in New York in 1925, his son Wellington was nine years old. It was hardly an overnight success. Wellington (who ultimately took over the football end of the business while his brother, the late Jack Mara, handled the financial affairs), remembers well the days when the Giants played before thousands of empty seats in the Polo Grounds while standing off a number of challenges, beginning with an upstart league headed by a hustler named "Cash and Carry" Pyle, who had signed the spectacular Red Grange as his bell-wether.

From the clubhouse of the Polo Grounds, young Wellington had trained his field glasses out the window and across the Harlem River to nearby Yankee Stadium, where Pyle's New York team was playing on the same day as the Giants. "Don't worry, Pop," he told Old Tim. "Nobody's watching them either."

Today those same Giants, playing in the Meadowlands, fill more than seventy-six thousand seats each week and have a waiting list for season-ticket vacancies of sixteen thousand names. Season tickets are rarely relinquished. It would take flood, famine, and the kind of pestilence never seen before on the continental land mass for that list to be accommodated.

That isn't all that's changed. On the basement level of Giants

Stadium, a modern television editing studio goes full blast throughout the season. Each practice session is taped. Game footage of other teams is available. Tony Ceglio, the head of video operations, supplies video outtakes of offensive plays, defensive plays, and even composite reels of individual pass receivers' moves.

"Back in 1935," Wellington Mara says, "I shot the first game films we ever had. My parents had given me one of those old bulky Bell and Howell cameras for my birthday and I would climb up on the rickety press box roof at the Polo Grounds, shoot on Sunday, rush them in for special developing that night, and then we would show them at the hotel the next evening.

"But the coach was a rough, tough character named Steve Owen and most of the time he'd look at them for a few minutes and walk out, although he did show them in the locker room to the players. But it was so different then: no offensive and defensive meetings, a single scout named Jack Lavelle who would watch next week's opponent and come back with a written report, and a bundle of newspapers from the next opponent's town so Owen could study the game accounts."

Mara is having lunch in the Giants' press lounge. Once, before the eruption of the most famous family feud in all of professional sports, he was extremely active in the football end of this business. In 1969, at a time when the club had not had a winning season in five years, he was still working the coaching booth telephones along with the offensive and defensive assistants. When the Giants finally played their blood rivals, the Jets, for the first time in an exhibition game in New Haven, Wellington feverishly called a play down to the sidelines. Except there was one small problem.

Nobody picked up the phone. It just rang and rang.

Within a week, Allie Sherman, the head coach, was fired.

In 1978, this NFL showcase franchise reached its nadir. The

Giants were no longer merely awful. They were horrendous. Here they were in a magnificent new stadium, hopelessly disorganized, working on their third coach since Sherman and showing no signs of respectability, let alone winning.

Jack Mara, Wellington's brother and co-owner, had long since died and Jack's 50 percent of the stock (the Giants are one of the last enduring family-owned operations in pro sports) had been split among his wife and children. As the team continued to sink further into the quicksand of ineptitude, Tim, owning or representing an even 50 percent of the team, supposedly challenged his uncle for decision-making power. The feud grew so volatile that even the other owners were taking sides.

And in that year, the single most ignominious moment in Giants football history transpired. Ironically, it happened against the Philadelphia Eagles. On November 19, in the waning seconds of a game which the Giants had all but won, they were attempting to run out the clock. With twenty-six seconds left, instead of taking the ball and falling down to end the game, quarterback Joe Pisarcik wheeled to hand off to fullback Larry Csonka and tripped. Csonka's knee hit the ball, knocked it free, and the Eagles' Herman Edwards picked it up and ran it in for 26 yards and the winning score. It was the fumble that almost broke the franchise's back.

The rage that gripped the customers in that stadium was as ugly as it was passionate. Never before had a crowd turned against a home team like this one did. Within a week fans were organizing opposition. Management kept coach John McVay but fired his offensive coordinator. It didn't help. On December 10, with the Cardinals in town, a small number of hard-core fans stood outside the park and burned their tickets. It got nobody's attention.

But during the game, a small plane suddenly appeared over the stadium, dragging behind it a banner which read, "Fifteen Years of Lousy Football."

Both Wellington and Tim Mara were traumatized. As angry as their intramural feud had become, neither man could conceive of this kind of embarrassment being heaped upon the glamorous franchise and family heirloom of the National Football League. The feud threatened to paralyze the franchise by season's end when McVay was fired with agreement from both sides. There was no coach. There had never been a general manager as such. Now there was no operation at all.

Wellington Mara agreed to hire a general manager, but he and Tim, who had stopped speaking, could not agree whom it should be. As the days dragged on through January, Wellington called a press conference to announce that since no agreement had been reached, he felt compelled to hire a coach.

"Then all hell broke loose," he recalls.

There are two versions of what followed but what is important here is not who won but that it was settled—and settled in a manner which today makes this one of the best-run franchises in the business.

Both agree that Pete Rozelle, then commissioner of the NFL, did indeed step in. He advised them to get a general manager and let the new man run the operation and hire the coach. Working off separate lists, the two interviewed several candidates jointly. They agreed on a talented man named Jan Van Deuser, who then worked in the league office.

"What I think happened," says Tim Mara, "is that he worked in the city and every day the papers were filled with this battle and he must have taken one look at the headlines and said, 'Who needs this? Thank you but no thank you!' "

The Maras went back to the drawing board. Rozelle told them he would draw up a list of five names for them. Wellington's version of what followed goes like this:

"I called Bobby Beathard, then the Redskins' general manager, and he endorsed George Young without reservation. I knew a lot about George because I got to read his reports at the scouting combine. George was then working for Don Shula down in Miami. So I called Pete and he said to me, 'What do we do now?' And I said, 'You make sure that George Young's name is on that list.' They [Tim and his advisors] didn't know about my telephone call.''

Meanwhile, Rozelle had independently contacted Ara Parseghian, the retired Notre Dame coach, who immediately declined. In any event, we do know that, for whatever reason, Rozelle did call Tim about Young. "I want you to choose between two people," Rozelle told him, "George Young down in Miami and Frank Ryan, the Browns' quarterback, who is now the athletic director at Yale."

"This was on a Friday and Rozelle wanted it wrapped up by Wednesday, which, incidentally, happened to be Valentine's Day. 'Think about it over the weekend,' Rozelle told him. "I had Frank Gifford check Young out for me. He called Bobby Beathard and got a glowing report," Tim says, "and he told me that he was definitely the man. Now we go on Wednesday to the Drake Hotel and we interview Young for two hours. We're impressed and we all go over to Rozelle's office.

"Now remember, the press conference is scheduled for that night. We're sitting there and we have to go over the new resolutions about how the club shall be governed and who has right of first refusal in the event of a stockholder's death and things like that. It also placed the football operation in the hands of whoever would get the general manager's job.

"George wants to go home and talk it over with his wife but Pete wants it settled tonight. So George is in the other room and we're dotting i's and crossing t's. The contract was for three years but the commissioner said, no, it should be for five. The money was X number of dollars but the commissioner said, no, you should make it this much more.

"Now it's like 7:00 P.M. and nobody is left in the league

offices, so Pete walks over to the typewriter and he starts to type out the press release for that night. It's probably the first one he wrote in twenty-five years and the last one he ever wrote. While he's writing, he suddenly looks up and says, 'This is a great way to spend today. It's my wedding anniversary.' ''

So peace came to this franchise and the truce has held together remarkably well. George Young got the job and hired a bright young assistant coach from San Diego named Ray Perkins as his new coach. When the Giants broke the huddle on opening day with their shirts tucked inside their pants, it was the most progress the franchise had made in fifteen years.

As for Young, he would be the first to tell you that in no way has either owner seriously attempted to interfere with his duties. Ironically, some of this is due to the simple fact that Wellington is far more interested in the football end of the business while Tim, like his late father, is primarily interested in the financial end. "I imagine it gets tough for George at times," Wellington says, "but he has very broad shoulders."

2:30 P.M., general manager's office

George Young is talking about David Meggett, the sleeper find among a very good crop from last year's Giants draft. He explains about the standard grading system of college prospects which has been effectively refined by Tom Boisture, the Giants' personnel director. He talks about grading the individual skills and characteristics position by position. Meggett, who played in relative obscurity at Towson State in Maryland, drew Young's personal attention because of the general manager's strong roots in the Baltimore area.

But the essential question is, how did he manage to get on the prospects list in the first place, considering that he is only five feet seven inches tall and listed at 180 pounds.

"Let me tell you a little story," Young says. "I remember in

April of 1968 I was working as an assistant in the player personnel department for Don Shula and the Colts and I went to Gram-
bling and there was a cornerback down there and he was a little
short. So I say to Eddie Robinson, the coach, isn't that guy a little
short to be playing corner and he just looked at me and said,
'George, speed makes him seven feet tall.'

"So that's my answer to what anyone says about Meggett's
size. Speed is a great equalizer and it's one of the few things that
will alter the rigid grading system.

"Now just before the draft Washington traded up ahead of us,
and for me, that was an 'oh, shit' because, first of all, Towson is
in their area and, secondly, they worked him out four times,
including the Saturday before the draft. But they wound up taking
a different cornerback.

"We thought we were getting the kick returner we desperately
needed but it turned out that once he made the team that way, his
skills opened up all other kinds of possibilities for him.

"But if you look at last year's draft, you have Myron Guyton,
who wound up starting at safety. You have Brian Williams, who
already is a player on the offensive line, and Bob Kratch, who
looks like he is going to be, Howard Cross, who gets to play a lot
at tight end now with Bavaro gone for the year, and Lewis Tillman, who should wind up being a hell of a back. Now that's not
too bad.

"The key for these guys is to prove early to the coaches that
even though they're rookies they have skills that must get into the
game. Listen, major changes in pro football don't come along
because some coach is a genius with a pencil. They come about
because he recognizes the talents in people. We used to have a
shotgun with Tony Galbreath as the other back. Now he was big
and it was clear that his job was to protect the quarterback first
and then do other things. But along comes Meggett and Bill
recognizes what he can do and suddenly it's a very different kind
of shotgun.

"Nobody changed the approach to linebacking and then went out and got Lawrence Taylor. Lawrence came in here and the coaches saw the talent and they said, 'OK, now this is what we can do with him.' "

The sermon has been delivered in the precise manner of a skilled educator, which is not surprising. Young holds twin master's degrees and taught history and political science. He also won six Maryland state championships during fifteen years as a high school coach. With the pros, his experience has run the gamut from offensive coordinator to director of player personnel.

The skills have shaped him as a contract negotiator, an organizer, and a manager.

"I can honestly tell you that dealing with the two owners here is a lot easier than most people think. I'd have to say there hasn't really been a serious problem with it."

The selection of Valentine's Day back in 1979 would appear to be straight out of central casting.

4:00 P.M., Giants' dressing room

Phil Simms does not practice. The ankle has been slow to respond to treatment and Jeff Hostetler, the number-one backup, took all the snaps from center this afternoon while Simms and Jeff Rutledge, the number-three man, shivered in the cold and watched. The wind, ripping through the empty concrete stadium, gives the cavernous place all the charm of a frozen-food locker. "It was one of those days," Hostetler says, "when you wish you could have worn gloves. I was having trouble feeling the ball."

Hostetler is twenty-eight years old and last year was the first time he took a snap from center in a regular-season game since he was drafted in the third round out of West Virginia in 1984. The waiting has not been easy for him. It never is in such situations. The emotional gap between what was in college, where he was a football hero, an academic all-American with a 3.85 grade point average in finance, and a Rhodes Scholar nominee, and what has been here for him thus far with the Giants is enormous—but he has handled it well.

The competition in this business is unlike that in any other. There is a bond born of the fact that in the aftermath of a single instant of physical contact, one career could end and another one begin. It is the reason why veteran Ottis Anderson, one of the oldest players on the team, will help a rookie who will eventually take his job—perhaps as early as next season. It is the reason that earlier in the day, Hostetler and Rutledge stood in their corner of the locker room and Rutledge shook his head in unspoken agreement when Hostetler asked a reporter, "Do you think it's fair the way they [the press] are down on Phil? They don't know . . . they don't understand all he's going through now."

When Simms went down on the sixth play of the Minnesota game this year, Hostetler replaced him and played the entire game against Phoenix the following week as well. The Giants won both of them. Parcells says that if Simms is not close to 100 percent this week, he will not hesitate to start Hostetler. It is unclear whether he says this to motivate Simms, motivate Hostetler, or perhaps both.

The coaches do not correct many things as the offense runs through its allotted plays from the new game plan. They are more interested in seeing the videotapes of the session tonight. Now the defense takes over and begins to work against the scout team, a blend of varsity and backup defenders who wear red tank tops over their practice jerseys with the numbers of the Eagles they represent across the chest.

As the defense works, Hostetler and Erhardt are discussing a problem that surfaced quickly when the offense ran a play called 62 wolf. The pattern calls for two wide receivers on one side with the tight end coming over on a short underneath pattern and another back clearing out to the same side. The object is to have four receivers on the same side, trying to "stretch" the corner (i.e., give the cornerback so much to do that he can't do anything). But the formation the scout team threw against them out of the Eagles' past-performance chart sets up an insurmountable traffic jam.

"I don't feel comfortable with it," Hostetler said.

"I'm not either. You might as well forget it," Erhardt responded, "because it sure doesn't look as though it can work."

Simms has disappeared for more treatment and then drifts off to watch some film of the Eagles. Hostetler cannot be sure whether he will have to start in his place. Just before he leaves, he picks up a tape of the Eagles game against the Chargers. He will study it at home this evening.

Meanwhile, across the locker room, somebody has neatly placed three large strips of white surgical tape on the floor in front of Johnie Cooks's locker at right angles so that, in conjunction with the edges of his locker, they form a large rectangle. The "somebody" was Johnie Cooks. "If you want to speak to me, men," he says to an approaching group of reporters, pointing to the tape, "you'll have to step into my office."

A gun, a whip, and a chair couldn't keep them away. Daily practice sessions are open to the press at Giants Stadium and today number 98 was running in number 56's spot when the defense practiced. It is a clear message to them that Superman just may miss this one.

As for Cooks, well, he's thirty-one years old and this is his second season with the club. Things did not quite work out the way most folks thought they would back when the Indianapolis (née Baltimore) Colts (he played in both cities) made Johnie their number-one draft choice. It is no secret that the Colts viewed him as a "locker-room radical."

Early last year, they released him and he was glad to go.

"I'd really much rather that Lawrence be here but it's not the way it is. We just gotta pick up the slack and go on. I'm no superstar. I just gotta go out and play football and if I can do that, we'll win the game. What's so great about it is that we get to play them here, and once we get them inside these blue walls it's an entirely different game with the fans we got. They're gonna get us over the hump. Right now I've been playing inside [linebacker] and now without Lawrence I'll have to go outside so I gotta go back and make all the adjustments.

"But I've been in this league awhile. I'm not impressed with starting. I just want a job. When I came on this team I realized I didn't come here to take anybody's place. I understood they wanted me to back people up. When you get to my age you don't worry about stardom and all that stuff. You just want a chance to play. Monday night when LT went down, if it had been a fight, I'd have been the main attraction. I was real emotional. When they took him off and I had to go in, I just wanted to hit somebody because of what they did to him. When you lose your leader like that, it really hurts.

"Now we get Cunningham and we got to figure something out for him. We got to treat him like he's the sixth receiver or the third running back because that's what he can become. Today I stayed after practice to get some extra pass rush work in. Look, this is the NFL. You just can't go out there and say it's all gonna come back to you if you haven't worked on it.

"Am I replacing Lawrence Taylor? Are you kidding? How you gonna replace Lawrence Taylor?"

Then he knelt down to untie his shoes and somebody said, "Headline: Cooks praying for Lawrence Taylor's return."

"Hey," Cooks said when the laughter died down, "if I could find a pill to heal him I sure would get it to him."

5:00 P.M., Bill Parcells's office

He sits behind the desk with his coffee, his pack of cigarettes, and a stack of phone messages in front of him. Earlier in the day he had received a call from a man named Charley Jarvis. "The best running back I ever coached," Parcells said, "and I'll bet you don't remember him. Army . . . twenty-seven games . . . twenty-seven hundred yards. He was a great player but in his junior year his fumble cost us the Navy game. The following year he damned near won it by himself. He just called to tell me he'd seen the game Monday night and I ought to put it out of my mind now. I told him, 'Yeah, just like you didn't carry that fumble around for a year until you could get to play them again.' He was a hell of a competitor."

He riffles the stack of messages and says, "Tony LaRussa [the Oakland A's manager] called. He heard about Taylor and he just wanted me to know what he had told his team when they lost [Jose] Canseco in spring training. Al Davis called. He knows. Yeah," Parcells said, nodding his head, "he knows what it feels like. Of course I spoke to Bobby [Knight], too. I called him."

When Bill Parcells first met Bobby Knight, their world was young and their work was a magic kind of challenge. Knight was the hot young basketball coach up at Army and Parcells was working as an assistant for his old high-school coach, Tom Cahill. It was a time when both knew where they wanted to finish but neither knew the route they would take to get there. You cannot live and coach at West Point for any significant period of time without being moved by it. The castlelike architecture, the tradition, and, of course, the athletes, like the rest of the student body, who project a maturity that comes with self-assurance.

The two naturally gravitated toward each other. The friendship remains a force in both their lives.

"Yeah, we talked about a lot of things. He has to play Kentucky this Saturday. And he pointed out that here we are—two coaches, with athletes, some of whom are about to play the biggest game of their lives—and here we are trying to find a way to motivate them. Makes you wonder, doesn't it?''

Then he held up a message from a former player named Kenny Hill and smiled.

"He was something. A black kid, comes out of the deep South, beats all the odds and goes to Yale, has a mind that's as sharp as hell and all kinds of ability. We're really friends now but he had a temper that was something awful. I called him aside one day and told him that if he didn't get hold of it, one day it was going to get him in a situation that was really going to be trouble for him. He understood what I was talking about. I used to tell him that when his playing days were over he had the kind of a mind that could make a difference in other people's lives.

"But every once in a while he'd get that look on his face and I'd get really pissed off and I'd yell at him to get that Goddamned trout-fishing look off his face and get his head into where it was supposed to be.

"He watched the game on television. He saw LT go down. He understands. Look, here's the message he left.''

Parcells held up one of those standard pink while-you-were-out memos. The message simply read, ''Forget about the trout.''

5:30 P.M., coaches' conference room

They are all there, assembled around the long conference table, and they have started to review the tapes of the day's practice session. Parcells walks in and takes the seat nearest the door. He is wearing a white Giants sweater, tan slacks, and coaching shoes. The tape continues to run as he begins:

"All right, here's what I did today. I told the press that Taylor is out of the game. Now just so you guys understand, he may not be out of the game. I didn't say that there was no chance he wouldn't play. I just said he was out. Like I said yesterday, I don't want the defensive players running in the dressing room and looking in his locker to see if he's gonna play this week. OK? I want them to think he's out and if he plays let 'em be surprised.

"Jumbo [Elliot] is going tomorrow. Simms is gonna try to go but I'll tell you I'm worried about him. If we play him and he's less than 100 percent he'll have cabin fever so fuckin' bad that he will not give us what we need to win. Does anybody disagree with that? Seriously, speak up. I think he'll try to but . . . but . . . I'd rather go with the other guy if that's the case. I just think we have to do some things."

"I think I agree with you," says Erhardt.

"Is Simms that badly hurt?" Leachman asks.

"Well, I don't know how bad he's hurt, Lamar, but if he can't move around and he don't have no confidence, we're gonna have one of them Rams deals (the Giants lost that one, 31–10, two weeks earlier). He could be throwin' the ball . . . just get it and throw it, and, you know, that ain't gonna beat these guys."

"So, . . ." and Leachman leaves the sentence unfinished.

"I think we'd be lucky to have Taylor," Parcells continues. "Mike Ryan thinks he can have him ready, though. I know Taylor will do everything he can."

"He'll be ready. If anybody can make it," Leachman says, "he'll make it."

"All right, now, here's what we're gonna do tomorrow and you ain't gonna like this, Lamar," Parcells says to Leachman, who much prefers physical practice time for his defensive line. "We'll meet at nine o'clock until 9:35. The team talk will take five minutes. Then 9:35 until 11:30 we'll meet offense-defense. That means you got an hour and fifty-five minutes to meet. That makes up for some time we lost. Then, 11:30 we'll go to lunch and twelve o'clock we'll have a walk-through until 12:20. Bring 'em back in and meet 'til 1:15. That gives you three hours of defensive meetings, Lamar, you got me. Then . . ."

As he details the rest of the schedule the coaches take notes. He outlines how the offensive and defensive time is to be used down to how many blitzes to work against and how many plays will be run. Then he returns to personnel.

"Now one of the big things we have to decide tomorrow," he says, "is where to practice [Eric] Moore. Look, Jumbo's gonna try to go on Sunday but tomorrow without pads we ain't gonna know how good he is. So you better give Moore half at left tackle," he tells Fred Hoaglin, the offensive line coach, "and half at right guard. Give [Brian] Williams the other half. I want to make sure that Maurice [Carthon] gets enough heavy work. Has [rookie Bob] Kratch learned that other stuff we talked about?

"I think Lionel [Manuel, who has a bruised thumb] will be all right. I'm gonna dress all three quarterbacks on Sunday. I don't know which two players we'll make inactive Sunday but we might have plenty of choices the way things are going. One more thing. I don't think practicing in pads is gonna do us any good. I know you don't like that, Lamar," he says to his defensive line coach, "but the way we're banged up and with the short week I think it will only set us back.

"All right, now put the offensive stuff from today up there." The videotape of practice appears on the monitor.

"Who is that at center? Oates?"

"Yeah," Handley replies.

"Well, isn't he supposed to—"

"Yeah," Erhardt says, "we ran it over. Somebody jumped offside."

"Hey," Parcells says, staring at the screen, studying the blocking scheme of the offensive linemen, "do we have some other kind of code word they can call out in that situation?"

"Yes, coach," says Hoaglin. "We already got it worked out because they [the Eagles] know all our calls."

"Hell, they ought to by now," Parcells says.

"If they double Meggett, we got to go to Zeke [Mowatt, the right end] here," says Erhardt.

"Well, they got to double one of 'em," adds Mike Pope, the tight end coach.

"What the hell is going on with this guy here?" Parcells suddenly asks, leaning forward as the next play jumps up on the screen. "I mean, can anyone tell me what he's trying to do?"

"Who?" asks Erhardt.

"Turner."

"Bad pass. Hostetler's fault."

"Oh. OK. I see now. Listen, how's that Runager kicking now?" Parcells asks of the Eagles' recently reactivated punter.

"About like in preseason," says Romeo Crennel, the special teams coach. "Not too great. He's trying to get a little more hang time."

Given the weather forecast and the treacherous Meadowlands wind, Parcells makes a mental note to see that Meggett is told about Runager. Under these conditions a punt just might decide this game.

Now the defense comes on with the scout squad emulating the Eagles' offense and Parcells begins a stream of consciousness monologue.

"You tell Banks to rough this guy up," Parcells says to Groh, the linebacker coach, as the scout team player—in this case it's Zeke Mowatt imitating Keith Jackson—breaks off a pattern in the middle. "You understand, Al? Rough him up."

"We're gonna jam the hell out of 88 [Jackson]," Belichick interjects, watching as the play is rerun.

But Parcells, whose mind is racing ahead, is looking for a basic running play with Keith Byars as the ball carrier; a play he knows the Eagles will try to make a living with on Sunday. "All right, there it is . . . right there. This is the play they're gonna run, fellas. John Washington [who has been playing for the injured starter, Eric Dorsey]. They'll pick him out again," warns Parcells.

"That's it right there," says Leachman. "Can we see it over?"

"Listen, Lamar, you better tell that Washington he's got to get his ample ass out there," Parcells warns. He's frustrated by the fact that he knows Eric Dorsey, a solid defender who led the team in tackles last season, has been out for several weeks now and will not be there when Byars hits that hole on Sunday, and Washington, who has played up-and-down football, will be. "Understand? Tell him to run straight down the line. He's got to do that, Lamar."

And then he sees another pass play and his eyes dart to Jackson (who is really Mowatt) and he asks, "You gonna have him overrun that tight end, Al?"

"Which one?" Groh asks.

"[Giants linebacker Steve] De Ossie," Parcells says. "Because that's what he's doing. See? See? Right there."

"We're trying to bracket Jackson with two guys . . . maybe get him out of the pattern altogether. And on this next deal here," Groh says as the scout squad running back slides out of the backfield on a pass pattern, "we're asking Cooks to do the same thing as you want Banks to do. If Byars is a problem, he's got to handle him."

"Let me ask you a question," says Parcells, pondering all the attention being given to Keith Jackson, the multitalented Eagles tight end. "Do you think we ought to put Banks to the tight end side all the time?"

"Well, we talked about that," Belichick says. "But—"

"I'm just talking about trying to get a little more pressure on him," Parcells says. "Johnny Washington can't chase him down. Cooks can't chase him down. [Leonard] Marshall will have a hard time chasing him down. At least Banks might be able to chase him down."

"Well," Belichick answers, "we talked about that. One problem you got is putting Cooks and Washington on those left-side runs, which is where they ran against us last time. The ratio was 17–4. We might have a little problem there."

"But they might change their minds without Taylor in there."

"Yeah, but if you put Cooks and Washington over there and Banks and Marshall over here," says Belichick, "there's not much doubt where they'll go. I know where I'd run if I were them," he adds, clearly referring to Cooks and Washington as the weaker set.

"Well, here's what we do," Parcells says. "You just tell 'em to be ready and a couple of times during practice, tell 'em to do it. You with me, Al?"

"What you're saying," says Belichick, "is that in passing situations, be ready to flop 'em but not on the run."

"Yeah," Parcells replies. "And if—wait a minute. What's this? What's going on with Collins? What's he doing pouting around out there? Why is he twisting like that?"

"He says he hurts."

"Well, then why wasn't he in for treatment?"

"I don't know if he was," Belichick says.

The rest of the sequences flash by to the end without comment, and then Parcells suddenly says, "All right. I don't want a word about Taylor. He's out. Everybody got it?"

Then the offensive and defensive staffs head back to their separate meeting rooms. Their evening is far from over.

8:30 P.M., Bill Parcells's office

"Today," the coach is saying, "I told the team after practice that I was tired of hearing about the Eagles because they had never beaten anyone or done anything of any significance. I said all they did is win one division and lost the first playoff game. There's a lot of guys here who have done more than that.

"I said I'm just tired of hearing about 'em and the way they do things. I don't really care whether they received it or not as long as they knew my mind was completely on Philadelphia. That's all I cared about today. That immediately puts all the other things away. If you don't watch it, the press will come in and start talking about the San Francisco game and I want their minds on the Eagles."

There is, of course, no question where his is.

"I got a better chance to win without Simms than without Taylor," he suddenly says, not knowing whether he will have either one. He will agonize over those options all the way home.

9:30 P.M., West Paterson, New Jersey

Erik Howard is thinking about the Eagles. "They have a pretty basic offense," he says. "No fancy blocking. Technique at its best. That's a coach's dream, to be able to put our guys against your guys—gladiator stuff. You think about a game like this and you wish you'd never put yourself in this situation [the San Francisco loss]. I'm sore all over. Thank God we didn't wear pads this afternoon. My back is sore, my knee is sore, my hand is sore, and I have bruises on both feet."

11:00 P.M., Franklin Lakes, New Jersey

Phil Simms did not practice. In the morning and in the late afternoon they treated him with ice and with electric stimulation. He and the trainer discussed using a knee brace on Sunday—not so much to help the knee but rather to keep the ankle stiff so that he cannot turn it with a false step.

The last thing he is aware of before sleep finally comes is its steady throbbing.

3. THURSDAY, NOVEMBER 30, 1989

6:30 A.M., coaches' wing, all-purpose room

Phil Simms and Lawrence Taylor are not the only football players in Al Groh's life who are nursing injuries this week. Al Groh's son, the quarterback, is going to miss the big game. Just like Mark Bavaro and Joe Morris, who have spent most of the year in rehab for disabling injuries, seventeen-year-old Michael Groh has dealt with his share of ice packs and exercise. Michael, the quarterback on the Randolph Township, New Jersey, high-school football team, has recovered from a knee injury well enough to dress for Saturday's state championship final against Morris Hills Regional. But he's not expected to play.

"The kid has a great attitude," Groh says. He has just filled a Styrofoam cup with coffee and is about to join Belichick, who already has both his notebook open and his tape machine rolling down the hall in the defensive coaches' conference room. Michael's coach has told him that if they get in trouble and he needs a stronger arm at quarterback, he may use him. But the chances are Michael Groh won't play. He understands that he's only a junior and he knows that his time will come next season.

"After practice on Saturday I'm going back home and pick up

the family and we're heading out to the game," says Groh. "Randolph has won thirty-eight straight and the state title is at stake. They expect five thousand people."

And then he laughs.

"How many crucial contests can I take on one weekend?" Groh is in his first season as linebacker coach with the Giants. He has held assistant jobs at Army (where he spent one year on the staff with Parcells), Virginia, North Carolina (where he helped recruit and coach Lawrence Taylor), Air Force (where he rejoined Parcells, who was a head coach for the first time there), Texas Tech, and the University of South Carolina. For six years, Groh was the head coach at Wake Forest, where he became the second-winningest coach in the school's history.

Of the eleven assistants on Parcells's staff, four—Groh, Erhardt, Pope, and Leachman—have been head coaches at one level or another during their careers. It appears to be no accident.

In terms of coach-player contact, this is a difficult week for Groh. With Lawrence apparently down, some of the Xs and Os on the blackboard are more accurately portrayed with question marks. Although the short week has allowed for only one day of practice thus far, Groh has already begun to reinforce the switches by seeking out individual linebackers in the locker room and dropping a thought, a hope, and sometimes a warning here or there. He spoke with Carl Banks about the added responsibility for big-play leadership if Taylor doesn't play.

"Carl Banks is a remarkable person," Groh says, "and because Lawrence is on the same team, a lot of people don't know just how good a linebacker Banks is. You have to remember that Lawrence came here three years before Carl and had that spectacular season as a rookie. So in a real sense he's always been in Lawrence's shadow. They're two very different types of player. The way I like to explain it is that if they were Indians back in the early days of this country, Lawrence would be the emotional war counselor who leads the braves into battle. But Banks would be the tribal chief. When you have two personalities like that in one linebacking corps, it's a coach's dream.''

Then he spoke to Pepper Johnson, an inside linebacker, who has some outside linebacking experience and who may have to reinforce Cooks if the patchwork plan doesn't work. Johnson normally plays part-time as weakside inside linebacker on the regular defense and the left defensive end in the sub (third-down pass) group. Now, on Sunday, he'll become full-time inside linebacker and retain his sub duties. The net result is that unless hurt, he probably will be on the field for the entire game, which poses something of a problem since the whole idea of the sub defense is that it's supposed to throw fresh bodies into the assault on the quarterback.

"It's the way it has to be,'' Groh tells him. "You're all we have now, so you have to get it done.''

And on Wednesday night, just before he went to sleep, Pepper Johnson kept telling himself, "It's the Eagles. It's the kind of game that you want to be in. It's like back in college when Michigan would come to town and Coach [Earl] Bruce would tell us that this game should be the reason that we came to Ohio State. It's the kind of game you want to play. It doesn't matter about the changes. It's a game where you have to do whatever it takes.''

Then there's Cooks himself, an early season pickup a year ago, an outside linebacker with a reputation as a blitzer at Mississippi State which did not quite hold up in the pros. Cooks knew the Giants picked him up as a fill-in but never in his wildest imagination did he dream that one day he would be called upon to replace Lawrence Taylor in the biggest game of the year.

"You want to shut down lanes against Cunningham,'' Groh was saying now. "You want to make sure that he doesn't scramble out of there and go. So we have to be careful. We don't have

Lawrence Taylor here—we have Johnie Cooks. Now, he's playing out of position and he's a guy whose strong suit isn't rushing
the passer in the first place. If he were one of our very best rush
guys he'd have been on the sub team [used on third down and in
obvious passing situations] from the start of the season. Yesterday I was explaining to him that the first thing he has to do is give
it a shot—give it a shot because he might be able to do it—but if
the first shot doesn't lead you to believe that you have a chance
to get him, then don't fall into the trap of continuing to rush so
that they can do what they want to do.

"All you have to do is watch the way the Eagles operate and
you'll see that they like to push rushers out of their lanes to give
their number 12 [Cunningham] a quick escape route. So I told
Johnie he has to do something about that, and if he sees he can't
get to the quarterback, then he has to stay cool, use his head, and
make sure that his lane is closed.

"Look, they're a team whose production is basically a production of people. What they have is a nice scheme and they
execute it perfectly. They give the ball to three guys—
Cunningham, Byars, and Jackson—Carter on that touch pass
down in the red zone. Basically the other people are role players.
I can't look in his head but I'm willing to bet you there are times
in the huddle when he says to, say, Jackson, who's their best
receiver, 'Look, I'm going to throw you the ball whether you're
open or not so you better get there.'

"There's no mystery about who he wants to hit. On first downs
the order is Byars and Jackson; on third downs it's Jackson and
Byars. And in the red zone, it's Carter and Jackson. We're gonna
double Jackson a lot. If you could really shut down Jackson, they
could never put together an 80-yard drive.

"At this point in his career, he [Cunningham] is not beating
people every week with his arm. But he is beating people every
week with his running. That's a constant for them right now. You

look at our first game with them and you'll see that's how they beat us.

"I explained to Johnie that if he takes his shot and if he doesn't get there, then he has to calm down, break it off, and get under control because the guy's still coming and you can count on it. Now you do that against other quarterbacks like, say, Joe Montana, and they have the time to sit back there and pick you apart. But this guy isn't going to do that. He's an unconventional quarterback and to apply conventional defenses to him is going to be a mistake. Unless you have dynamic rushers, you can't just put four guys up there and tell them to go. You know the saying about what happens to those who fail to acknowledge the lessons of history and how they are doomed to repeat it? Well, we have enough history to know that's not the way to play him.

"You know what this would be if we played it that way? It would be a repeat of the old Trojan horse. That's what this guy does to you. He Trojan horses you to death. He can be a quality thrower which makes you say, 'Bingo! This guy's a good passer, so we better rush the passer,' which you have to do to some extent. But as soon as you do that, they jump out of the horse and kill you.

"Now if Taylor were to play . . ."

And then he moved off down the hall to join Belichick and Leachman.

6:50 A.M., Bill Parcells's office

It is suggested to the coach that he is a little late. "I'm not late," he says. "I've been sitting in the car for twenty minutes listening to the radio. Stan Walters [the ex-Eagles tackle] has a sports show in Philadelphia and he was analyzing this game. He said pretty much what I've been saying all along. He thinks the weather is going to be important. So do I."

Outside the wind chill is down around ten below but the forecast for later in the day calls for temperatures in the mid twenties, making it a far better day than Wednesday when Reyna Thompson thought he was going to die in the wind at practice and said, "Please don't tell me I'm getting used to this. I'm from Texas. I don't ever want to get used to this." Erik Howard had trouble generating feeling in his toes. But Parcells, who has already made his first call of the day to the weather bureau ("976-1212," he says automatically, with less effort than a man reciting his own street address), is smiling. The long-range forecasts for Sunday would please the Abominable Snow Man—winds gusting up to forty miles per hour, wind chill perhaps twenty below. Possible snow.

"This is the kind of game," he says, "where we cannot fall too far behind this team. I mean if it gets, like, 20–3, then forget it. It's over. I'll tell you, at this moment with Taylor probably out, I'm more worried about the defense. Our defense has handled them before, sometimes very successfully, but we had more athletic people," he says, thinking back to his Super Bowl team. "Marshall, George Martin, Taylor—guys like that. And when you have three or four more athletic guys that compounds Cunningham's problems.

"Hell, we started the mirror and we've been doing it for four or five years and sometimes very successfully. But when the athletic ability of your athletes deteriorates, then you have problems.

"We picked this guy [Adrian White] as the mirror because we didn't have any choice with the injuries. We could have put [Greg] Cox in there but then we'd have to use White to cover Byars and we didn't feel like he could do it—he's too stiff . . . just not quick enough. He [White] is more of a straight-line speed guy so we're gonna try to get Cunningham to go in a certain direction and Adrian knows what direction we're trying to push him and he'll try and close on him at an angle from there.

"We're out of people so it has to be him. And then we get hurt on the sub unit because instead of bringing in fresh bodies for that play, most of them are already in the game. And if it doesn't work, there's nothing else we can do. The only alternative plan is if we have Taylor and I can't count on that.

"I don't know. . . ." And then his voice trails off as though it were struck by the frailty of all those Xs and Os when you cannot program the human factor into any of those equations. "The whole damned thing will probably come down to one play here or there, a tipped pass, something. If it does, well, then it's our turn."

On November 20, 1988, Lawrence Taylor blocked an Eagles field goal try in an overtime period but the ball bounced into the hands of a Philly lineman named Clyde Simmons, who picked it off the artificial turf on one bounce and ran 15 yards for the winning touchdown. In their next meeting down in Philly earlier this year, Cunningham dove toward the goal after faking a hand-off. Videotapes show that his knee touched the ground before he reached the goal line. But it was ruled a touchdown and the Giants lost. Thinking back on those two games earlier this week, Erik Howard may have voiced Parcells's thoughts when he said, "It's like they've got a deal going with some evil spirit."

"We really outplayed 'em both times," Parcells says. "Go back to the Monday night game down there last year. That's the night Bavaro dropped the pass and we should have won. Then we play 'em up here later in the year and they're ready to quit. We got 'em beat. Then Simms gets hurt. We had a lead and we're driving for another touchdown and it's over if we score. We don't. They win. But we really outplayed 'em.

"Then this year, down in Philly, we easily outplayed 'em most of the way and then we just let 'em have a couple of things that got 'em back in the game quickly. We even had an additional opportunity at the end that would have put us in position for the field goal to win it, but we miss the receiver and Simms throws an interception instead—a guy open and he tries to throw it to the wrong receiver.

"In 1986, we were killers in the last part of that season. That Giants team would have won both of these games. But this team goes down to Philly and we got 'em hanging on the ropes and we just can't knock 'em out.

"And now it looks like we have to go without Taylor."

8:00 A.M., special teams coaching office

Romeo Crennel is looking for a seam. This is not to be confused with the previous week or the week ahead. For Crennel, whose players call him Rac, much of life is spent looking for a way to create that critical opening within the armor of a wall of flesh just wide enough to get the quickest six points in the game. He is forty-one years old and holds a master's degree from Western Kentucky, where he once captained the football team. As a coach he worked at Western Kentucky, Texas Tech, Ol' Miss, and Georgia Tech. He came to the Giants in 1980, a year before Parcells, and is their special teams coach. Only Belichick (eleven years) and Leachman (nine) have been with the organization longer.

This year, he is like a kid with a new toy. Its name is David Meggett. Because the Giants stuck with a "safety-first" policy on punt returns ("you can't return it if you can't catch it" is not necessarily illogical) and couldn't find the burner they needed on kickoff returns, they had not returned either for a touchdown since Crennel joined the staff.

Going into this season, it had been seventeen years since they stuck one in the end zone off a kickoff (Rocky Thompson, 92 yards) and thirteen years since they got one off a punt (Bob Hammond, 68 yards). Now, with David Meggett, it has simply become a question of when and how many.

"When I first saw him in the preseason minicamp for rookies, I knew that he had return ability, but there was no pressure on him. Then in training camp, he was making the catches and that's the first thing you have to do. In the preseason, we really knew what we had. I was a little concerned in his first exhibition game when he lost balls in the lights and he fumbled. Maybe I should've been more concerned, but it's a long time since we had a guy back there who could break a game open.

"And that's what he has going for him.

"On Sunday, we might be able to do something because of the guys they have covering on kickoffs. They don't have tremendously fast guys covering. Their kicker [Roger Ruzek] is not going to be able to get the ball into the end zone too often, so that means we have something returnable. With a returner like Meggett, if you can kind of halfway get him started, he's gonna make some people miss and you'll have a chance to have a decent return.

"The Eagles use a strong side and a weak side. That doesn't mean more people or fewer—it means a division between physical strength on one side and their smaller, faster people on the other. They try to do what we call directional kicking—kick it to the side where their stronger people are. They usually kick to those guys and then have the smaller, quicker people on the back side so that if you try to outrun the strong-side guys, they still have their speed on the back side and they can run a guy down and make some plays.

"We're gonna try to return the ball to their quick side"—that is, they'll see where they line up and make the determination.

There's no mystery to the theory. What it boils down to is pitting Meggett against the smaller people and counting on his speed and his moves to get past them into the open field.

But the prototype special teamer is not the returner. Rather, he's the man who makes the blocks or beats the blockers and makes the tackles. In situations when the Giants are kicking off, you will find him at L-3.

That's three spots to the left of the kicker out toward the sidelines. His name is Reyna Thompson and he has made himself a serious special team force. Like all special teamers he dreams of the day when he will have other duties. Thompson has been used in certain pass defense situations but for the most part, his duties are limited to special teams on kickoff coverage, punt return, punt coverage, and the field-goal-blocking unit.

"He's a good athlete. He's got strength," says Crennel. "He's also got other qualities which you can't create through coaching—speed and desire. That's why he's here. He's a major asset to us and, let's face it, playing mostly on special teams still beats the alternative." The alternative?

"Yeah, like sitting at home and watching the game on television."

10:00 A.M., trainer's office

The walking wounded have already received their morning treatments and Ronnie Barnes is between appointments. "Simms will practice today," he says, somewhat relieved. "He won't be 100 percent but he's a lot better and this morning he told me it felt pretty good. Of course, some of that is brought on by Bill's announcement that if he [Simms] isn't 100 percent, then he'll start Hostetler. All of that gets involved in my job, too. Sometimes it makes it easier. Sometimes it makes it more difficult. If a player's stressed out then he's on me about 'Is there anything else I can do? I gotta play.'

"Manuel's thumb has come around. The others ache but they should be ready, although we do have a problem with Jumbo's ankle. Zeke [Mowatt] was in the training room for a wrist contusion. I didn't know he had it, but I shouldn't have been surprised to see him. He's been in the training room every day since the season began. I think he thinks he's on a trainer-maintenance program. Lawrence was still a major, major problem this morning. We're battling our asses off to get him ready if there's any way possible. Right now we've listed him as out for Sunday's game.''

Under NFL rules, the coach has the option to upgrade that to questionable or doubtful later in the week.

"You have to know Lawrence to understand that," says Barnes. "In his mind he still thinks he can put the Superman outfit on and surprise the world. He loves it like this. He's convinced he's going to play. Yesterday, he asked about DMSO. He can't get it from us but I wouldn't be surprised if he went over and got some from the track. I'll know because I'll smell it."

DMSO (dimethylsulfoxide) is an antiinflammatory which is used very successfully on horses. Barnes says it has been experimentally approved for humans in a couple of states. Rubbed on the skin, DMSO is absorbed directly into the bloodstream. Some years ago, Warren Moon, the Oilers quarterback, who suffers from tendonitis, used it when he played in the Canadian Football League and continued to use it when he came to Houston. The substance has a side effect that gives the user's breath an odor which has been charitably compared to rancid garlic. This caused some of Moon's teammates to look at him strangely in the huddle. Barnes does not stock it, recommend it, or use it. In his heart of hearts one suspects he subscribes to the Jewish Grandmother Theory in this matter: It probably couldn't help, but then again, it probably couldn't hurt.

"Today he told me, 'I want to play. Let's do whatever we have to do. They don't need me at practice. They need me Sunday. Bill says I have until 11:45 on Sunday before I'm really out.'

"I brought in a podiatrist yesterday and he brought a number of braces with him but they didn't seem to help. He told Lawrence he'll probably be sore for about three weeks and he didn't expect him to play. Meanwhile, Dr. Warren sent him for more X rays. We want to make sure the ankle isn't broken.

"It's tough to get an appointment for an MRI so I sent him over in the middle of practice and I got my ass in trouble with Bill, who wanted him to watch the new stuff we put in just in case. So Bill called me over on the field and he said that it was the stupidest thing I had ever done in my life. He says, 'How is he gonna be ready for the game if he doesn't know the plays? Couldn't you get it done this morning or later tonight and what's the difference anyway? If he can walk on it, he can play and if he can't, he can't.' So I took it all and said, 'Yes, sir . . . yes, sir . . . yes, sir.' And he said, 'Don't yes-sir me! Can he play Sunday or not?' I said, 'Well, I think there's a chance' and he said, 'You think there's a chance? Do you think I need to know?'

"Now, this morning, LT was in here for an hour. He got electric stimulation, ice, and massage. He's taped and he seems to be walking better. He's not on crutches. We ordered a brace from California on Tuesday from a place called Action Dynamics Brace Company. It was supposed to be here by now but we're still waiting. That's just as well because if it were here, he'd talk me into fitting him and he'd put it on and try to run and probably set himself back to where there was no chance. If you ask me, I'd have to say it's no better than fifty-fifty and you have to understand that Lawrence's fifty-fifty probably is somebody else's thirty-seventy.

"Later in the day [but sure as hell not during practice] he'll go for more tests—tomograms and a CAT scan—at St. Mary's Hospital in Passaic. You can't take chances. Not just because it's Lawrence. We would handle it this way for any player. To our organization it's a game but to the player it could be a career.

"Meanwhile, he's still taking Endocin, but the way I have to deal with Lawrence is like a child. You give him ten pills, he will lose them in his car or forget which pants pocket he put them in. He's so preoccupied with everything else. Every day I have to say, 'Lawrence, did you take your pill?' and he'll say, 'No, I lost them' so I have to say, 'Put this in your mouth now. Take this one home with you. Make sure you take it tonight.'

"But I'll tell you one thing that might surprise you. Nobody on this team is going to get a shot of painkiller so he can play. Bill won't permit it. He's very strong about that, always has been. Players come here and they can't believe it. But it's a firm rule here. Dr. Warren feels the same way as I do and Bill simply won't permit it."

10:00 A.M., locker room

The team meetings began an hour ago. Parcells spoke to the entire squad for about five minutes. He told them they wouldn't practice in pads. "You are going to be physically ready for Sunday. I'll see to that. It's up to you to get mentally prepared. You have to study these films no matter how many times you've seen the Eagles." He did not exhort them, cajole them, or inspire them. He knew they were wondering about Taylor. He knew they were unsure about Simms and he knew that the linemen and linebackers were still healing physically from the nightmare in San Francisco. This was Thursday. Parcells is a master at pacing. He will begin to strike the emotional chords tomorrow.

The quarterbacks and the special teams broke off for private meetings. Most of the others went to the trainer's room to have their ankles taped. In the quarterback meeting, yesterday's doubts about 62 wolf were translated into today's modifications. Erhardt asked them how they thought that play and five others would work if the quarterback were to take a five- instead of a seven-step drop.

The concept was to get the ball off quick enough to frustrate the Eagles' rush line and to prevent the secondary from having the time to handle those plays as the scout squad indicated they could on Wednesday. Simms, Hostetler, and Rutledge agreed they preferred it.

The quarterbacks would meet three more times before the long day ended. One of those meetings would be devoted to the hunt for something careless in the Eagles' alignment. Erhardt and all three of his quarterbacks have been watching the Eagles for a long time and nothing major has yet to develop over the past several years. But the personnel changes, so you keep on looking.

"You watch," says Hostetler, "to see if anybody on their side is going to tip off what they're going to do. Sometimes you can find something like that. With some defenses, one or two players will tip off whether it's a man-to-man or a zone just by how they line up. Sometimes you can get a read on the defenses by the cornerbacks—whether they're up or off. Sometimes you can tell when a blitz is coming because some teams have a designated blitzer, and if he lines up in a certain spot you know it's coming."

This last review is as helpful to the quarterback's life and limbs as it is to the game plan. If the defensive play call puts an extra man into the rush and the quarterback doesn't change the play with an alternate audible call, he could find himself with an unblocked pass rusher on his hands—and ultimately on his chest. Football people refer to such a defender as the "hot man."

This often sets in motion what coaches call a "sight adjustment." With a hot defender bearing down on the quarterback, there's no time for the affected receiver to run his pattern. He must see the quarterback's problem, break off his pattern, and cut to the spot the defender has vacated and the quarterback must throw to that spot. The whole process is as much feel as it is sight.

"Sometimes," Parcells will tell you, "you have to make sure that they aren't trying to bait you. Sometimes, the blitzer will come and at the last second a safety may move in there and beat your guy to the ball. This is something that the Eagles do."

But pretty much as expected, nobody picked up anything new in today's film session.

When the full squad broke into offense and defense, the offense watched tapes of Wednesday's practice. In another meeting room, the defense was doing the same thing but the defense got an extra added attraction.

It began routinely enough. In the back of the room, Erik Howard is watching himself in action against Brian Williams, the Giants' 300-pound first-round draft choice, who is trying to imitate the Eagles' center, David Alexander. There are times when Howard fantasizes about squeezing his 268-pound nose tackle's body into a 195-pound frame and roaming the secondary intercepting passes. But like Cyrano seeing the profile of his nose on the wall, reality sets in on Howard. "The fact is," he says, "God gave me this body and I was destined to be a nose tackle."

Now Belichick is discussing what the Eagles generally do in the red zone and the Eagles themselves are flashing across the screen, doing it to the Giants in the taped version of their last meeting. Erik Howard is concentrating on the task at hand, and by his own account doing "reasonably well up until they busted Leon."

But from his seat in the rear of the darkened room, Howard thought he heard the sound of music. A moment later, he *knew* he heard the sound of music. What made it so eerie was that it was coming from Leon Cole's head.

Leon Cole was a free-agent defensive end out of Texas A&M who gained a measure of fame as a high-school star in East Orange, New Jersey, not far from Giants Stadium. He's a member of the Giants' development squad—a sort of lineal descendant of the old taxi squads on which teams stashed players who probably would never play for them or anybody else. Development squad players attend all meetings and often work with the scout team.

"When the lights go out," Howard says, "Leon usually pulls his sweatshirt over his head and goes to sleep. To break it up today, he smuggled a Walkman radio in under his sweat clothes. So I heard the music. Rob White's sittin' next to me and he hears it too. Belichick sits in the opposite corner of the room so I didn't think he could hear it.

"All of a sudden, Belichick goes, 'Hold on a second. Will someone please turn on the lights?' So I kick Leon—and he doesn't move. Then I kick him again—and it's too late. The lights come on and suddenly, Leon's fumbling desperately inside his shirt and instead of turning the volume off, he turns it all the way up and blows his earphones off his head. Then Belichick shoots poor Leon a look."

The room rocked with laughter. For a moment, you got the feeling that twenty guys were going to jump up and holler over to Leon, "Thanks. We needed that."

11:00 A.M., locker room

The special teams are discussing Eagles punt returns in their unit meeting. Up on the screen the Eagles return team is putting on a return. As it forms, Romeo Crennel is taking it apart, player by player and block by block. As always, Reyna Thompson is listening intently, following the narrative and not allowing himself the luxury of focusing in on those individual Eagles whom he will meet up close and ungently.

"Now watch Gizmo [Williams, the return man]," Crennel is saying. "See—he's kind of a darty runner who will try and make you miss. He isn't going to try to run over you."

Now the tape backs up and Crennel is zeroing in on the Eagles at the line of scrimmage. "Pressure," he says. "They try to put on a lot of pressure . . . more than a lot of teams who will just try to hold you up and then peel back to set it up for the returner. Now we can't miss any assignments here. We've got to block and hold the blocks longer because of the pressure. If we can't do that, then we'll have to bring Reyna or Adrian [White] back in from the outside to help out."

Thompson is thinking, "Adrian and I have to get down there faster . . . a lot faster to secure that guy and bring him down. The troops are gonna be busy back at the other end keeping those guys off Sean [Landeta, the Giants punter]."

Now Thompson's looking at Gizmo and he's thinking, "He's no Brown," meaning Ron Brown, the devastating Rams punt returner. But then Crennel is saying, "His longest this year was 20 yards and, in case you've forgotten, it was against us."

Thompson hasn't forgotten.

He missed a tackle on that sequence.

11:30 A.M., locker room

Lamar Leachman has gathered his defensive linemen together to discuss the third-down pass rush. Like most of the Giants' staff, Leachman has coached in a lot of places, primarily in Canada and the South. But back when something called the World Football League jumped off the drawing board with more ambition than money and immediately landed on its nose (within two years, two teams, including the league champion Birmingham Stallions, had their equipment impounded by the IRS), Leachman was the defensive coordinator for the New York Stars.

They played their games before thousands of people disguised as empty seats in a crumbling municipally owned stadium on Randalls Island in the East River off Manhattan under a lighting system that looked as though it were powered by a large safety match. But no matter where he coached, Leachman's direct style of approach hadn't altered much from what he himself had heard as a linebacker-center at the University of Tennessee.

His players say he is the master of the coaching cliché. They may laugh at the maxims, but they must get their attention because they discuss them so much. "Toughness always wins the battle," Leachman is fond of saying. "Every time you do not chase the ball, you give the other team a better chance to win. Every time you pass up a hit you give the other team a better chance to win. Whatever the mind can envision, the body can achieve. Life is like an echo: you get out what you put in."

On the practice field, it is his voice that comes across the loudest.

In today's meeting, there is a genuine determination. In their first game against the Eagles down in Philadelphia earlier this year, the Giants' defense had played its guts out as the red zone shrank around them. At one stage it took the Eagles five plays to get a touchdown from inside the 5—and they needed an interference call and a highly questionable judgment call by the official on the goal line where they had apparently stopped Cunningham.

As Leachman talked about the third-down pass rush and what Cunningham has done to rushers in situations like that, there was complete attention. It wasn't so much that they needed reminding. It was more the fact that each of them had finally begun to believe that number 56 would not be busting through and over blockers to help bail them out.

12:00 noon, press room

The press contingent is the largest of the year, swollen by camera crews dispatched by TV assignment editors who have tapped their infallible unidentified sources (they read the news-papers) and discovered that there is a big game Sunday and Lawrence Taylor and Phil Simms may not play. The regular beat men and columnists from about a dozen New York area news-papers and a full press and television brigade from Philadelphia are all there as well.

Parcells generally likes these sessions more than he admits because of the repartee involved with the regulars. But today there are too many faces, too many cameras, and too many prob-lems which he is not prepared to fully discuss. He hasn't decided on the answers to his own pressing questions, much less theirs.

The coach is wearing a blue Giants windbreaker and tan slacks. As he walks to the head of the oblong work table and takes a seat, somebody asks, "Is Simms taking treatment?" and Parcells half-smiles and shoots back, "No, he's goin' fishin'."

But he is reasonably relaxed under the circumstances. When he is asked about Elliot's ankle and whether he'll practice, Parcells replies, "Yes, Jumbo is out of dry dock and Simms will practice, too."

"And Taylor?"

"As of now his chance to play is zero."

"Could that change?"

"I can only tell you what I know."

A barrage of questions follows about Simms, who has told Parcells he can practice today, and the coach holds up his hand and says, "Let me explain something here, fellas. My choice is not whether Simms can play the game or not, you understand? That's not the point. The point is how functional can the guy be. That's the point. I'm not deciding whether he's gonna dress for the game. That's not the problem. Whether he's functional is and I have to determine that in practice by watching him perform. If he performs in a way that makes me think he won't give us the best chance to win the game, then he won't start."

"Is this an opponent where mobility becomes more important than anything else in your quarterback?"

"Only if you don't block 'em."

"They're pretty tough to block."

"Hey," Parcells pauses for an instant and then says, "that's life in the big city."

Another question about Simms and another about Taylor and then he says, "Look, fellas, you're makin' too much of this— what if this guy . . . what if that guy—it's out of our control. We're playin' for the division championship. That's the bottom line. That's it. Who's there? Who's not there? You can't dictate those terms. You play the guys you got and hope that you can get it done and if you can't, then it doesn't make any difference. And if you do, it doesn't make any difference."

Somebody brings up the Buddy Ryan bounty issue again and while Parcells will not get involved in that, he does say something about the whole concept of cheap shots.

"I don't know of very many football players who go out there with the intent of deliberately hurting somebody. You try to teach your team to be aggressive within the framework of the rules and I think that's the way 99 percent of the players in this league play the game. You know when you have fifteen hundred guys there's always gonna be some perverted sick bastard out there who doesn't adhere to them. Every once in a while you see one of those guys around. You know who they are. It doesn't take long to take 'em on. They don't last too long. Their life expectancy goes down.

"Hey, we had a couple guys here like that I had to talk with and straighten out.

"Anything else, fellas?"

"Yeah," a reporter says, "we were talking with [Bjorn] Nittmo yesterday after what happened with Zendejas and the Eagles and he says he would like some physical contact."

"He said that?" Parcells asked. "My Swedish kicker said

that?'' And then the coach laughs and shakes his head and asks: "Listen, how many guys we got in this league—1,500? Well, that means there are 1,495 guys he can't lick."

"So who are the five he can whip?'' another guy asked.

"Well, two of them have to be that little five-foot-three kicker at Cincinnati, what's his name [it's Jim Breech and he's really five-foot-six), and my own punter."

For the second straight day, he leaves them laughing.

1:30 P.M., on the field

The Giants are spread out on the stadium floor while the wind slams against the empty stadium seats in repeated gusts. For a brief time, the unexpected sunshine takes some of the curse off the cold, but then it sinks from view beyond the stadium wall and the refrigerator cold sets in. Meanwhile, Ed Wagner, Jr., the equipment manager, has lugged a stationary bike out to the edge of the practice field so that Lawrence Taylor can pedal and watch practice at the same time.

All through the offense and defense run-throughs against the scout team, Lawrence peddles ceaselessly and ferociously. "When is he gonna stop?'' one of the reporters asks the frozen group around him. "I don't know,'' one of the others replies. "I think he made a vow not to quit until he gets as far as Peoria."

The offense is working on a list of offensive plays from the game plan. Simms is taking the snaps against the scout team. Earlier in the quarterback meeting, Erhardt had said that Phil and Hostetler would divide them.

As the offense works against the scout team, those regular defensive players not involved in the drills stand around and watch. "That's the hardest part,'' Howard says, "because you've loosened up and now all the sweat you worked up starts to freeze in the wind."

Basically, both offensive and defensive practices go fairly smoothly. Harry Carson, the ex-middle linebacker who retired at the end of last season and is now a sportscaster, walks over to talk with Lawrence. As Carson talks and Lawrence continues to peddle, several reporters rush in that direction. "Get the hell away from him," Parcells shouts across the field. That ends that. Now the punt team is practicing returns and coverage. Each time Landeta punts, Thompson talks to him about the wind and where Landeta thinks the ball will go.

The winds of East Rutherford, New Jersey, have been kind to the Giants this season. They have a will and a personality all their own so with each Landeta practice kick, Thompson studies the trajectory of the punt. "I want to see," Thompson says, "the way he's kicking, whether the nose of the ball is dropping soon enough or whether it's staying up there. The timing makes a big difference—especially on this field."

After practice, Johnie Cooks gets a volunteer to help him on his pass rush, which he will need much more on Sunday on the outside than he would normally utilize as an inside linebacker. At the other end of the field, Thompson and Meggett pair off. Renya gets the ball downfield and Meggett tries to run it back and beat Thompson's coverage and tag. It is something they do a lot of. But today the wind is impossible. After three sequences, they surrender and return to the locker room.

3:00 P.M., general manager's office

The rapport between the general manager and the head coach is not what either would have you believe it to be. In moments of stress, the coach will say, "George doesn't have a clue about our real problems at this end of the building [the coaches' planning sessions] and how we have to make decisions about personnel each week." Then he will hastily add "he doesn't have to."

Next, Parcells will say that Young is too conservative, that he has a kind of "it's better to do nothing than make a mistake attitude." He explains what he calls the general manager's conservatism by saying, "engineer mentality . . . schoolteacher mentality. He is more comfortable putting people into groups—coaches, scouts, players—he sees them as stereotypes."

And having said all that, he will immediately add the key and most candid part of his analysis: "Because he's very conservative, he makes me rethink why I want to do certain things. I have to admit that's valuable. You want to take risks but you don't want to be a fool. I guess the balance our thoughts create is a good thing for this franchise."

Now Young is talking about his coach. At the end of the 1982 season, Ray Perkins dealt what could have been a crippling blow to a franchise that was just recovering from both intrafamily warfare and artistic ineptitude. Having brought the team from spectacular ineptitude when he was hired in 1979 to a wild-card playoff berth by 1981, Perkins advised Young near the end of the 1982 season that he planned to return to the University of Alabama, his alma mater, as head coach the following year.

It is arguable that, contracts being contracts, Young could have taken serious action but the last thing he wanted was a head coach who didn't want to be there. Despite having signed a new deal recently, Perkins had always made it clear that the Alabama job was something he had wanted and would continue to want.

To compound the agony of this confusion, 1982 had been a season of labor unrest and the players' strike cut the schedule to just nine games. With what a general manager has to do during a season like that, the coaching change could not have come at a worse time.

But if George Young is conservative by nature, then it must be said that his very conservatism enabled him to save what the franchise had already accomplished. It also got the head coaching job for Bill Parcells. He had no intention of organizing a search for a new coach. The day all this happened, Young said, "The whole future of this ball club rests with the notion of continuity. We started something. We have a system. We cannot go back to square one. There are guys on this team who survived some horrible seasons. I'm not going to have them wonder whether they are going to have to start all over again and go through the same kind of thing. Bill Parcells is solid. As defensive coordinator, he coached half this team. I see no reason why he can't coach the other half."

Young immediately called two separate press conferences for the same day. He wanted things to move along with as few distractions as possible. No two-a-day sessions at the old Palace Theater were ever staged any more smoothly. Within hours, the press had been shuffled into the upstairs press lounge to say good-bye to Ray Perkins and then shuffled into the downstairs press room to witness Parcells's promotion. With the Eagles still to be played in the final game of the season (Perkins's Giants would win it, 26–24), Young designated Parcells as coach-in-waiting.

Given the history of the recently settled war between the owners (settled in Giants matters but not with each other), it could have been an explosive situation. Totally overlooked in the confusion was the fact that each owner expressed total confidence in their general manager by not attempting to interfere with his decision.

Today you can speak with either Mara and the one thing they'll agree on is that, no matter who engineered it, George Young's step into the Giants' hierarchy created the viable franchise that exists today. And Young's selection of Parcells was a critical part of that process. He does what a general manager is supposed to do; he does not interfere with the coaching process. He lets the coach coach.

"We have to get the personnel and I have to try to make sure we stay within the discipline of our own grading system when the draft rolls around," explains Young. "Sometimes that's not so easy. What helps is that we have good scouts and good personnel people. But you have to bring the coach in on this. It makes no sense to force a player on him and give him a player he doesn't want to coach. And regardless of how much you like a guy, you draft him, sign him, and then turn him over to the coaches. You can talk but you can't lobby. If your judgment is right, the coaches will eventually see it.

"But it takes time. Meggett made the big jump because he had that returner's skill which caught their attention and got them to thinking about how else to use him. But we've got some kids here who have not been able to force their way into the lineup and that's all right. Lewis Tillman [rookie running back] is a good example of that. But he'll get there. So will [Bob] Kratch [third-round pick]. We know Brian Williams [first pick] is a player. Howard Cross [sixth pick] has had to play more than we thought with Bavaro down. Myron Guyton is a starter. And you know what Meggett has given us. All told, that group isn't too shabby.

"Bill is a coach. He'll complain like a coach. He'll see traumas the way a coach does. It doesn't bother me. That comes with the territory. Philosophically, we agree about what makes a football team. We agree that the starting point is good, tough defense and the ability to run the ball. For the rest of it, I take him as he is.

"He's a coach," he adds, inferring that that explains everything else.

As for Young's territory, it has some broad brush strokes behind it. The coach does not have to sit down and negotiate contracts with players—or to be more precise, their agents. Young and assistant general manager Harry Hulmes do. Young sees things in players' demands that Parcells cannot because his think-

ing is colored by immediate needs and production. The job is
brutal because each time a salary negotiation stalls, much of the
press castigates the Giants and Young. What most people don't
consider is the fact that Young, according to Tim Mara, is trying
to balance the second-highest payroll in the league. The very
conservative background that Parcells cites when talking about
Young is what makes Young an excellent general manager.

3:30 P.M., ticket office

Wellington Mara remembers vividly when the Giants waded
through a sea of red ink which, on several occasions, threatened
to critically wound the franchise. It is fairly common knowledge
among insiders that the salary bidding during the desperate war
between the NFL and the short-lived All-American Conference
cost the Giants dearly. What is not so well known is the fact that
in the battle's aftermath, the Giants' franchise came perilously
close to folding and had to borrow a large sum of money from a
private source in 1949. The amount of the loan is unknown but it
must have been a healthy chunk for its time because, according
to Tim Mara, the family did not get back all of that portion of the
stock which had been put up as collateral until the early 1960s.

Tim Mara recalls that in 1965 when New York City radio
station WNEW expressed interest in airing the Giants games,
Tim's father, Jack, told him: "We are going over there and we're
going to tell them the price is $50,000." Jack Mara was amazed
when he got it. Measure that against the millions of dollars involved in radio and television rights now.

Today, people are dying to see the Giants play the Eagles. But
then people die every week to see the Giants play. "My mother
[or father or brother or aunt or uncle] is dying," the phone calls
go, "and her last request is to see this game. You have to help
me." It is remarkable the number of times the same people can

die. If you didn't know better, you'd swear they weren't people
but cats with nine lives. Sooner or later, everyone in the ticket
office fields such calls.

There are 76,891 seats in Giants Stadium, including the luxury
boxes. All are sold out. The waiting list for season tickets has
16,000 names on it. By the time you finish reading the list, it will
probably have more. "Each day people call to ask why they
haven't qualified," says a secretary named Pat Emanuel, "and I
have to explain to them how long the list really is. One day a
couple of us looked at the tiny number of people who do not
renew and we figured out it would take about forty years for the
bottom name to get to the top. Sometimes people call and put
their children's names on the list. That's all right if the kid is five
days old and even then he'll probably be a grandfather by the
time he gets his tickets."

Jim Gleason is on the telephone. He has been the Giants' ticket
manager since 1973. Before that he was with the Yankees for
twenty-five years. It doesn't matter what time of the day you drop
by, it will be an out-bet that he'll be on the phone. The job is
massive and it deals with every aspect of the box office. On game
day, Gleason will arrive early in the morning. By actual count,
the Giants average fifty legitimate crisis cases on any Sunday:
"My wife washed my pants and my tickets were in it." "We had
a big fight at home and my wife tore up my tickets." With a click
of the computer, the veracity of the claimant and the seat loca-
tions can be confirmed. New tickets are issued at face value. A
refund is granted when the original tickets are located and returned.

At halftime, Gleason will add up the receipts, deduct the rent,
and draw up a statement for the Philadelphia general manager
showing precisely how much the standard visiting split of 40
percent comes to in dollars and cents.

In the outer office, John Gorman, the assistant ticket manager, is explaining that he is never alone at a cocktail party. "What line of work are you in?" somebody asks. "I'm the assistant ticket manager for the Giants." The mob that surrounds him and its requests are inevitable.

More than once, season tickets to the Giants have been bitterly contested items in divorce cases.

4:00 P.M., Giants' locker room

Pepper Johnson is waiting to see his old college roommate, Keith Byars. He is going to have to wait three more days. Within the past twenty-four hours they have exchanged messages with each other's answering machines. Much of the week, Johnson has watched Byars on film. But on Sunday, they'll be in very close touch—or at least Johnson hopes so. Keith Byars is the Eagles' bread-and-butter back. They will run him through quick opening holes on the inside. They will run him wide. And they will throw to him coming out of the backfield. Sometimes, when Johnson thinks about it, it still seems strange to him that he and Byars are playing against each other.

"I probably see more of the Eagles than I do of the Giants in the off-season because of Keith. I play basketball with them in south Jersey. I work with them at Keith's youth camp—Keith, Anthony Toney, Cris Carter, Andre Waters, Wes Hopkins, and Reggie White. I talk to Keith every week.

"You know I'm a talker and I talk a lot of bad trash to taunt guys from other teams on the field, but with Keith, I'm just jokin'. I mean, I might make a good hit on him and help him up and say, 'You gotta run, you gotta run,' and he'll say, 'I know,' and then wink.

"The thing is that when I first came here we beat the Eagles regularly, and so Keith was always coming into this locker room because I had the press and it took me longer to get dressed. Now

I find myself going over to his locker room three straight times. I got to use this game to bring him on back in here.''

Across the room, Myron Guyton, the rookie safety, is expecting company on Sunday, too. Guytons, Guytons once-removed, and Guyton in-laws have created a ticket demand from him that won't quit.

"My sisters Betty and Ann are coming up from Georgia along with Betty's husband and their two kids. Then I got two cousins from upstate Connecticut who will be here with their two kids. There's two more coming and I don't even know where they're coming from.''

Guyton is the biggest surprise of the season for this team. If David Meggett was a sleeper, then Myron Guyton was Rip van Winkle in shoulder pads. He was only an eighth-round draft choice out of Eastern Kentucky, primarily because nobody could figure out what he was. At Eastern, they played him at linebacker, at safety, at rover back, and at a variety of other spots. Every time a pro scout showed up he was playing another position.

But Belichick scouted him and liked what he saw enough to convince Parcells to fly down and look at him. After an hour of drills and lunch with him, the Giants coach decided if they didn't have to bypass some blue-chipper and he was still available late in the draft, he wanted him.

After he made the selection later in the year, Parcells wandered into the stadium press room where a beat reporter immediately asked him, "What's a Myron Guyton?"

"Somebody who's gonna make this club," Parcells shot back.

At twenty-two, Guyton and reserve tight end Howard Cross are the youngest players on the team. Nobody expected him to learn so fast, but by the second game of the year he was a regular. For a long time he felt overwhelmed. On Sunday, only the thirteenth professional game in his brief career, he will play in the biggest game of his life—and he knows it. The thought of the number of Guytons who will be in the stands only adds to the pressure.

Belichick walks up to his locker with a videotape of the Eagles-Vikings game in his hand. "Jackson caught twelve passes in this one," the defensive coordinator says. "You better see as much of him as you can now, because you'll see a lot more on Sunday."

Guyton has already watched a half hour of Keith Jackson on his own today. Earlier in the year when he played against them in Philadelphia, the talented tight end was injured and did not play. That only compounds his urgency today. "I don't think I had a good game against them down there. Nobody said much about that but it bothers me. I played terrible. I looked at the films and I was too deep sometimes. It was almost like I was scared.

"I'm not gonna let it happen again."

Guyton will spend tonight with Keith Jackson live and in color.

4:30 P.M., Giants Stadium parking lot

Lawrence Taylor, wearing his long black coat, black loafers, and no socks, walks slowly to his car, his ankle heavily taped and his limp barely noticeable. He is on his way to St. Mary's Hospital in Passaic just up the highway for more X rays.

The general feeling among the medical staff, as confirmed by two previous sets of pictures, is that the tomogram he is about to take is routine. There is no medical evidence to indicate he has suffered anything more than a highly painful and serious sprain.

5:00 P.M., utility room, coaches' wing

The offensive coaches are having dinner. The table is a sea of cardboard containers and aluminum takeout pans. In a real sense it is the only time of the day when the pressure is off. So what do they talk about?

Football.

They are discussing a shift they have put into their red zone attack which is designed to confuse the Eagles defense, draw them offside, free up receivers, or goad them into calling an unnecessary time out to sort things through.

"If their guy jumps," Ray Handley asks, "can he [Simms or Hostetler] get rid of it fast enough?"

"They're gonna have to cover your receivers," Tommy Coughlin, the receiver coach tells Erhardt, "and then you got two guys left."

"Well, it'll be hell," says Handley, "if they adjust and we're the ones who get confused and we're the ones who have to call a time-out." And for the first time this week all the coaches are laughing.

"I'll tell you one thing," says Erhardt, trying to return to business, "I thought our scout squad handled that play pretty well against our offense in practice this afternoon. They covered it pretty good."

"The problem is . . . the problem is . . ." and now Handley is laughing so hard he can barely finish the sentence, "they were in the meeting when we put the play in."

"Those suckers," says Coughlin, as the laughter fades again, "are always trying to pull something."

"I'll tell you what," Handley, who coaches the backfield, continues. "My guys were all saying, 'Now wait a minute. The wrong guy is running the quarterback keep' "—a reference to the fact that Simms, who is far less mobile than Hostetler, was taking the snap when the play was called. "Is he [Simms] playing? Because if he is, I'm gonna wipe that play out. I'm not gonna call the signal for it."

"You know what Hostetler told me?" says Erhardt. "If I don't call that quarterback keeper if he's in the game, he's gonna be pissed. He wants to bet a hundred dollars he'll score.''

"Shit," says Mike Pope, the tight end coach. "I'll bet him a hundred. If he scores on that play I'll give him the hundred. Put me down for it.''

"Damn, this guy's loaded!" Coughlin hollers.

"Anybody else?" says Erhardt.

"It sure as hell would be worth a hundred to me if he scores," Handley says over the laughter.

"Tell you what," Erhardt says, "he's already got Rutledge bet. He went off on him so Rut bet him. Hostetler's convinced he can do it. You bet him," he says to Pope, "and Ray, you bet him."

"I'm seriously considering it," Handley says, "because it's easily worth a hundred dollars if we get a touchdown on that play.''

All Hostetler has to do now is score.

Well, not all. First he has to get into the game. At the joint staff meeting with Parcells, which begins in ten minutes, the head coach will confirm that Phil Simms will start at quarterback.

6:30 P.M., Bill Parcells's office

The evening coaches' meeting with Bill Parcells and the obligatory critique of the afternoon's practice session is over. The offensive coaches have done some homework on how to present their Xs and their Ys a little differently to the Eagles than the first time these two teams met.

In the Giants' terminology, the X is the split end and the Y is the tight end. Parcells is explaining the changes.

"Philadelphia is a team that [defensively] plays a lot of things—man-to-man things—and they're not really an intelligent defense. They can become confused sometimes. Now, they're gettin' better at it. When he [Buddy Ryan] first went there, they were always confused because when you formation 'em or move people or change people around after you give 'em a certain appearance they become confused and make mistakes and turn guys loose.

"There's a lot of ways to mix them up . . . motion to certain spots, for one. They switch off on people. We have to get 'em into a gray area. Make 'em indecisive on the switches. To do that, we have to spread out offensively. But when you spread out you become more vulnerable, so you try to pick the right time to do it. Field position pretty well determines it.

"But when you think about last game, there were too many times we threw to the wrong receiver."

Parcells has not mentioned Taylor since he sat down. But there is no way to avoid the subject. In their hearts, the players think he will play. In his, Parcells thinks logic says no. But Taylor is, well, Taylor.

"I don't know what he'll do if we let him play. I know right now he's just focused on three hours, what will it take to get through three hours of that pain. And I won't let anyone inject him. I don't believe in that.

"See, if he did get the doctor's OK, I'd have to look at him on Saturday and then we'd sit down and I'd ask him to tell me what he really thinks he can do. He's very respectful. Very polite. He's not gonna tell me, 'Well, I can do this or that,' because he might not be able to do this or that. I know him. He'll come up with some kind of proposition that he thinks I might agree to.

"You know, I been through a lot with this kid—a lot of things. With him, there's a lot more involved. The thing he responds to most is competition. He's easy to coach because he responds to competition. That's the easiest kind of guy to motivate. I did it to him this year, called him What's the Matter With because the press kept asking, 'What's the matter with Lawrence Taylor?'

"So I call him What's the Matter With and he still gets just as mad as he ever got and then tries to go out there and prove me wrong. Then he comes in the dressing room after he plays that great game against Minnesota and I'm talking to the team and he stands right up and before I can say, 'Nice going' or anything else he says, 'Well, they ain't gonna ask you what's the matter with after you see that film tonight.' See, he knows what he did.

"He's always said he wants to win two Super Bowls. You know . . . we're gonna win two. He's always said that when we're alone and neither of us knows how many more chances we're going to get. He knows it. I know it. And we each know the other one knows it. That's basically what's motivating him right now. He's an amazing guy. He is one of the few you'll ever meet who understands what a team really means. He's very bright. He knows a little bit about handling money and he's got some street smarts. The drug thing? We talked a little about it today. You want my honest opinion? He's come back so far I don't think he's going to throw it away.

"On strength of will I'd put him up against anyone I ever met. Just strength of will. Relentless. Focused. Zeroed in. He wills things to happen. That works against him in other things. That worked against him in his drug problems—'I can do this . . . I can stop this'—but I think he's taking the right steps to remedy that.

"Now if you ask me, I have to honestly say I don't think he can make it this week. Right now, structurally his ankle is sound. But he's got a lot of pain.

"Last year in New Orleans we were in desperate trouble. Simms was out and Lawrence had a shoulder that he just couldn't take a hit on. But he just kept hitting with it until the game was over. He was great. And we won. I told him after the game—I remember he was huggin' me and he put his head right on my forehead and his nose was right on my nose—and I told him,

'You were great tonight,' and he said, 'I don't know how I got through it.'

"I know what he's thinking right now. He just thinks he can will it to happen this Sunday. I know it because I know him better than anybody else does.

"I'm downplaying this injury in the press because I know what Buddy Ryan will do if I don't. He'll say, 'Oh, those crybabies up there.' He's just waiting for me to make a mistake that he can use. But he won't get it. He won't get it."

And then the talk naturally drifts back to the coach and the team that comes to town on Sunday.

"Buddy Ryan is a Neanderthal and he attracts Neanderthal players. Neanderthals can win certain kinds of wars, but they lose some they should win if you find a way to make them make enough choices." And across the hall, the offensive coaches are trying to create situations which force those kinds of decisions. One of the people they are hoping will serve as a catalyst in that situation is David Meggett.

Evening, various places

WOOD RIDGE, N.J.—Reyna Thompson is doing his homework. On the television screen, the Eagles are about to return a punt against Minnesota and in his mind's eye, Thompson inserts himself into the action in place of the Minnesota end. He sees himself spread wide to the left. The Eagles are double-teaming him with Eric Everett and William Frizzell. A moment earlier, spread wide right, he had imagined himself facing Sammy Lilly, an ex-Giant, and rookie Jessie Small.

This is the second time this evening he has seen the tapes. He watched them for an hour shortly after he came home. Then he returned to join a number of teammates at a hotel near the stadium where they gather each Thursday night for a Bible-study class. Tonight the group included Jeff Rutledge, Zeke Mowatt, Robb White, Mark Duckens, Eric Dorsey, Howard Cross, and John Washington. Now he's back home in his apartment, staring at the screen, lost in a number of thoughts. None of them have anything to do with turning the other cheek.

"The first time I watch, I'm looking for the strength. Like Eric might get beat at the line but he's a great effort guy. He'll come back, still hustle, and get in my face to try to give 81 a chance to run the ball a little better." Football players always talk in numbers; 81 is Gizmo Williams.

"As far as Lilly, one of his strengths is his ability to change pace. One time he would shuffle off. One time he would attack. One time he would angle off to keep the end guessing about what he'd do at the snap of the ball. Lilly hustled more, but Everett was a little better at sealing you off.

"What I'm gonna do is try to break free and get them behind me. Once I get directly in front of them, then I can hurt their pursuit because if they get to block me, they'll have to do it from behind and maybe we can draw the clip.

"I noticed they like to stab jam—one arm out, right at the shoulder, that's called a stab jam. I'm gonna try to use that to my advantage. I'm gonna slap at them. I'm gonna be expecting it. They like to let the runner get about two strides and then they stab and once that happens I'm gonna use my hands to keep 'em off me. I think I'll be able to accelerate and put 'em behind me."

It is 10:00 P.M. He'll watch the tapes one more time before he turns out the lights. Tomorrow morning, Thompson will get up early and look at them again.

RIVER VALE, N.J.—Jeff Hostetler is taking a break from football. After practice, he returned home, picked up his wife Vicky (whose father was his head coach at the University of West

Virginia), and drove into Queens to watch a taping of "Cosby."
Before the show, they met the star and posed for pictures with
him. The indications all day were quite clear to him. He is not
going to start and he is unlikely to play.

By 11:00 P.M., he was sound asleep.

RUTHERFORD, N.J.—Just like half of his own team and half of
the Philadelphia Eagles a turnpike away, Myron Guyton is watching tapes. "You have to study them over and over," he says,
"because each time you're looking for a different thing. I watched
these same tapes last night, too. Now I'm looking at the quarterback. I'm trying to see if I can learn anything from where he
looks . . . anything at all that can help."

WEST PATERSON, N.J.—A major crisis has just been solved at
the apartment Erik Howard shares with Jumbo Elliot. Howard
was unsure whether he had given the pizza delivery boy the right
directions. Then when the pizza arrived and Howard opened the
box, there was nothing but pepperoni on top of the cheese. The
peppers he had ordered never made it.

"If I had known that," Howard says, "I never would have
tipped him."

Logically, food gets a high call here. Jumbo Elliot is six-foot-
seven and weighs 305 pounds. Erik Howard is six-foot-four and
weights 268. Together they are capable of devouring any two
Chinese restaurants east of Shanghai on the same night. That they
have yet to succeed is not for lack of trying. They are not fussy
eaters, which is to say it is less important where they eat or what
they eat just so long they can eat when they want to eat. And
sometimes, the takeout containers take a little time getting out of
the apartment.

"We're not into the *Better Homes and Gardens* bit," he explains. As he speaks, Jumbo is asleep. The throbbing ankle is

giving him less trouble now but it's still bothersome. He will play on it Sunday with little complaint.

Much of the soreness which Howard has experienced has dissipated. But he will be in a half hour early again tomorrow for more ice—which he refers to as the "trainer's penicillin." This afternoon, he lifted for about a half hour in the weight room. Under the building pressure of the season's biggest game, each player, in his own way, reacts quite differently. Erik Howard will not think much about the Eagles as individuals tonight.

"I try not to think much about them," Howard says. "There's no point in getting too uptight too early. What happens with me is that this is only Thursday. I know that on Saturday night, everything will hit me. On Saturday night, I'll be into it and thinking about it, and then on Sunday morning the butterflies will be back.

"But tonight, it's not going to bother me. Tonight I'll sleep."

UPPER SADDLE RIVER, N.J.—Tomorrow morning, Bill Parcells will say he slept well. Generally, he does. After dinner, he sits in the same brown chair in the family room, which is where he goes when he wants to be alone. In the evenings he does not stay there long. He is basically a morning person and his body clock has long since set 5:15 for an almost automatic wake-up call.

Head coaches, as everyone knows, are loyal, trustworthy, cheerful, brave, and totally candid. But one suspects that no matter what he reports tomorrow, he will not have slept all that well tonight.

He has just received a telephone call. Lawrence Taylor's right ankle is broken.

4. FRIDAY, DECEMBER 1, 1989

6:00 A.M., Garden State Parkway, southbound

They were both still asleep when he nosed the big Lincoln out of the driveway and headed for Elmer's and the first coffee of the day. The big Colonial house in Upper Saddle River had begun to put on its game face the night before. The Parcellses' oldest daughter, Suzy Schwilley, who is married to the trainer at Temple University, is up from Philadelphia to see the game. Tonight, Dallas, the youngest, will be home from Gettysburg College for the weekend. Jill, the middle daughter, will probably stop by. All of them, along with Judy Parcells and Dallas's boyfriend, will be at the game on Sunday.

"The papers say," Judy Parcells had started to remark at dinner the night before, "that Lawrence and Phil—"

"Don't believe everything you read in the papers," the coach replied. Judy Parcells does not press the point. Like most wives of head coaches, she is a good soldier. By her own account, a long time ago her husband had told her, "Don't ask me and I won't tell you. You never know who you might tell by accident. This way, you can't tell anyone something you never knew in the first place."

She, like everyone else, will have to wait until the Giants' first defensive sequence on Sunday for the answer to her particular question.

The coach has already finished his coffee. Traffic was light on the parkway. The only sound he heard as he rolled down the window at the toll booth was the wind as it ripped through the car like a giant left hook and slammed against the unopened window on the passenger side. Now he begins to slow down for the exit ramp that leads from the parkway to State Highway 17. The sky has turned from coal black to a faint dishwater gray. Despite the weight of the big car, the bronze Lincoln has begun to sway slightly in the wind. Parcells does not need the weather report to tell him that what he hopes for at game time has already begun to happen.

The temperature doesn't interest him. The Eagles will not exactly be leaving the garden spot of the East tomorrow when they head up the turnpike to check into their hotel headquarters. And they are no strangers to either cold or snow. But the wind—the Jersey Meadowlands Wind—is something else. A gale, he thinks, would be very nice.

And then there is Lawrence.

After three different types of X rays since halftime last Monday evening, Parcells finally learned last night what he feared the most. The ankle is broken. But it is a peculiar type of break. As usual, nothing is quite what it seems with Lawrence. In layman's terms you could describe it as a hairline fracture of a non-weight-supporting bone. Dr. Russ Warren, the team orthopedist, explained that it's impossible to do further damage.

But the pain factor is something else.

The brace is expected to arrive from California this morning. It is a slim hope at best. But maybe, just maybe . . .

Until they can find out, there is at least some comfort to be derived from the fact that only Dr. Warren, trainer Ronnie Barnes, and Parcells know the truth.

But that assumption is wrong. Last night, a hospital technician placed a call to Vinnie Di Trani of the Bergen *Record*, the most knowledgeable writer on the Giants beat. His peers and even Parcells refer to him as "The Sage." Di Trani is the group's pool reporter—the designated writer where either the coach or the game officials have agreed to utilize one writer as a conduit in situations where they cannot or will not deal with the press as a group. From the coach's viewpoint the leak will be the worst and best of distractions; the worst because the secret is out. The best because at least it is in the hands of the most responsible, thoughtful writer on the beat.

And as Parcells noses the Lincoln down the ramp and to his parking spot beneath the stadium, another thought occurs to him. None of the writers and sportscasters who will pack the press room this morning know anything about medicine beyond how to affix a Band-Aid. None of them, therefore, will understand the nuances about this injury.

How will the general public receive stories written by people with no medical knowledge? If the brace works, will it still come down to people saying "Parcells is playing a guy with a broken ankle"? He winces at the thought.

7:15 A.M., defensive coaches' conference room

This is the day Bill Parcells calls the most important workday of the week. Now, with Lawrence Taylor a long shot at best, it becomes even more so. Both offensive and defensive game plans are in and for two days they have been run in practice. Because of the closeness of the last three games between these two teams, the red zone, the last 20 yards before the goal line, is getting even more attention than usual.

Now the full complement of defensive coaches, including Romeo Crennel and Mike Sweatman, who run the special teams, is trying to retrace every possibility before they go downstairs for the first team meetings of the day. They have spent hours in this very situation dissecting Cunningham, Byars, and Jackson. Now Belichick reminds them of Cris Carter, who generally is far less a factor in other areas of the field. Carter, a wide receiver, and Cunningham have developed an uncanny knack for getting six points out of the far corner of the end zone on a play where Cunningham throws to a spot and Carter simply goes and gets it.

"So what are we gonna do about Carter?" Belichick asks.

"He [Cunningham] is gonna throw him that fade to the corner where Carter can jump," Groh says, voicing what everybody else already knows.

"How tall is Carter?" Leachman asks. "Is he just a good leaper?"

"He's six-two, I guess," Belichick says. "One thing we don't want to do is get up too close to him. Why don't we just back off and be in position to take the jump?"

"Well," Groh says, "they're just gonna throw it to a spot whether you're up tight or back off."

"Well, we're just gonna have to cover it," Belichick continues. "And there's one other thing down here. Last time they burned us on a slant pattern. The guy caught it out of bounds so we got off the hook but it shows they can do it. We played it up hard during practice that week. Remember? Kinard was bitching about the indecisiveness of the flat route but it was decisive in the game. Our guys [the scout team] just couldn't run it right, so we were pretty shitty against it in practice. This time why don't we try to see if . . ."

The discussion continues. Each of them knows the clock is racing toward Sunday.

7:30 A.M., utility room, coaches' wing

Mike Pope, the tight end coach, is on his way to an offensive meeting just down the hall. Early in the season, he lost his star pupil when Mark Bavaro, an all-pro, went down with a bad knee. Bavaro was already what trainer Ronnie Barnes referred to as "the team's bionic man" because of all the anatomical repairs he's had since he joined the club in 1985. He's a good receiver but of even more value is his ability to run with the ball after making the catch. At six feet four inches and 245 pounds, Bavaro is a force to be reckoned with in the open field. The coaching staff still marvels at the memory of a Monday night against San Francisco when he caught a 10-yard pass and carried four separate tacklers on his back for another 20 yards before they wrestled him down.

Going into the season, Parcells had put great emphasis on an offensive wrinkle that would feature three tight ends. Bavaro's loss was a major setback. Pope was left with Zeke Mowatt, the starter whom Bavaro had replaced, and Howard Cross, a big rookie out of Alabama whose magnificent blocking abilities were utilized in college more than his work as a receiver.

Maurice Carthon, a crossover from the defunct USFL in his fifth year as a Giant who had been primarily a blocking back with the kind of work ethic that coaches would kill for, often lined up as the third tight end after Bavaro went down. In the red zone, the Giants have also used William Roberts, a veteran guard, at the spot. Roberts will tell you that in his most desperate dreams, he yearns for the day when they will throw him the ball. Thus far, cooler heads have prevailed.

It would be nice to have Bavaro this Sunday. But then it would also be nice to have Simms at 100 percent or Taylor or the injured running back, Joe Morris, who hasn't played a down this season. Pope's job, of course, has no time for that kind of reverie. The only reality is Sunday and it is rapidly approaching.

The tight end coach has been through thirteen previous meetings with the Eagles. Eight of them were decided by six points or less. Three of them went into overtime. Just two months ago, the Eagles beat them, 21–19. The winning score came with just 2:18

left in the game. Ask him if there is a common thread to these games and he will tell you, "Just about every one of them has been like watching two body punchers landing shot after shot in the center of the ring for twelve rounds. Physically, we're alike in many ways. It's the kind of game where the hitting is so hard and the sequences so demanding that somebody has to wear down. What happens is that 30-yard runs in the first quarter could become 80-yard runs in the fourth."

Small wonder that his counterparts in the other room, who have not yet learned that Taylor's ankle is broken, are still privately hoping for a miracle from number 56.

7:45 A.M., Bill Parcells's office

The coach is thinking ahead. He sits behind his desk in a blue Giants windbreaker and doodles on a yellow legal pad. In his mind's eye, the Giants have the ball and the game is on the line. With or without Taylor, with or without Simms at 100 percent, with or without the wind, whether or not their prayers are answered and they get Meggett one-on-one with anybody, the conduct of the game keeps coming up the same way over and over again in his mind.

"To win this game," Parcells says, "we're going to need some big plays—not home runs necessarily, but big plays, 30- or 40-yarders—because they're a team that it's difficult to sustain long drives against. They have a good defense and if you're trying to execute fifteen plays to get the ball down the field, there's a good chance you're going to make a mistake. They have enough guys to force you into it. And then we need touchdowns, not field goals. You saw that in the first game when we didn't get them."

And then he shakes his head as though he still can't believe it. "That game we should have won, 30–14. But I don't know about now. We're just not the same team we were. They're better now and I don't know whether we're even as good as we were then."

He sees this as a very basic football game—*slam, bang . . .* and the last one standing wins. In such situations, given the closeness of the talent spread ("If you held a draft off the two starting rosters," he figures, "you'd probably wind up with a team that was just about half Giants, half Eagles"), attitude coupled with determination usually prevails. It is the kind of game cuteness or mystique cannot win. The simplest approach and the most determination to get it done is what makes you a winner when the sides are this even and this physically tough. In games like this, Parcells clearly believes, there comes a time when all the rest is frills.

"In situations like that," he says, "all the film guys in the world aren't worth a shit. I remember a couple of years back when we'd stop 'em on three plays and out and the next sequence, we're doing something entirely different and I scream at Belichick, 'Are you watching the game? What the hell are you doing?' And he says he just wanted to give them a different look and I yell, 'What the hell for? We're stopping 'em, ain't we?'

"See, this kind of game is just like playing baseball. If your fastball is getting them out, you just keep on throwing it until there's twenty-seven of 'em gone and that's it because there's no innings left. It's that kind of thing. If you get away from that in a game like this, it's only because you want to show everybody how smart you are as a coach. That's like carnival football: jugglers to the left, seals to the right, high-wire act in the center, and then everybody says, 'Look how smart the coach is. This is really exciting.' But you're not a coach at all, then. You're a carnival barker. And don't think we don't have coaches in this league like that.

"It's not that complicated. You have to understand what will work and why it will work and get it done. I had a kid down at Texas Tech when I was coaching there named Mike Mock;

he went on and played for the Jets for a couple of years. He was a rough, tough, beer-drinking Texas kid—one of those guys that every time you had a problem, he could solve it. So I moved him around pretty good and in his sophomore year, I had him playing eight positions. Now he's a junior and we go over to Arizona to play them and they're riding high. We've got a pretty good team but we're not better than them. So we get ahead but now they're going for a score that's gonna beat us. It comes down to fourth and goal on the 5-yard line. They score, they win. We stop 'em, we win. It's that simple because there's six seconds left.

"Mock intercepts the ball in the end zone. Now we're in the locker room and the press is all around him and a reporter asks, 'Is that the biggest play you ever made in your life?' and the kid says, 'Yep.' Now the guys asks why and Mock says, 'Because if I don't make it, they win, but I made it so we win.'

"I knew right there I had that kid. I knew he understood. That's how simple it is. You get your coaches and your players to understand it, you win. You don't get anything for being smarter or flashier. All anybody wants to know is if you won. In a game like this, well, like I told you and I tell them, you don't get any medals for trying."

As he speaks, Eddie Croke, the team publicist, enters the room. He is wearing a gray sweat suit and a blue ski jacket and is waving a yellow speeding ticket.

"They got me this morning," he says.

"Who got you?" Parcells replies. "The Westchester Police? Come on, you oughta be smarter than that. They got poodles in their canine corps, for Christ's sake. What's the weather report?"

"I heard four to six inches of snow on Sunday—maybe mixed with rain or sleet."

"What, are you dreaming? Where did you pick that up—in the Atlantic Ocean outside the three-mile limit?"

"No, I was listening to radio, CD-101."

"What have they got, three amps? Get real."

And then Parcells picks up the telephone, dials the weather bureau, and repeats the forecast as he hears it, word for word all the way through Sunday, which calls for extreme cold and high winds.

"You want me to give you high and low tides, too?" he says, "just in case we have to go out to sea and hole up somewhere to get out of this one?"

Now Croke is going over a list of appointments. On those occasions when he adds "we need to do this," Parcells writes it down. The rest Croke will handle for him.

"All right," Parcells says. "Now I got something you won't like. No television cameras today. No still cameras today. All they want to do is film this fuckin' kid [Taylor] limping. Yesterday, they even filmed him in the fuckin' tunnel. I don't want 'em filming here on the field, in the tunnel, or in the fuckin' locker room. That's it. And you'll have to deal with them as best you can about it."

"I don't blame you," Croke says. "I'll handle it. Fuck 'em," he adds. "I just got a speeding ticket."

8:30 A.M., publicity office

Ed Croke is sitting behind his desk thumbing through additional working press requests. The home writers already have their tickets. Earlier in the week, Ron Howard, the Eagles' publicist, has picked up and distributed the tickets for his regulars. Now Croke is juggling the size of the press box against the volume of requests. Because working space is working space— and there is just so much of it—a number of ad agency and non-television types are not going to get in out of the cold.

Croke looks up and says, "I'm no doctor and I don't know how bad it really is but I wouldn't count LT out. He's the most competitive person I have ever met in my life. Here's a guy who takes up golf and overnight he becomes a four-handicap player. And determined? Hell, nobody here wants to play with him because he's so intense from the minute he steps up to the first tee.

"One day he hears a couple of players talking about going bowling, so he says, 'I never went bowling in my life. I'd like to come along.' The first game he throws a 180. Then he starts talking about how he doesn't see any challenge to this so he's leaving. He gets to the front door and he discovers somebody has stolen his Porsche.

"He's furious. He's jumping up and down and somebody tries to calm him down by reminding him his insurance will cover it. 'Damn the car,' he says. 'My golf clubs are in the trunk. The best set I ever had.'

"Nobody wants to compete as hard as he does."

Just then the telephone rings. In the middle of the busiest week a team publicist can have, at a time when the phone is jumping off the hook with calls about Simms's and Taylor's conditions and incredible requests for impossible interviews, this call tops them all. It is from Bill Cosby's agent who says that Cosby's daughters are big football fans and they want to see the game.

"I can't help you. I only handle working press. I have no tickets."

"Well, that's not exactly fair," Croke is told. "I mean we have your players over here all the time to watch the tapings. The least you could do is reciprocate."

"Let me get this straight. You have had our players over there?"

"Exactly," comes the confident reply.

"Good, then go call the players for tickets."

9:00 A.M., trainer's office

Dr. Russ Warren, Ronnie Barnes, and Lawrence Taylor are huddled in a semicircle. Through the glass half of the door they are visible to Bill Parcells, who has just turned the corner into the treatment area. Parcells bangs the door open, races into the room, and screams:

"I know what you're doing in here and I won't stand for it. If you think you're going to get a shot on Sunday," he yells at Taylor, "then you better think again because I won't allow it. And you," he says to Barnes, "don't think for one minute that you're gonna get away with doing something crazy."

Russ Warren, who hasn't a clue to what this is about, stares at Parcells as though he were a madman. Ronnie Barnes, who knows exactly what is going through the coach's mind, says, "What are you talking about? I'm putting a cast on his ankle."

"A CAST?" Parcells shouts.

"Well, his ankle is broken."

"Oh, well, sure . . . yeah . . . I see."

After he leaves, Barnes says, "He does get a little carried away. But then he knows players. The irony is that guys come here from other teams where the trainer did shoot them up and they come to me because, as far as they know, that's the easy way. But I think the very fact that we don't do it eventually gets them to have a lot more trust in the trainer and the doctor.

"On the other side of the coin, people tend to forget that Bill has been through some very hard personal times here. We've had deaths; John Tuggle [a player] and Bob Ledbetter [backfield coach] died. We've had players contract life-threatening diseases. These are people he cares about. People forget it hasn't been easy for him."

9:00 A.M., locker room

The team meeting is called for 9:30 but already the quarterbacks and Erhardt and Belichick and his defensive signal-callers have gone their separate way for preliminary talks. Erik Howard is sitting in front of his locker with a container of tea, reading the newspaper. This is the first morning that Howard did not have to be in early for treatment. He is one of those most grateful for Parcells's decision not to practice in pads this week. His major problems have faded away into a single familiar dull ache. His swollen hand is all that visibly remains of them. He's in early because his roommate, Jumbo Elliot, has his car in the garage for repairs and he must report early to have his badly swollen ankle attended. Because of his size (305 pounds), Barnes is concerned about the healing process but Jumbo indicates that he will play.

Myron Guyton is early, too. He has come to meet with Belichick along with selected other defensive players to go over signal changes they will be called upon to make during the game. Also present are Carl Banks, Johnie Cooks, Gary Reasons, Adrian White, Pepper Johnson, Greg Cox, and Greg Jackson.

Meanwhile, Simms, Hostetler, and Rutledge have joined Erhardt to discuss both the red zone and the two-minute drill, which teams employ at the end of each half when their offenses are trying to beat the clock.

"The Eagles," Erhardt reminds them for what seems like the 567th time, "are very, very tough in the red zone. They pack it and they hit. Most of the scores against them down there have come on passes."

Then he puts the Eagles back up on the screen. The quarterbacks are averaging four meetings a day this week, with film at every one of them. Hostetler makes a mental note to remind himself not to let his wife talk him into taking her to the movies for another eight years.

By 9:30, the entire squad has assembled to hear Parcells. "Six plays," he tells them, "six plays, that's all. Six plays going the way they should have gone the last time we played these guys and we would have won it. Think about that."

Then the special teams break off to meet on punt returns. More films. Another lecture from Crennel. And now Reyna Thompson hears Crennel say, "The guy they reactivated, their new punter [Max Runager] is very erratic, so they'll try to get their cover guys down much quicker than usual."

As the Eagles punt again and again and again up on the screen, it occurs to Reyna Thompson that nearly an entire week has elapsed since Monday night when he lined up offside on the 49ers' critical field-goal miss, giving them another chance. And yet he has not heard a word about it. Nothing from Crennel . . . nothing from Mike Sweatmen, the assistant special teams coach . . . nothing from the players . . . no criticism . . . no needling. "It's so strange," he thinks to himself. "I almost feel left out."

The teams have now broken into full offense and defense meetings and Howard is half listening to Belichick point out that the Giants have had good success on the goal line defending against the Eagles. Primarily, the big nose tackle is studying the moves of David Alexander, the Eagles' center out of Tulsa. Although Alexander is in his third season, this will only be the second time Howard has faced him. The job previously belonged to Dave Rimington, who presented a totally different problem. Alexander is large at 282 pounds, but Howard notes that he is not a "strength player."

"On run blocking," Howard thinks to himself, "he's there. He'll take a side shuffle step and try to hook you instead of coming straight off the ball and trying to drive you back. That's the problem. The solution is I've got to be concerned about my lateral movement, make good use of my hands, and make sure he doesn't move me to create a seam for the ball carrier."

Belichick is talking about the slants they will throw to Keith Jackson and the fadeaway pass to the corner of the end zone for Cris Carter. But in the darkened room, the down linemen are staring at the screen and fighting private wars of their own.

10:30 A.M., promotions office

Tom Power is about to perform his happiest task of the week. Power is the director of promotions for the ball club and his office is next door to Croke's. Many of Power's duties deal with routine—the Sunday catering for the coaches' wives, setting up the Sunday will-call booth for ticket pickups, various press box routines involving the stat crew, and assorted problem-solving along with Croke for the working press and the logical daily promotional type things you would expect.

Tom Power is about to make his favorite telephone call of the week. He is calling a man named Cy Fraser, who has been listed as the franchise's halftime entertainment director since 1934. Cy was a Giants fan, a friend of old Tim Mara and actively engaged in the retail uniform supply business. Almost from the beginning, he was a Giants fan. He would also like people to remember him as the author of "Go, Giants, Go"—a fight song which some say hasn't been played publicly since the Mohawks listened to tom-toms on the night before their big games against the Onondagas.

Cy no longer books the entertainment—Power does that—but he still gets the starting lineups, cues the National Anthem singer, and makes sure that the designated high-school band gets early morning rehearsal time and gets on and off the field on schedule at intermission.

Power is calling Cy to tell him that Sunday's entertainment will be provided by the Immaculata High School marching band of Somerville, New Jersey. This is merely a detail. Actually, he is calling because he likes calling him.

Since 1934, Cy has only missed one halftime. He is eighty-four years old. Some years back in the middle of a ferocious snow storm, Cy called Power in a panic.

"I can't believe this. I can't believe this," he said. "I'm stuck, Tom. My car won't start."

"Listen, Cy," Power deadpanned, "if you can't be more responsible about this, we don't need you."

11:00 A.M., trainer's office

The X ray the Giants hoped they'd never see is on display against the square glass panel just inside the door. Ronnie Barnes is pointing to what looks like a small, thin scratch to the untrained eye. There is bad news and good news and news that nobody can still quite figure out.

"He's got a small, nondisplaced fracture just off the tibia—a chip fracture," Barnes says. "It's about six centimeters long. He's also had an injury there before. By comparing X rays, we now know that he had some kind of fracture in the same region in 1983. By nondisplaced, we mean it hasn't moved. It is also a non-weight-bearing situation. If you broke it off there, it couldn't do any additional damage and we would still treat it in the same way. What the problem is is pain and a lot of it.

"Am I surprised? Yes. Remember this is the third time he's been X-rayed and without the tomogam we never would have picked it up. Russ Warren was in to look at it this morning and he told Lawrence that if he limps on Sunday he's not going to let him play.

"He's doing very well. He's even walking well. We've given him a lot of electric stimulation. We're probing this one spot. But the real fear is that no matter what we do, with a broken bone, he's gonna have pain. Russ says the guideline is if he can't play or run without limping, he's not going to let him play."

Then Barnes laughs and says, "Like I expected, he's using DMSO on his own. I'm sure he got it at the track. But he's up-front about it. He told me as soon as he came in this morning. I guess he thought I'd smell it. A couple of other guys have used it, too, and they make the room smell like a stale pizza parlor.

"It's the kind of thing that either helps right away or it doesn't help at all. Now what I've got to do is figure out what I can do for him, if he can play. He'll wear the new brace but maybe there's some way I can figure out to tape him differently and give him a little extra help.

"What I'll probably do is use elastic tape which is more sturdy and binding than what we normally use. We'll use some moleskin, which is a very sturdy strap that we'll use side to side. We'll tape his Achilles tendon and his arch. It'll probably take half an hour. It normally takes about three minutes to tape a player.

"I'll give him a little heel lift in his shoe to take some pressure off. I'm gonna try to do a little dress rehearsal tomorrow just in case.

"Of course, you know Lawrence asked if we could shoot him up but you already know how that turned out. The funny thing is that with all the other drug problems he had, I know needles could never be involved because Lawrence hates them. Any time we put a needle in his arm for an IV or to take blood, he almost faints. Now he wants to play so badly that here he is asking for a shot which he isn't going to get.

"Simms, meanwhile, is fine. He's not going to wear a brace but he'll be heavily taped."

Just outside in the treatment room, Mike Ryan, the assistant trainer, is putting away the hot gun. He is explaining the composition of the brace, which is made of carbon filament, the same stuff they use on the stealth bomber. It looks very much like a boot.

"The secret of a good brace is controlling the motion in the ankle. The ankle is so mobile that to stabilize it with this kind of injury is very difficult. First I had to measure him," Ryan explains. "The size you see marked at the bottom of the boot is only a kind of general guide. First I had to have him walk around and tell me what was loose and what was too tight. Then I turn the gun on and start to shape it with heat.

"I had him put it on so it would cool in a weight-bearing position. With Lawrence, I don't think it's a question of saying he won't have any pain or willing himself not to have it. What he does is accept it and force himself to live with it. Is there too much pain to do it this time? I don't know, but I do know if he can't, nobody can."

11:30 A.M., locker room

All week Fred Hoaglin has been working on William Roberts and Eric Moore. Just as he did in the trenches against various opponents as an all-pro center during an eleven-year career with four teams, he varies the technique but the goal is always the same. Both are scheduled to start at guard on Sunday. Each, because of Jumbo's aching ankle, could wind up playing some tackle. With the Eagles, they are matched up front against raw power and a hell of a track record.

Roberts was a first-round draft pick out of Ohio State in 1984. He was slow to develop, then missed all of 1985 after surgery. For a long time he struggled but the shift to guard has benefitted him. Moore was a number-one pick last year but reported late to training camp and was on the inactive list at the start of the 1988 season. He came on well late in the year. The Giants think he may well be a player, but there is still a lot to find out.

This is not going to be an easy Sunday for either of them, based on what the Eagles plan to throw at them. Because of the difference in age and experience, Hoaglin has decided to challenge Roberts and encourage Moore.

Much of Roberts's time will be occupied with trying to displace six-foot-two-inch 295-pound Jerome Brown. When they met in October, it was Hoaglin's contention that Roberts played very well in the first half, but then missed a block in the third quarter and surrendered. This dovetails with a thought that has bothered Parcells for some time. For one reason or another (injuries, lack of bodies, and his own potential) William Roberts has figured prominently in the Giants' plans in various ways for several years.

"There are just certain guys," Parcells says, "you just can't do much about. William Roberts is a good kid, not a bad pro, gregarious, happy-go-lucky. The talent is there but he doesn't have the mentality to cope with adversity well. I have several like that. They get destroyed before they can rectify a mistake. Now, sometimes they can start all over again, but not always. They're very fragile that way. Whereas I've had other players like [Jim] Burt, Taylor, a lot of others, the worse it gets the better they like it. When the task is greater, their level goes up right away. Now I hope William Roberts can do it on Sunday but if you're asking me, I'd have to say I don't know."

It is up to Hoaglin to try to find a way to make it happen. All week long he has told Roberts, "You must be aggressive. If you miss a block, then you must come back and be just as aggressive on the next play."

With Moore, who will also figure prominently when the blocking scheme doesn't call for Bart Oates to go up against Reggie White alone, the approach is different. "Two years from now," Hoaglin says, "I would challenge him just like I do Roberts and Oates. But now I have to do more explaining, more encouraging, and show a lot more patience."

Before he leaves to meet with his unit, Hoaglin pauses, thinks a private thought for a moment, and then shares it: "Last Monday when we played the 'Niners, that was your basic television fan's game . . . the glamour, the slickness. But this game," he says, "this game is the kind of game I used to love when I played. This game is a player's game."

A moment later, he is meeting with the offensive line in its regular meeting hall—the team laundry room.

"We've talked about who they are and what they do all week," Hoaglin is saying. "There's no mystery here because you have already faced them and they're going to be the same people you know. They may be the best defensive unit in the league. So you know the way it's going to be, and the only way you can win is to establish yourself right from the start. It won't change much in the red zone. They're going to play a basic defense. You're not going to see a lot of blitzes. They jam you down in the middle and let their backers hit up in the hole. You have to stay on your blocks and control them. This is the kind of game where you buckle up your chin strap and go to work."

Then they put the tapes on and William Roberts is staring at Jerome Brown and thinking, "He's low, he's powerful, and he's coming straight ahead." And in the back of his mind he hears the echo of Hoaglin's voice saying, "You can't quit because you miss a block. You have to challenge him, William, challenge him."

11:30 A.M., locker room

It is lunchtime for the players, a tradition which for some is more honored in the breach than in the observance. Jeff Hostetler has brown-bagged it of late. Some of the players use the period to slip into the weight room and work with the strength coach, Johnny Parker, to chip away at their weekly quota. Even Erik Howard, who spends this half hour sound asleep on the couch in the players' lounge, brought in leftover turkey on Thursday. Jumbo Elliot, probably the least fussy luncheon guest at Chez

Mara, complains half-heartedly about the day's fare and then disposes of what has become his obligatory three hot dogs.

It is also meet-the-press time, phase one. This is another ritual more honored in the breach than in the observance. Parcells has declared the locker room open territory for the press from 11:30 until noon. He knows very little interviewing will take place here. Most of the players have already been taped and are at lunch, lifting, or secreting themselves in the lounge. All three areas are out of bounds to the media. Hostetler and Rutledge are sitting in front of their lockers as usual. So is Johnie Cooks. But for the most part, the players have scattered.

And then along comes Lawrence, dressed in trademark black.

During an earlier press briefing down the hall, which was much shorter than usual, Parcells had restated his ban on cameras for the day; said he thought this was a battle between two tough defensive teams and the one that couldn't keep the other from becoming an offensive one would lose it; announced Simms would start at quarterback; and refused to deny or confirm what Vinnie Di Trani already knew.

So here was Lawrence walking stiffly but with no noticeable limp through the locker room toward two reporters.

"How's the ankle, LT?" one of them asked.

"It's broken," Lawrence said.

Surprisingly, no alarm bells sounded as the steel curtain of mystery dissolved right on the spot.

12:30 P.M., locker room

Lamar Leachman has decided to pour on the emotion in today's defensive line meeting. He begins by reviewing the entire Eagles offense by formation. "What you got to do," Lamar says, ignoring the obligatory Xs and Os which they have heard all week long, "is to knock those sons of bitches backwards." He senses the room beginning to react. He has, after all, in a single sentence put this whole game into perspective from their standpoint. "Have any of you forgotten the last game of the year against the Jets last season? Have you forgotten how we went in there with a playoff spot in our pockets and came out with nothing? Do you remember how low your heads were hanging after that game? Hell, this one is for the division championship."

"He got me fired up," Howard says. "I mean it wasn't like I was distracted from the task by his voice. Hell, let's face it—you don't have to be no rocket scientist to play nose guard. There's a guy that's gonna hook you left or he's gonna hook you right and sometimes there's going to be two guys coming at you. It's a strictly reactive position.

"I don't think watching a lot of tape can really help me. When you're sitting there six inches from bad breath and leather, it doesn't make a whole heck of a lot of difference what you're looking for because all you're going to see is the center's face. Sometimes it's hard to pay attention in meetings to motion and formation and all that crap. Even when you say, OK, it's wing formation and they like to play slant 18, I still can't play the play, I have to play the block.

"For me the whole game is right in front of me in my own little world. The Triangle we call it. The Nose Triangle—I see both guards and the center and nothing else.

"Sometimes I try to get a good blow and start breathing real hard and puke on the center's hand. I did that in college once. That really discouraged the guy."

2:00 P.M., Giants Stadium

The wind never quits. It hammers them from the time they get out there until Parcells mercifully calls a halt. As the offense begins to run its plays, Phil Simms is under center and throwing the ball well. The defensive players stand around in a large semicircle, trying to keep warm. Off to one side, they have brought out the stationary bike and Lawrence Taylor, newly braced and taped, peddles at a furious rate. Jeff Hostetler claps his hands in the cold almost as though he were checking to see if they are still there.

When the offense finishes, he will quarterback the scout team. Then he will hold for Bjorn Nittmo when the field-goal team takes the field. When Raul Allegre, the regular placekicker, pulled a groin muscle, it took some hard work for Hostetler to deal with his other role as holder. Nittmo, unlike the vast majority of kickers, is left-footed.

"I held for him in preseason camp so it wasn't totally new," Hostetler says, "but I hadn't done it in ten weeks by the time Raul went down. It really didn't take long to get it together again. People ask me what's the most important thing about holding for placekickers and it's so basic I want to laugh.

"Catch the ball. Just catch the ball and he'll do all the rest. He comes over to me and marks the spot he wants with his foot. Then I just concentrate on it, catch the ball, and set it up. Outside of a bad snap, all you have to worry about is rain or snow and the ball getting slick."

As the offense finishes and the defense takes over, a lone figure appears briefly in the tunnel, fronting the ramp to the dressing room. His compact frame is hooded against the wind. A broken foot, suffered in an exhibition game, put Joe Morris in dry dock before the season began and a management decision on a roster move deactivating him before the opener precludes him from playing until next year. If the Giants make the playoffs, all he will be able to do is watch.

In his eighth season with the Giants, Morris holds nine club rushing records, including a career mark of 5,296 yards gained. At five-foot-seven, he is small for a pro running back. All through high school, college, and finally with the Giants, he had to battle to convince his coaches that height had nothing to do with his ability to carry the ball. The intensity of that battle has left its mark on him. Angry over what he considers the Giants' haste to deactivate him, he is, by his own admission, a bitter man.

Out on the field, the defense is starting to get into position to face the scout team. Myron Guyton has spent so much time watching Keith Jackson on the tapes, he can almost detect his skin blemishes. Now he watches Zeke Mowatt, the starting tight end, line up with the scouts to emulate Jackson.

"He [Zeke] was perfect for me to work against today," Guyton will say later in the locker room. "First of all, he takes this seriously, even though he really runs with the starting offense. He takes it seriously, I guess, because he likes to work on his moves no matter what the reason. He pushes off with his hands just like Jackson. He's so much like him coming off the ball, you'd almost swear they were the same guy."

Suddenly, the sound of Parcells's voice cuts across the field in anger. "What the hell is going on here? Please, can somebody tell me what the hell is going on out here? You got twelve men out there!" he shrieks at the defensive coaches. "Can anybody count over there?"

What is going on is that Lawrence Taylor has slipped off his bike and sneaked into the defensive alignment. Nobody has noticed it. Now people are bumping into each other and the coaches are trying to figure out what has happened.

"Get him out of there," Parcells screams. "Lawrence, are you crazy?"

Nobody dares even considering an answer to that one.

5:00 P.M., classroom area, locker room

The newly crowned commissioner of the National Football League has come to town. Paul Tagliabue has been making the rounds of as many teams as possible to introduce himself. For nearly thirty years there had been Pete Rozelle and the NFL and the NFL and Pete Rozelle. When the first league contract with television was signed, changing forever the face of all professional sports in America, Rozelle was there as its architect. When the antitrust exemption necessary to make it happen was steered through Congress, Pete Rozelle as there to steer.

Through expansion, through the war between the rebel AFL and the old-guard NFL, through the creation and anointing of that Roman-numeraled, overpromoted, and often underartistic money machine called the Super Bowl, through strikes and lockouts, good games, bad games, and scab games, Pete Rozelle was the first, fortieth, and final word on everything from which city got a team and which one didn't to which city got a Super Bowl and which city didn't.

But now he had retired and the new man, Paul Tagliabue, whose rebounding record still stands back at his old New Jersey high school and whose legal career was tightly wound within the framework of the league, had become the new man.

Eager to answer all questions, soothe all doubts, and hear all suggestions, Tagliabue played to an audience of no more than a handful of players. From the locker room, just a doorless archway away, came the sounds of music, banter, moaning, groaning, and "Who the hell stole my deodorant?"

Gary Reasons, the Giants' players union rep, is there. So is Phil Simms, perhaps eight or nine other players, and, mystery of mysteries, Lawrence Taylor. The commissioner spoke briefly and then Reasons had a few union questions. At that point Taylor took the floor.

"I was wondering," he asked the newly minted Lord High Commissioner of Autumn in America, "if you could reinstate Dexter Manley [the Washington defensive end who had been suspended for drug abuse] right away. I think you ought to do it."

The commissioner thanked Lawrence for his suggestion but felt at the moment it was impractical.

Then Simms raised his hand. "What's the most important thing in every professional football game?" he asked innocently.

"I don't know," the commissioner affably replied. "I'm kind of new at this. Suppose you tell me."

"The ball," Simms replied triumphantly. "The ball. And it's got your signature on it and it's a lousy ball. You have to do something about the ball, commissioner. It really isn't a very good football. I wouldn't want my name on it the way it is now."

Staggering under the weight of such massive input, the commissioner thanked the troops and fled the building.

5:30 P.M., locker room

The room smells like the Last Rose of Sorrento. In the 100-yard folklore of Giants football tradition, Friday is Let Us Not Forget Tom Owen Day. You can pore through the team's 225-page press guide and all you will find to show he ever existed is a single line in agate type on page 218 as part of the club's all-time player roster, which reads: "Owen, Tom (QB), Wichita State, 1983."

So who was Tom and what was he?

Further research with the Elias Sports Bureau, keeper of all NFL statistics since leather helmets, shows that Owen was born on September 1, 1952, and had a ten-year career during which he occasionally even played.

In 1974, he broke in with the 49ers and threw 184 passes—or more than half his career total. He was also on the rosters of the New England Patriots and the Washington Redskins. In 1983, Bill Parcells became head coach of the Giants and Phil Simms, trying to throw the ball before an on-rushing lineman could do major alterations on his anatomy, banged his thumb against a lineman's helmet and went down for fourteen games.

With only one ambulatory quarterback, Scott Brunner, available, Parcells remembered Owen from the Pats and installed him as the backup. He had not thrown a football in anger since 1981. He would not throw one during his lone active season with the Giants.

But Tom Owen's momma didn't raise no fool. He had been around long enough to know that the quarterback who wants to keep all his moving parts in working order damned well better get a little help from his friends.

Consequently, he began what has become a long-standing tradition at Mara Tech. Each Friday, he had fifteen pizzas and enough hero sandwiches to feed the Chinese Eighth Route Army delivered to the Giants' locker room.

Phil Simms, who has held the quarterback job without serious challenge since 1984, has picked up the tab ever since. A sea of white pizza boxes strewn around the locker room stands as evidence of diligence.

The Giants are eating as though they have come off a ten-day fast, but Ottis Jerome Anderson is otherwise occupied. He is stripping the tape from his body.

If all the tape that was used to hold OJ together this season were stretched end to end, the Giants could follow it all the way to Denver, where they will play again a week from Sunday. There is double tape on his left wrist and double tape on his right. There is extra tape on his ankles. There is protective tape next to his groin. If the late Andy Warhol were still around, he'd probably collect all the discarded tape, roll it into a ball, call it "Portrait of a Resurrected Running Back," and hang it in New York's Museum of Modern Art.

When Anderson comes in to get taped, Ronnie Barnes yells, "Shut the saloon. Here comes the old gunfighter."

OJ goes through life with a perennial wound on his forehead. "He gets hit and his helmet spins on him," Barnes says. "At first, I thought maybe the equipment man wasn't putting enough air in it. But it's his head. It's shaped like an egg. It's impossible to get a helmet to fit him."

He is thirty-two years old and in this locker room only Phil Simms at thirty-three is older. But OJ is a well-worn thirty-two. In another incarnation he was the wunderkind of St. Louis, Missouri, a town that, before the Cardinals fled the scene of their crimes, had precious few wunderkinds when it came to professional football.

In 1979, the year Giants' management and its then horrendous football team were to struggle back from the nadir of their twin crises, Ottis Anderson came rocketing out of the St. Louis backfield like a bomb in search of a fuse. In his rookie season, he rushed for a magnificent 1,605 yards. Ten years later, clinging desperately to a job as a bare roster survivor with the Giants, he carried the ball two whole, entire times for an aggregate total of 6 lonely yards.

What happened to him was after five 1,000-yard seasons in seven years, the Cardinals tied a large can to him and the Giants got him during the early part of the 1986 season for virtually nothing.

He had what management termed an attitude problem. The following summer Anderson fought desperately for a job with the Giants. It was a sobering experience.

Gone was the attitude. In its place rose the good soldier. "Run down under kicks? OK. Tell me what it takes and I'll do it." That year he became a short-yardage-situation ball carrier. He was quietly minding his own business when Joe Morris broke his foot.

They gave him the job by default and waited for him to break down. All he did was run like hell. Halfway through the season, Bill Parcells gave him an award as the half-season comeback player of the year.

Says OJ: "That's why he calls me Old Red and talks about the resurrection. He calls himself tryin' to motivate me. I been in this league twelve years. How's somebody gonna motivate me? The truth is, he's probably tryin' to motivate himself.

"Besides, I got all the motivatin' I need from Maurice [Carthon, the blocking back in the next locker] over there. He's on me all the time. Ask him."

Maurice Carthon just smiles back and points to a large piece of tape he has plastered across his mouth. He says this is a big-game week and he wants to stay focused, so no interviews. Now he is waving his arms as though he were answering in sign language.

"When Joe [Morris] went down," Anderson continues, "he [Parcells] told me I was going to get a little more work. He told me I'd probably carry the ball fifteen times a game. So what we know from that is either Bill Parcells is a big liar or he can't count. Most games it's twenty-seven carries."

He says he thinks the Giants will beat the Eagles. He says it will be a very difficult game. Two things can be said with certainty about the new world of OJ Anderson. He still can run a little bit and he says the right things.

At the opposite end of the room, David Meggett is quietly thinking about the biggest football game of his life. Three weeks ago, Parcells was all over him. It wasn't the occasional but extremely costly fumble that bothered the coach. Parcells will tell you, "That's going to happen and you live with it as long as it doesn't happen too often, in which case, you don't live with it at all." What rankled at him was the fact that the rookie was trying to do too much and, consequently, achieving too little.

"Don't try to make ten men miss you. Just start with one," Parcells told him, "and, for a change, will you please try to run north and south instead of east and west." Then he stopped talking to him for a week.

David Meggett may be a rookie but almost without warning,

this single season has made a lot of people sit up and take notice. Not the least among those interested are the Philadelphia Eagles. In the first game against the Eagles, Meggett played more minutes than ever before as a pro, caught more passes (six), carried the ball more times (seven), ran back four punts and one kickoff.

He knows that he will not come to this rematch without receiving a little special attention from the other side of the ball. "That's all right," he says, "because what I do, I will do because Phil [Simms] throws a great pass or Bart [Oates] picks up a blitzer. I'm not any more nervous for this game than I am for any other."

They are modest rookie answers, said with all the right rookie inflections. But when you ask him how he will react if the Eagles forget their homework and he breaks the huddle and knows he is going to catch a linebacker one on one, he smiles and says, "Why, then, my eyes will light up."

Immediately, three eavesdroppers in three nearby lockers turn loose a storm of howls that drowns him out.

Meanwhile, Joe Morris dresses quietly in front of his locker. Ever since he was ten years old, autumn has always meant being part of football for him. Suddenly, nineteen years later, for the first time he can remember, Joe Morris is without a team. Four weeks ago, they took the cast off his foot. He has lifted in the weight room since then. He will begin to run alone in the empty stadium on Monday.

"I think their decision was medically correct," he says slowly, "but as a player in a time cycle, I'm very frustrated. You say to yourself you'll do anything to get in shape. If I have to run until I drop on Monday, I don't care if it helps to put me in shape.

"You start out and you can't begin to believe you're not playing. You try to rationalize in your mind why God picked you out of all the people to miss a whole year. I talked to a lot of guys who missed a whole season and they all say, 'Joe, one thing you're going to find is that to a lot of people, you're not going to exist anymore.' I found that to be true with some people.

"Most guys here still treat me like a teammate but you feel like you're invisible sometimes. It's so frustrating to watch a game where you could play for a team and have some control over the outcome of a game. My performance really did some things to help the Giants win.

"I watch a game on television, I can watch maybe five plays and then I can't take it and I switch to a movie. Then I turn back and I feel worse . . . helpless . . . because you're not a part of it. For a while, I became a demon at home. I did a lot for this team. I think they should have given me a chance to come back this year.

"When you work out three times a day in the summer to get ready for a season and they take it away from you the first week of the regular season, there's a lot of frustration. Now we have this week and this game. What do you live for? I'm a ball player.

"One of the things that happens is you watch the team and suddenly you're saying 'they' instead of 'we' because in the middle of it all, you feel invisible again.

"I'll be at the game Sunday. I'll watch and I'll cheer."

Then Joe Morris finishes dressing and leaves. The laughter in this room has nothing to do with him.

6:30 P.M., Giants Stadium field

The crew moves slowly through the teeth of the wind and across the empty stadium. Inch by inch they begin to unroll the heavy tarp across the stadium floor. Parcells has decided to cover the field and forego outdoor practice tomorrow. The last forecast he heard calls for snow flurries, high winds, and plummeting temperatures for Sunday. Tomorrow, there is a 40 percent chance of snow. In his public thoughts he vacillates as to what role the weather can play in this game.

But in his heart of hearts, he knows what he wants and he knows why. He wants to take the teeth out of Randall Cunningham's long bombs. He wants to keep as much of this game on the ground as possible. He knows that in the very heart of the treacherous winds of the Meadowlands, the Washington Redskins came into this stadium and their punt return team lost their handle on its game. He knows that Washington did not or could not field those punts as they danced without reason or pattern through the air, struck wildly against the artificial turf, and began to roll. He knows that Washington lost well over 100 yards in field position after those balls rolled crazily toward its own end zone.

And he knows something else.

Strictly off what he has already seen, the Giants have both the punter and the returner to do it. Strictly off what he has also seen, the Eagles do not.

7:00 P.M., coaches' wing

The offensive coaches have shut down for the night. Before Erhardt leaves, he says he is satisfied that the game plan and the practices have put Meggett into every situation that could be exploited. Most of all, he would like to see the Eagles offer a defense at some point that will set up a play called zero slot out 76 double in. Cutting through the Giants' code, that would boil down to Meggett going one-on-one against Andre Waters, the free safety. As soon as he explains it, Erhardt quickly adds he doesn't think there's a chance in hell the Giants will get it.

The Eagles may be physical but they aren't stupid.

Tommy Coughlin, the receiver coach, says they have done just about all they can do if they are to take advantage of the basic coverage they expect to get from the Eagles in terms of creating confusion when the Giants put two receivers in the slot. Basically, this would involve either Odessa Turner or Stephen Baker at the X back and Mark Ingram or Zeke Mowatt at tight end.

Most of the others have already left. From across the hall, you can still hear the clack-clack-clack of the videotape machine in the defensive coaches' conference room. Bill Belichick is staring at the tape. He will be the last to leave.

Bill Parcells is sitting in the large easy chair in front of his office television set watching the videotape of today's practice. "There's Taylor now," he says. "See? See him sneak in there in the jacket?" Then Kim, his secretary, sticks her head through the doorway and says, "I don't know about you but my stomach is in knots."

"Why?"

"Because I want these guys. The Eagles. I want them humbled."

As she leaves for the evening, it is clear she has rendered the most concise pep talk of the week.

Now Parcells is watching Adrian White, the mirror, and he is saying as he stares at the screen, "I don't know. He's just too slow." Then he pauses and adds, "But we can't cancel the game."

Then Al Groh walks in holding a pair of enormous winter sideline gloves, which are standard December gear for the Giants. His son will wear them on his high-school bench tomorrow.

"How about this Cox on this?" Parcells asks, pointing to the screen.

"He's the shakiest guy on it," Groh replies.

"Those mittens for Michael? Is he playing tomorrow?"

"Well, he's activated. He's in if there's trouble. That's what they told him. They're playing Morris Hills and they're 10–0. This is it. They're 10–0 and Randolph is 10–0. This is it, the finals. The last game. Plus the winning steak we got going and plus it's probably the old coach's last game. Michael called today and he said they expect twelve thousand. I'm supposed to relax tomorrow but it's harder being the quarterback's father than the linebacker's coach."

"You got another session with Taylor tomorrow just in case?" Parcells asks.

"Yeah, what we're gonna do is, we're not gonna change any of the terminology for anybody else. We're just gonna teach him what to do. We're just gonna meet and I'll tell everybody the contingencies and then hange loose until tomorrow night so that Adrian and Cox don't have too many things running around in their heads."

"Well," Parcells says, as though he has just come to a decision after watching the practice film, "if it's snowing and it's blustery, we're gonna blitz 'em. We're gonna make that guy throw and take a chance."

"I think it could work," Groh says. "This guy [Cunningham] is good enough so that he can beat you once in a while passing, but he hasn't shown he can do it every week out of the box. Like a guy like Montana, he'll be there every week throwing. But this guy's gonna be there every week running."

Now Parcells is watching the screen again and Groh says, "Cox's job is pretty simple but his concentration is bad."

"Bad?" Parcells says. "He's like the highway wanderer. Now Adrian is trying. Look, we just got to beat them on offense. If we got Simms thinking the right way, we might have a chance to make ten big plays, and if we make three out of ten, we'll win."

With that happy possibility voiced by the boss, Groh says good night while he's still optimistic.

"You know, if we get snow," Parcells continues, "we'll blitz them on every third down. And if we don't get it, well, I want wind. Just give us wind and we'll be all right. See, when it's windy, your punt returner can hurt you. Remember when we played the Redskins in '86? We got that really vicious wind.

[Phil] McConkey [then the Giants' punt returner] won the game. Nobody knows it. But he did it. They punted six times. We never let one ball hit the ground. They let four balls hit the ground and it cost them 119 yards in field position.

"So a lot falls on Meggett Sunday. I was trying to teach him that if it was windy and he let the ball hit the ground, the ball was gonna roll down the field. We lost a game like that one time in New England. Ball rolled about 60 yards.

"That's why I spent a lot of time working with Meggett on this. See, their punter is not very good. Kicking into this wind, well . . . If we win the toss, we'll take the wind. This is a very tough park when it comes to wind. I'm not sure they'll know how to read it.

"If you asked me what one thing I'd like to be able to do in this park, it's run the ball. Particularly when you don't have the wind at your back.

"You know, this is gonna be a vicious game. I don't think a team can get too possessed on defense. Offense, yes. Defense, never. That kind of mood makes defenses happen."

8:30 P.M., Upper Saddle River, New Jersey

Everyone has come home tonight. For this evening, the big house is not too big at all. They talk some about the game but not very much. They have been through nights like this too many times in too many places not to know the rules of the game. They make the most of dinner. Nobody will be awake tomorrow when the coach leaves. None of them will see him on Saturday and the chances are that he will not even telephone from the hotel the Giants make their pregame headquarters for home games. If the Giants win, Judy Parcells will leave the stadium and drive directly to nearby Manny's Restaurant to wait for him. Whenever they win, she meets him there.

If they lose, she will return to an empty house to wait. He will come straight home, eat a sandwich ("He says he never eats anything on the day of a game," she says), fall into the big easy chair in the family room, and stare at the television screen where the second game of a network doubleheader is just ending or an ESPN Sunday night game just beginning. Within a half hour he will climb the stairs to bed and begin the weekly cycle all over again the next morning.

The two ritual options are as unspoken as they are chiseled in stone.

10:00 P.M., West Paterson, New Jersey

This is Erik Howard's last night to forget. He has already become a little anxious. For most of his life, first at Bellarmine Prep in San Jose, later at Washington State, and now as a fourth-year pro, he has been able to hold off the tension until the night before the game. "Otherwise," he says, "you burn up too much anxiety too fast."

Tonight, the tension surrounding this biggest game of the year has begun to nag at him. But he wills the demons to sleep for another twenty-four hours, knowing that in this game he will need them at their wildest. Through sheer force of habit, he has managed to keep the task in perspective. Tomorrow night will be something else.

After practice today, he left his car for Jumbo and he and Steve De Ossie drove over to the linebacker's apartment where "I kicked his butt in video football and hockey. Then we went out and got something to eat. I had filet mignon," he says. "Why not? It was the house special.

"Now tomorrow night . . . well, tomorrow night, it won't be this easy."

11:00 P.M., Rutherford, New Jersey

Myron Guyton is starting to feel more comfortable in the Big Apple. It is, of course, a far cry from Thomasville, Georgia, but he anticipates living here in the off-season to take part in the Giants' winter-spring conditioning program. "I want to become more involved in the community," he says. "I want to be useful. This evening I called a guy over at the sheriff's office and he told me I could start to volunteer in late January. I want to speak to the kids in school and help out all I can."

Tonight, he and wide receiver Stacy Robinson have been to see the New Jersey Nets play at the arena just down the road from the stadium. They spent most of the night comparing Keith Jackson and Zeke Mowatt.

Now he is back home and for the first time this week he has no plans to study film. "I pretty much know what I have to do now. I'll be better than the last time we played them. One thing, I won't have trouble sleeping. I've had too much to learn and so much to remember, I'm just too tired to stay awake."

11:30 P.M., Wood Bridge, New Jersey

Reyna Thompson and a few friends went to the same Nets basketball game. They did not talk football. Thompson is a basketball buff and tonight's matchup between the Nets and Miami was somewhat disappointing for him. On the way home he stopped by Sheldon White's apartment and shot some pool.

"Earlier in the week," he says, "I think everybody was tense. There's a lot at stake here. But today, I could really feel the confidence level building. We know the game plan. We've studied them. We played them before.

"I think we're going to be all right."

5. SATURDAY, DECEMBER 2, 1989

6:30 A.M., offensive coaches' conference room

Fred Hoaglin is sitting alone in front of the tape machine, notebook open, ballpoint pen at the ready. He is staring at the strangers on the screen. He is fighting off a head cold. His eyes are watery and his nose is running. For the first time this week, he sees no Reggie White powering his way across the line of scrimmage; no Jerome Brown clawing his way through the pass blocking. The defense he's watching now does not radiate the muscle and stampede approach which he has studied all week long.

This time, the guys are wearing orange jerseys and defending their territorial imperative in a stadium where the air is so thin an Inca would gasp for breath in the fourth quarter. Pro football is a game of tomorrows and unlike the tomorrows of Macbeth, they do not creep forward at a "petty pace." They fly by as though the days were only fifteen hours long.

Even as Hoaglin lectures, cajoles, and challenges his offensive line with the specter of the Philadelphia Eagles hanging over them, he has other tomorrows with which to deal. In eight days, the Giants will travel to Denver, where the Broncos have already clinched their division title. In the solitude of the coaches' end of

the building, Hoaglin has already begun to identify the potential
for nightmares as yet unborn.

"I'm looking," he says, "at who does what and how to get
them blocked. I'm looking for defensive line stunts and linebacker movement. These guys [the Broncos] are totally different
from the Eagles. Their defense is simple, but now we're dealing
with finesse instead of power."

Then he cuts off the machine and puts down his pen. Long
after practice has ended today, he will continue to dissect this
other football team which has now intruded on his life. By Monday, he must be able to present his report on tendencies to
Belichick. Now, as quickly and as smoothly as an automatic
transmission shifting gears, he is once again talking about the
Eagles, as if talking about them will help him to find that one last
golden nugget in that worked-out creek bed.

"Yesterday we had to do some reminding on our pass blocking. We usually area block everything. The scout squad ran an
Eagle formation where their middle linebacker and their nose
guard crossed. We can block it two ways. If the guard [Eric
Moore] has the linebacker over him, he can stay where he is and
also help the tackle and the center, and if the backer crosses
behind one of them, they should pass him off.

"At practice, Oates should have been passing Pitts off to
Moore. He didn't. They have to communicate with each other.
You can't make those mistakes against them. The Eagles are too
physical."

He makes this last comment with a kind of open admiration. At
the height of his eleven-year playing career as an all-pro center,
these were the kind of opponents he relished. For him, his game
of games was always Bob Lilly and the Dallas Cowboys.

"He was my Reggie White. The Steelers were physical and the
Raiders were physical, but for me, Lilly made the Cowboys
special. He was a big, strong guy who played hard every play.

Against him, you could measure yourself. Players know if they are getting the job done. When you play against the best in the league like Lilly, you get to look at yourself. Remember he was 270 and back then, that made him the biggest at his position by, say, 15 pounds. Sure, he was really strong, but it was his technique that put him years ahead of every other down lineman of his time.

"I remember he played from a four-point stance with both hands on the ground and the first thing he did was shoot his hands up to your shoulders with such force that he seemed to gain total control of you almost before you could come off the ball. It took a couple of years before any of us could figure out how to play him. The coaches finally figured out that with his hands raised to control either the guard or the center, he was open below and the free guy could come over and chop him.

"There's an answer for everyone. What I have to do now as a line coach is to identify the technique and show my players what they can—must—do against guys as strong as they are. With Reggie, Bart's got to make up his mind to go out there and take him on closer to the line. Against a great player you have to have your mind made up what you are going to do, maybe two or three approaches, and then you have to say, 'I'm going to do it. I'm not gonna let him change my mind. I'm not gonna guess.' No matter what happens and no matter how great he is, you wipe out the last play in your mind and you keep on doing what you know can work if you do it right.

"With Jerome Brown, he's inconsistent. I don't know if he's lazy or tired or out of shape or just trying to lull you to sleep. He can make great plays and he's made the majority of big plays they've made against us. William [Roberts] has to establish a fast pace and keep it fast. He has to make Jerome work when Jerome doesn't feel like working. He has to make him the reactor rather than the initiator. Can William do it? I wish I knew."

Then the old player in him surfaces and in a single short burst he strips away all the Xs and Os and reduces this Giants-Eagles game to its basic elements:

"If you like football this is the place to be tomorrow. It's physical . . . a war . . . a battle . . . hittin' and cursin'. If you like the nasty stuff of pro football, this is the place to be. This is the kind of game I love."

7:00 A.M., Bill Parcells's office

The coach is sitting at his desk, the obligatory coffee cup and the pack of cigarettes at the ready. All week he had hinted at a possible quarterback change. The general manager had cautioned that "what the coach says on Wednesday may not be what he will come to believe by Friday." He now knows that Simms will start and, although he has not communicated this to his quarterback with any flat statement, in his own mind-set, Simms fully expects to be given the ball. He is not unaware of the coach's role as head psychologist. He will even grudgingly admit that it is often effective.

"I put in the paper on Friday," Parcells says, "that I wasn't sure whether he was gonna start or not. I did that as much for Philadelphia as I did for him. But I told him, 'Don't buy the papers tomorrow. You're not gonna like what you read.' Phil's very, very competitive, but he's human like everybody else. It could be that he may have lost a little something but that has nothing to do with his desire. I don't think anybody in the organization wants to face that possibility. But I will if I have to.

"The players are all paranoid," Parcells is saying. "They know that I believe that sooner or later, God takes it away from all of them—all of them. I had a kid here named Tony Galbreath [running back, 1984–87] and the hardest thing I ever had to do was cut him. He was one of the nicest kids you'd ever meet. He was ten years in the league and he was making $250,000 and he didn't have a thing to show for it. His finances were all screwed up. I sat down with him and I told him things like 'Pay your taxes.' He didn't have a clue. He worked hard and he played hard and he was gonna wind up with nothing.

"Tony was a guy I wished I'd had earlier. He was talented. I think if I could've had him earlier in his career, I think he would've been great. He was very shy and introverted until he got to know you. He had this one thing he could do. When he came here, I told him he'd have to be a role player and he was stubborn and he didn't like that. But once he understood, he accepted it.

"So now I could see his skills starting to slip. But the one thing he did—and he's still going to be able to do on the day before he dies—he could run out of the backfield and catch a third-down pass. But that's a trap. It makes you think you can do other things when you can't. I kept him as long as I could and I'm not sorry about that. Hell, we didn't find a guy for that role until Meggett came along.

"I worry about Galbreath now. He's shy. He didn't want to ask anybody for a job. He lives in a little town in Missouri. George Martin [perhaps the most financially successful of Parcells's ex-Giants] is trying to help him now.

"It happens and it hurts because there's nothing much you can do about it. One of the nicest kids who ever played for me was a big, old country boy named Curtis McGriff [defensive tackle, 1980–86]. He was almost illiterate but a good human being, good values, do the right thing. Same kind of case—only worse. I brought him up here last year and sat him right in that chair and screamed at him. I mean I chewed his ass off. Yelled at him to make something of himself. He just didn't have any confidence.

"McGriff never made that much. He goes down to Alabama, spends thirty-five, forty thousand a year. Well, in eight years or

less, you know it's all gonna be gone. He doesn't work. He
drinks beer during the day and rides around at night and that kind
of thing. But there's not much you can do about it.

"You stay in touch. [Jerome] Salley [defensive tackle, 1982–
86] I don't worry about. He's got his degree. He isn't afraid to
work. He's doing all right. [Dee] Hardison [defensive end, 1981–
85] is another one. I worry but I think he'll do all right. He's
another great kid. His wife's in the army. They have a good
marriage.

"Players are like anybody else. Society is so different than
when I was up at West Point. That place has a lot to do with what
I believe: the work ethic . . . do the right thing . . . loyalty. Now
the kids in college, the kids who finally come here, are totally
different. See, I talk to my players about what I call the To Have
mentality as opposed to the To Be mentality. You work to have
money, to have cars, to have houses, to have things—and that's
logical. And they shoot back, 'Well, what are we supposed to be
working for?'

"I tell them you have the tail wagging the dog. You work to
be the best you can be and then the rest follows. It's not To Have
first. It's To Be first. Leonard Marshall? I tell him you're playing
to negotiate your next contract but if you play to be the best you
can be, the next contract will come. Some of them listen. They
know."

There is irony to this last part. Whether it is the cause and
effect of the coach's lecture or whether it was arrived at from a
totally different thought process, there is a speech by the late
Martin Luther King, Jr., affixed to the inside wall of Marshall's
locker:

> If a man is called to be a street sweeper, he should sweep
> streets even as Michelangelo painted and Beethoven composed
> music or Shakespeare wrote poetry. He should sweep streets so

well that all the hosts of Heaven and Earth shall pause to say, "Here lived a great street sweeper who did his job well."

Parcells says that it is the failure to be the best you can that angers him the most, along with the failure to do what he calls "the right thing."

"Back in 1986 I had a couple of guys in training camp who were late. We had a dental appointment for them and they don't show up. *We're* gonna fix *their* teeth and we can't even find them. I was pissed. And I told them, 'You know, you guys are so fuckin' irresponsible. We do everything for you. We spoonfeed you. And you don't even have the courtesy to show up or call somebody and say you're not coming. And all I ever hear out of any of you when it's time to do your contract is that you have to do the right thing for your family because your family comes first. Well, I've been on the road and a couple of you sons of bitches act like you don't even have families.' I tore their heads off.

"Ask the old guys. Ask Phil McConkey next time you see him. He can repeat those speeches word for word. His imitation is better than my original.

"I only get angry at halftime if we are not playing at the level we should be at. The maddest I ever was was in '86. We're playing the Green Bay Packers and they stink. We get up 24–0 and it's 24–21 at halftime. I come in there and I knock over every hot chocolate container. I'm screaming that we're playing a bunch of ham-and-eggers and we're letting them make a game out of it. That team of ours was so good it was going to going on and win the Super Bowl a month later. I was so mad I actually threw garbage at them. I mean I picked up a garbage pail and dumped it on somebody's head and said, 'Go on back out there with the rest of the trash.'

"But I only get that way when we're better than we've played.

This year we are not a great team but I think we've performed as well as we can most of the time. But if we lose this game tomorrow, I'll feel like a failure. See, I know that it just doesn't matter who can't play or who isn't 100 percent. You can't rationalize like that. There's a way to do it . . . a way to win. You just have to find it. That's the mentality that coaching is really all about. Nobody else understands. It's black or it's white. You won or you lost. Monday morning, they'll be sitting in the diner drinking coffee and eating their Danish and there's only one thing they want to know about when they pick up the paper. Who won. Not who didn't play or who tried, but who won.

"Mickey [Cochrane, his old high-school basketball coach] taught me that. He always said there was a way to win every game. Finding it is what separates some people from others. I remember a game. I was seventeen years old. And the score is tied and he calls time out. He says to me, 'Parcells, I'm gonna get you the ball in this location with your back to the basket with about eight seconds to go in the game. Your job is to get it in the basket.'

"All right, now he has to go through the technical part of it to get me the ball. He has to deliver the situation. That's coaching. That's what he's supposed to do. I'm just focusing how to get the ball in the basket because the rest of the job is his. That's being a coach. Maybe I didn't realize it at the time but he reduced it to the bottom line for me when I was only seventeen years old.

"So maybe we don't have Taylor and maybe Simms isn't 100 percent. But there's a way to put us in position to win that game tomorrow. It's my job to find it."

8:00 A.M., Dunkin Donuts shop, New Jersey State Highway 17
"Mr. Donut of 1989" wheels off the highway and into the parking lot. As he approaches the front door, he walks like a man

who has covered all the bases, laid all the groundwork, and is in the midst of a serious mission.

"I got 'em right here, ready to go," the guy behind the counter hollers when he spots him. "They're all here. Just like you ordered. I got some more Bavarian creams in there this time." He emerges from around the edge of the counter carrying a load that gives him the look of a baker in search of a truss. "They're all here . . . twenty dozen."

"You sure you got the bran muffins in there for the older gentlemen?" Mr. Donut of 1989 asks.

"Sure do. And you got some of those special cinnamon rolls there, too."

Later, when his locker room trail has been reduced to crumbs and empty boxes, Mr. Donut explains:

"I bring variety. I do the job. I only got ten or fifteen complaints today. That's not bad. I heard those stories about Eric Moore, Mark Ingram, and Eric Dorsey. They say Dorsey used to buy day-old Munchkins. Not me. I deal in nothing but quality stuff."

Brian Williams will be defrocked as Mr. Donut before the end of January. It is a traditional task which falls to the highest draft choice each season. He not only picks up the Saturday donuts, he pays for them.

"I take pride in my work," he deadpans. "Where it's tough is on the road. Did you ever walk into a donut shop in Dallas and say, 'Give me twenty dozen to go?' "

8:00 A.M., defensive coaches' conference room

The defensive coordinator, Bill Belichick, is making last-minute adjustments before he goes down to meet the troops. For once, the projector is silent. On the table in front of him sits an open blue loose-leaf notebook. He is clearly the most intense among the coaches. If you didn't know better, you would have sworn that he hadn't left this room since Tuesday morning.

"Yesterday afternoon," he says, "we thought we were about finished and now here we are the morning before the game trying to come up with some adjustments in case Lawrence plays. If he does, we'll probably try to use him as a starter. We'll still mirror with Adrian [White]. Yesterday we thought about converting everything back to the original plan if Taylor can play, but at practice some people got confused.

"So we're going to use the new calls and make sure Lawrence knows them. See, even if Lawrence plays, I don't see where he could run well enough to be the mirror. So we'll leave Adrian there and see what we can get out of Taylor. And we'll leave Gary [Reasons] where we put him on the goal line stuff."

For Belichick, the bottom-line challenge is different than for some of his colleagues. It is not the raised level of physical combat when these two teams meet. What intrigues him is the challenge of new Xs and Os for a totally different task than faced the Giants against San Francisco in the previous game.

"I like the newness of the challenge," he says. "Last week, it was Jerry Rice and those guys. No emphasis on the tight end. Montana, a real accurate quarterback; Rice, a great wide receiver; Craig, a good running back and receiver, just a well-oiled machine. Two weeks before that, it was the Rams and it was different. The tight end never caught a pass. The tailback never caught a pass. But they had Flipper Anderson and Greg Bell and Robert Delpino—a totally different challenge.

"With the Eagles, we have the scrambling quarterback [Randall Cunningham], an outstanding tight end [Keith Jackson] in the passing game, and a great leaper [Cris Carter] inside the 20. Planning is totally different. This is really much more of a matchup game. The teams know each other so well. They know

where we'll be. We know where they'll be. Neither side wants
a mismatch. It's almost like a basketball game. If you're playing against Magic Johnson or James Worthy and you don't
have a guy who can stay with them, they'll score 50 points on
you.

"But if we were playing a team like, say, Bobby Knight's
style of basketball team, that's the kind of team where one guy
goes out one night and scores 20 and the next night somebody
else does it.

"Play the 49ers and they're like that. Rice could catch eight
passes or Taylor could or even Craig.

"Here against the Eagles, it's fewer people involved in the offense, but you can't afford to make a mistake. So prior to the snap
you have to disguise as much as you can, you know, the same
initial look and then you switch at the snap."

"You know, when you look at that game down in Philly, we
did get ahead in the fourth period. We were ahead late enough in
the game. Whatever else did or didn't happen, we should have
held them. We should have won.

"Now I read in the press that since we lost three straight to
them, we're getting this thing about the Eagles. They're saying
the Eagles have our number. You can't let something like that go
unchallenged with your players. So I told them yesterday that if
we block a field goal and the ball rolls around loose and they get
a touchdown out of their own error, if Jackson catches a pass over
the middle and we strip the ball and it bounces back into their
hands for a touchdown, or if they can't do it legitimately because
Randall Cunningham still hasn't crossed the goal on that touchdown against us down there, if doing that means they have our
number and you believe that shit, then you better go back and
look at the tapes."

As Belichick spoke there was a commotion just outside the
door. Al Groh was dashing down the hall toward the defensive

coaches' room, shouting. As he burst through the door, he threw both hands above his head and shouted, "Hallelujah, a star is born! Lawrence is going to play!"

9:30 A.M., locker room

They have begun the meetings. Mostly, it's a restating of the lessons of the week with some added attention to special teams. The quarterbacks can repeat the game plan like honor students in a catechism class. The separate full offense and full defense meetings watch game films. Then they break into subunits. Back in the laundry room, where the offensive line always meets, Hoaglin is breaking things down to their most elementary level:

"You were good enough to beat them last time, but you forgot to play with the same intensity in the fourth quarter and it cost us. You can't sit there and look over your shoulder and wait and see if he [Cunningham] is going to beat you. So what does it come down to?

"We've got to win every short-yardage situation—third and one. We've got to win when we get across the 20-yard line. We've got to win when we get the ball down on the goal line. In those situations, we've got to win the instant you snap the ball on that play.

"And settling for a field goal isn't winning."

11:00 A.M., general manager's office

George Young is sitting at his desk, returning telephone calls and shuffling through paperwork. This is his half of the building. Here on this side, removed from the coaching offices, the player personnel people tap their computers and study their scouting reports all year long. Farther down and even further removed from the coaches are the ticket offices, the public relations and promotion offices, and the twin offices of the owner-president, Wellington Mara, and the owner–vice president–treasurer, Tim Mara, who do not speak to each other unless absolutely necessary.

There is a great deal of symbolism in the building's working geography. It is no accident that the general manager's office is where it is. The ample bulk of the general manager keeps the football and business operations totally separate.

There seems little reason to doubt that the family feud is without impact on the actual running of the organization. Football, after all, is the corporation's sole product and just as painters must be left alone to create and musicians left alone to compose, football coaches do far better without a crowd at their backs.

Parcells would be the first to concede that he is left alone to run his team. George Young is the primary reason.

The head coach and the general manager share very little in the way of common interests beyond the life and times of the New York Giants. But in a way that neither will ever admit— except as a casual, sometimes grudging, appositive clause— each gives a great deal of credit to the other. Parcells wonders only half in jest why Young is the most visible and most interviewed general manager. But it is Young who accords Parcells the very privacy and working elbow room the coach obviously craves.

For three straight nights the general manager has fielded telephone calls at home (mostly about Taylor) from reporters, calls which come as late as 11:30. They are calls the coach did not have to be bothered with, and he did not have to alienate anyone by not accepting them. Young, therefore, is a buffer for Parcells in many ways, not the least of which is that no problem involving either owner can ever get to the coach without a pit stop in the general manager's office. By Parcells's own admission, Young is also a general manager who lets his coach run the football team.

In return, Parcells has brought the franchise, and its general manager, its only Super Bowl appearance and title, a role as annual contender for the division crown, and a football team that has finally repaid what was at times the undeserved semireligious ardor of its fans.

Parcells's elevation to the head coaching job in 1983 was Young's decision out of Young's initiative, with the ultimate approval of the two principal owners. Now the general manager is talking about that decision.

"The first time I heard his name mentioned, I was still in Miami straightening up my affairs to come here. I went into the Dolphins office to clean out my desk and to fly out to California to interview Ray Perkins, who got the job. I was talking with Dan Henning and he said there's a guy you ought to be interested in named Bill Parcells. He had coached with Bill at Florida State and he told me that if I did hire him, he would be the best coach on my staff.

"I have respect for Henning but I didn't want to jam anyone down the new coach's throat. Then Perkins told me he wanted to hire a guy named Parcells and I was delighted.

"Later, just before Perkins quit to take the Alabama job, I had a feeling he would go. You know we're talking about succeeding Bear Bryant. All those former Alabama players—they're like the followers of Muhammad and they're all there following him and when he dies, each of them wants to be the anointed one to take his place.

"Now Bryant didn't die, but when the word got out that he was favoring Ray, well, that was even more impressive, so I really wasn't surprised that he'd take it. In the first place, he could immediately make more money than he was making here.

"So now I'm in Tulsa and I'm getting ready to fly home and

I know what I'm going to do. There was never another candidate in mind. That was on Monday and I called Bill Monday night from the Tulsa airport and told him I wanted to meet with him on Tuesday night. When I got back, Jack Pardee telephoned about the job but I told him I knew how I was going to fill it. Both Maras immediately agreed.

"On Tuesday night, Bill and I met down the hall in the conference room. It was a great meeting. I had him read the corporate resolutions that made him responsible only to me. It wasn't really an interview because I already knew him so well and I knew he was the man I wanted.

"The thing I remember most was that there was no real negotiating and no problems and then, just before he agreed, he looked up and said to me, 'Now, George, you're not gonna write anything in that contract that says I have to socialize or play golf?'

"I started to laugh but he was serious. So I told him that the last place I wanted him was on the golf course.

"There's no mystery to what happens here. I'm not looking for a genius coach. I'm not saying that Bill isn't one. What I'm saying is that we are not in the genius business. We have good people in the front office and good people on the coaching staff who will pay a price to win. What you have to do is make sure you make every effort in every way to keep them.

"If you're looking for a messiah in this business, forget it. That happened a long time ago."

12:00 noon, trainer's office

The first time Ronnie Barnes noticed Lawrence Taylor that morning, it was 8:30 and the linebacker was sitting in the locker room drinking coffee with Ron Erhardt, Phil Simms, Maurice Carthon, and OJ Anderson. His naked foot was resting on the table and he was wearing no bandage. He waved to Barnes, who just laughed and shook his head.

"He had been using DMSO and I could smell it," Barnes says. "Actually he loaned some to Phil Simms because I could smell it on him, too. I had told Simms that I thought he was a pretty bright guy, after all, he's the quarterback. 'Are you sure,' I asked him, 'that you want to put your medical future into the hands of Dr. Lawrence Taylor?' Simms just laughed.

"Anyway, Taylor really had a positive attitude. He can get up on his toes and he can walk on his heels. I taped him. I taped his Achilles tendon and then I taped the rest of his ankle up real good and he put the brace on. Essentially, the only place he said he hurt was in his calf and in just a little spot up in his ankle. Some of that's from the swelling and some of that's from the fracture.

"Then Dr. Al Levy [another Giants staff physician] came in to take a look. He's named me Oliver Hardy this week, what with all the medical problems, so the first thing he said was, 'Well, another fine mess you've gotten me into, Ollie.' Then Parcells peeked in and he watched but he told Lawrence just to shut up and not make any big deal of all this because this thing wouldn't be decided until tomorrow morning.

"Then Lawrence left and Bill was smiling and he was saying that he wanted this game so bad, he'd pay a hundred thousand dollars to win.

"After the team meetings, Lawrence went outside on the tarp and ran while Dr. Levy watched. I found something else to do. I knew if I went out there he'd start telling me about how he could play and try to get me to talk to Parcells. I didn't want to hear that and I didn't want to watch him. I just wanted to get to the point where Russ [Warren, the orthopedist] can come in and test him. Actually, right now I'm still a little worried about Jumbo's sore ankle.

"But wait until they pick up the newspapers tomorrow and see that Lawrence might try it," Barnes says and then smiles broadly before adding: "Everybody loves Superman."

1:00 P.M., Bill Parcells's office

This is the shortest day of the workweek and, slowly, the coaching staff has begun to drift off to reintroduce itself to its families. Belichick is heading for Chatham, where he will spend a little time grading the San Francisco tapes, put up the storm windows, and take a ride with his wife, Debby, his four-year-old daughter, Amanda, and his two-year-old son, Stephen.

Erhardt, Crennel, Leachman, Handley, Pope, and Sweatman have left. Groh is off to watch his son, the quarterback, play in that state championship game. Hoaglin will take his Denver tapes and notebook home for a while and then take his family to a mall for some Christmas shopping. Tommy Coughlin, one of whose daughters is a student at Auburn, pauses in the doorway to talk about this afternoon's televised Auburn-Alabama game, the first time the two ancient powerhouse rivals will play at Auburn stadium.

"Talked to my daughter down there last night," he says, "and she said they're going crazy. There's 150,000 people gonna try to get into that stadium today. She says they're paying five hundred dollars for a ticket."

"I'll bet," Parcells says. "They'll be eating that Brunswick stew today. Somebody should do a book on that culture down there. You could write a whole book on what happens from eight in the morning until noon on the highways. Just drive back and forth down the highways to the stadium. People trading bowls of that crappy stew through the car windows."

"Hey," Coughlin says, "it's the most poverty-stricken state in the union but money is no object when it comes to football. You ought to see the building they built to house the football players. A ten million dollar building. The only building in town higher than two stories. There's this little town and the stadium holds eighty-seven thousand people. Game day they have a pregame meal and then the coach leads them out and they march to the fuckin' stadium. All the fans are right there and the sidewalks are roped off and they're going fuckin' nuts. Here they come with the coach in the lead—General Lee is marching the troops into battle.''

"Do you remember in 1972 when that Strickland kid blocked those two punts?" Parcells asks. And now he is telling his kind of story. "Bear Bryant is the coach and Alabama is undefeated and they're winning the game, 16–3, with eight minutes to go. This kid Strickland blocks two punts, both returned for touchdowns, and Auburn wins, 17–16.

"They say that the kid could hardly get to the dressing room for the money people were running on the field and shoving at him. Now I know kids who played in that game and they said that by the time he got to the dressing room he had more than five thousand dollars. He started off the field with nothing. People are shoving hundred dollar bills at him. He didn't know where to put it. He could hardly carry it. He had to stuff it in his jersey and down inside his pants.

"Then they came out with that tune, 'Punt, 'Bama, Punt,' and it's on every juke box in the state. It's another world."

Coughlin is out the door to run his errands so he can get home before the game comes on television.

While Parcells retains the intensity that will build until there is nothing in his mind or his view or his world on Sunday but the quest expressed by his old high-school basketball coach as "finding a way to win," he is not unmindful of the spectacle that surrounds all football games great and small.

"It makes you feel like you're twenty-one," he says. "Sure it does. I wish that everybody who is forty-eight could have moments when they feel like they're twenty-one. I tell my team that all the time. I hope one day when they're forty-eight they'll have something that makes them feel that way.

"It's a tremendous range of emotion. Tremendous. Maybe not every Sunday, but I know it'll be that way this Sunday. It starts to build today. Today I'm ready. It's competition. You wanna

fight. The bullshit is over. Let's see who's best. Gimme that
Monday night in San Francisco . . . gimme that last-second win
over Washington . . . gimme that Minnesota game nobody
thought we could win.

"Let me tell you, those fans in Washington and Philadelphia,
I like 'em. They hate me so much that it's almost like an ac-
knowledgment. They boo me so hard, they yell at me. They call
me so many vile names that it's almost respect.

"It gives you something extra. Like going down there to Washington for that Monday night when I tell 'em, this is what it's
gonna be like down there. Don't take my word. Ask the other
players. You must prepare for the violent sound. We won down
here before. We always win down here. But there's only forty-
five of us. Nobody else. You have to stay together. We're out-
numbered. All that kind of stuff.

"I have never in my life heard a sound like on that Monday
night this year when [Raul] Allegre made that 52-yarder to beat
them. Never. It was like . . . well . . . first of all, they go ahead
down the stretch and the people are berserk. It's the most boisterous, rowdy, and violent sound you ever heard when Hostetler
kneels down to make the hold.

And then it stopped—dead . . . stone . . . silence—like you
just stepped into a cemetery. I could actually hear my players'
voices just as clear as we're talking in this room. And it stayed
that way all across the field. All the way into the tunnel. One of
the greatest feelings I have ever had in my life.

"Now," and he stops in midsentence to laugh, "wait until we
go down there next year."

1:30 P.M., Newark Airport

He walked through the terminal with a small overnighter in one
hand and a garment bag slung over his shoulder. The flight from

Dallas was on time, but he quickened his pace because there was a rental car to pick up and there were people waiting for him at the nearby Airport Marriott Hotel.

He is fifty-eight years old and for the past twelve years, he has been employed as a sales manager for a Cleveland manufacturing firm. But that has nothing to do with this trip. In a little less than twenty-four hours, Gordon McCarter will be the single most important man in Giants Stadium. He has come to referee the Giants-Eagles game.

The crew he was on his way to meet would include Ben Montgomery (umpire), a school administrator from Washington, D.C.; Dave Anderson (head linesman), an insurance man from West Virginia; Ron Baynes (line judge), a high-school teacher and coach from Alabama; Jim Daopoulos (back judge), a mortgage banker from Atlanta; Dick Creed (side judge), who owns a nursing home in Ohio; Jack Vaughan (field judge), who is in financial planning in New Orleans; and Chuck Heberling (instant replay official), who is the executive director of the Western Pennsylvania Interscholastic Athletic League.

Gordon McCarter came to the NFL off the playing fields of Western Reserve University (where he was a varsity fullback) and out of the high-school football leagues of Ohio and four years' hard time in something called the United Football League, where he was a whistle-blower. This last credential was a minor league with franchises in cultural way stations like Grand Rapids and Wheeling. It used the National Football League rule book as its bible and, because of that, McCarter's application was given serious consideration when he first applied to the NFL for an officiating job in 1964.

Two years later the NFL asked for a schedule of games he would work that fall and he was duly scouted. After a written examination, McCarter was told that sixteen neophyte officials were competing for six openings made possible by imminent expansion. He was hired for the 1967 season.

As he nosed the rental car away from the terminal and around the maze of traffic circles that led to the hotel, McCarter was thinking about his crew's work schedule for this afternoon and evening. One thing he was not thinking about was a long-ago period of time when he worked sandlot football games on rock-hard Ohio fields.

Those were games where the Marquis of Queensberry Rules were of far more value than the NFL rule book. "We never had more than two hundred spectators," he says, "but it seemed like all of them were related to somebody playing in the game. Crowd control was, to say the least, a problem." What they lacked in numbers, they made up in filial loyalty. The fights before, during, and after the game were beautiful.

With all the talk coming out of the Giants and Eagles camps, it was clear that if it came down to it—and it almost never does in this league—there was nothing new either side could show Sunday's Head Zebra.

2:00 P.M., various places around New Jersey

These are the toughest hours. The Giants have all been turned loose to wait and to think and to kill time. From shortly after noon until 9:00 P.M. tonight, when they must check into the Hamilton Park Center (a sprawling hotel and meeting complex in Madison, New Jersey, not far from where the team has its preseason training camp) for yet more meetings and an overnight stay, they are on their own.

The one thing they seem to have in common is that most of them have plans to watch the Alabama-Auburn game on television. Al Groh and his family are already out at the tiny football field where his injured son, the quarterback, will sit on the bench, wearing his official NFL Giants cold-weather mittens, and watch his Randolph High School try to win the state championship. Heavy clouds have rolled in. The forecast tonight is for a 40 percent chance of snow with temperatures plummeting by morning. This afternoon, the thermometer has already begun to dip below freezing and the winds are increasing.

In Wood Ridge, Reyna Thompson has been on a nonstop schedule. The hectic pace is by design. "I don't like to sit around and think the day before a game," he says. "I try to keep as busy as I can."

He's already been to the supermarket to lay in the week's supply of food and household necessities. Now he is on his way to make the first of several stops to see friends in the neighborhood. After that, he will return home to watch a complete tape reel of all the special team sequences in the last Giants-Eagles game. "I'll probably get to the hotel around seven to relax," he says, "but I'll keep on watching the weather reports on television." He is from Texas and played his college ball at Baylor and his previous pro ball in Miami.

"This will be my first supercold game," he says. "I wonder what it'll be like."

William Roberts, on the other hand, will not set foot outside his apartment until it is time to leave for the hotel. "I'm going home," he says, "to study my playbook. I'm going to close my eyes and try to visualize the different formations, the defensive fronts and my blocking assignments. Then I'm going to watch Alabama-Auburn."

He does not mention Jerome Brown, but after Hoaglin's constant reminders, it is not unreasonable to think that he will give him a thought or two.

Jeff Hostetler is at home playing with his two young sons. Tonight he will drive fifty-one miles from his River Vale home to the hotel headquarters. Unlike the others, he will duplicate that drive early tomorrow morning when he doubles back and picks up his wife Vicky and drives her to the stadium. It is a ritual they have observed ever since he joined the team in 1984.

Erik Howard is back in the West Paterson apartment he shares with Jumbo Elliot. This afternoon he will follow his regular Saturday practice of loading up on carbohydrates with a heavy pasta lunch. "Energy," he says. "There's more at stake here than any other game this season. I'll probably go to the mall and try to get in a little Christmas shopping later on.

"Tonight may be the only time of the week when it's a little tougher to sleep."

Myron Guyton will spend the afternoon visiting with his sister and other relatives who have come to town for the game. He says he plans to try to contact Jessie Small, his college roommate, who plays for the Eagles and whom he has unsuccessfully attempted to reach by phone several times this week. Usually, they speak on the telephone about once a week.

"I wonder if he's avoiding me?" he muses.

Phil Simms is busy teaching the facts of economic life to his son, Christopher, who feels as though he absolutely, positively cannot play another basketball game in his old basketball shoes.

"Well, let's go out and get a new pair," Simms says, "and then—wait a minute. You have a closet loaded with shoes. Go up there and put a pair on."

"They're too tight," the boy says when he returns.

"Let me feel them. They're fine, Christopher, just fine. Maybe you'd just rather not play."

"I guess they'll loosen up," says Chris Simms, who knows he has just been sacked.

And wherever Jeff Rutledge, the eleven-year pro third-string quarterback, is, you can take it to the bank that he is one Giant who is surely going to watch the Alabama game.

Rutledge was born and raised in Alabama, lettered four years at quarterback for the late Bear Bryant, played in four bowls as well as the East-West and Senior Bowl all-star games and broke Joe Willie Namath's school record for touchdown passes.

He never calls it Alabama-Auburn. Like the army of 'Bama faithful, which Parcells and Coughlin so accurately described, to him it is just "the Alabama Game."

3:00 P.M., Gordon McCarter's suite, Airport Marriott Hotel

The officiating crew is in the suite's sitting room, staring at the television set. They are not watching Alabama-Auburn. They are watching San Diego at Indianapolis and they already know who is going to win because they worked the game last Sunday. What they are doing is studying a detailed written review of their officiating performance. They will stay together as a crew all season and they will follow this same ritual on the afternoon before each game.

Each week, following the tape, one crew member is assigned to give a talk on rule interpretations. This week, because he had attended a special meeting for referees in Dallas on Friday, Mc-Carter has assigned himself to the task, using a topic discussed the night before. Now he will lecture on "the phantom call." It deals with accidental flags and no calls and calls without flags. Undoubtedly, it would be an interesting subject to the men who will play tomorrow and the men who will coach them.

The group will break for an early dinner in the hotel at 5:00 P.M., and during the meal, somebody mentions the Great Buddy Ryan Bounty Hunt, still under investigation by the league. Mc-Carter tells them that "the entire bounty thing is none of our damned business."

Before the evening ends, the group will meet yet one more time in McCarter's suite. Earlier in the week, each man had received an open-book examination in the mail from the league office—a weekly practice. This week's subject is Rule 12. In light of all the verbal muscle-flexing between the Giants and the Eagles this week, there is more than a little irony here.

Rule 12 is the unsportsmanlike conduct rule.

3:00 p.m., Eric Moore's apartment

Eric Moore feels as though a large blast furnace and an iceberg large enough to sink the Titanic are fighting for control of his body. Periodic waves of nausea override both feelings. If it's December and it's New Jersey, then you can take it to the bank that this must be the flu.

It began the day before. Barnes, in consultation with the team's medical staff, has provided Moore with the proper medication. The week has contained more than its share of private tensions for the lineman out of Indiana University who was the team's number-one draft selection a year earlier. For one thing, there is Jumbo's ankle.

For a time it looked as though the huge offensive tackle might not make it on Sunday, in which case Moore would have had to shift from his right guard spot to Jumbo's slot at left tackle and he, in turn, would have been replaced by Brian Williams, Mr. Donut. Now it appears as though Jumbo will play and Moore will be in more familiar territory when the Eagles rush comes at him. Still, the possibility remains that something will happen to Jumbo and Moore will have to move during the game.

Then on Friday, the flu grabbed his body and wouldn't let go. Right now he feels as though he does not need medication. What he needs is an exorcism. He feels no immediate relief from what Barnes has given him. This morning he began to use some over-the-counter remedies along with his prescription drugs in the hope it will speed the recovery process.

He plans to check into the hotel earlier than usual to rest.

3:30 p.m., Randolph, New Jersey

The Grohs are standing on the sidelines talking to their son, Michael, who is still wearing his uniform. Michael did not play. It wasn't an extra arm Randolph High needed, it was an in-your-face defense. It was the kind of hitting game that delighted the linebacker coach who lives inside the father of the quarterback's body. Randolph won it, 22–7, and with it, the state championship.

Now Groh will have an hour or two to spend with the family back home before he leaves for the hotel. In the back of his mind, the euphoria of this morning's meeting with Lawrence Taylor has dissipated.

In its place there remains the same series of question marks— can Cooks handle the outside? Did Cox do his homework and will it help? How effectively will Adrian White mirror the Eagles' number 12? Groh knows that the answers and number 12 are both rushing toward him.

5:00 P.M., Upper Saddle River, New Jersey

The three Parcells daughters are all home for dinner along with Dallas's boyfriend from college. The coach is not there nor will he telephone. This is simply the way it is in most households when the game is about to go on the line and the father-husband has reduced the focus of his thoughts until they are 100 yards long, bounded by a goal post at either end.

Judy Parcells is no rookie in this game. Even before she met her husband, she was working part-time as a student in the Wichita State sports information office. It was there their paths first crossed when he was a varsity linebacker and their relationship blossomed into marriage before either graduated.

The coach says she knows so little about football that she doesn't even know whether the ball is blown up or stuffed with feathers. But he would be the first to concede that she knows a lot about the endless hours the job swallows and the endless number of coaches it chews up and spits out.

"Actually," Judy says, "his hours are better since he became a head coach. Depending on the circumstances, he's usually home by eight or nine o'clock. When he was an assistant coach at

Wichita State, he'd work until one or two in the morning some-times. And then with college ball, there were always the recruit-ing trips. Even though the season is longer in the pros, he actually has more time at home.

"But football is never very far out of his mind. I remember a couple of years ago we were sitting around the house—I guess it was April or early May—and he said why don't we get out and take a ride up to West Point, have lunch at the hotel in Highland Falls and ride past our old house at the academy.

"We both have a lot of feeling and memories about West Point so it seemed like a great idea. It was very cold but I didn't expect to get out of the car so all I took with me was a light sweater.

"We were driving toward the old house and the stadium is on the same road when we saw all these cars parked there and the football team was inside practicing, so Bill wanted to stop for a minute and say hello to some people. Mostly he wanted to see the coach and the trainer and the bus driver, who he really likes.

"So we got out of the car and it was freezing. We sat in the stands and then he went down on the field to talk to some people and then he came back up and sat some more. We must have been there an hour and a half and the wind was blowing in off the reservoir and I was absolutely shivering.

"That's when I tapped him on the shoulder and asked him if we were having fun yet."

Except for the year in Colorado Springs when he left football and suffered—not always in silence—their life has been an un-broken chain of 100-yard victories and defeats in a span of ge-ography that stretches across the entire face of the continent.

And, of course, there will always be the biggest memory of the biggest victory of all—the Super Bowl.

"I somehow knew that Bill was going to get there. The year out in Colorado when Bill wasn't coaching and we both knew he was going to get back into it, he said to me, 'I'm going to go back and someday I'm going to be a head coach in the NFL and I'm going to win a Super Bowl.' I always believed he would. And when it all came true it was such an emotional experience for both of us.

"I remember that when they came running out of the tunnel for the start of the game, all I could see was him and I was trying to feel what he was feeling. The huge stadium and all those people and he was in the middle of it. Then with half the fourth quarter left, I started to realize we were going to win.

"When it ended, they played that song, 'New York, New York,' and it just filled the stadium. And to just stand there and listen to it, I got goose bumps. My parents and my three sisters were there and my daughters and my son-in-law. There were even some of the people who had played with Bill at Wichita State.

"And just before that the clock was counting down and I was looking for Bill on the sidelines. That was the year they were dumping the Gatorade on him each time they won. I found him just about the time the players were picking him up on their shoulders. And I started to cry.

"It was the happiest moment of my life."

5:30 P.M., Bill Parcells's suite, Hamilton Park Center
The coach is stretched out on the bed. Directly in front of him, the television set is filled with Auburn-Alabama, just as it had been filled with Texas A&M and Arkansas an hour or so before. The excitement that had marked him heavily during the afternoon has given way to reflection. Now he is talking about the business of football.

"It occurs to me," he says, "that in all of the NFL, I'm the sixth senior head coach and I haven't been here all that long. One of the problems with franchises in this league is the continual stream of new coaches with new faces and new philosophy. They continue to create chaos in their own organizations because, well, the scouts are used to doing things the way they do it and here comes a new guy and to them he's just another coach. And the coach doesn't get to stay long enough to where the organization will listen to him.

"See, there's only three ways to go for a coach in this kind of world. You can dominate—run your own team completely with absolutely no interference ever. You can migrate—move from team to team and make new beginnings each time like some coaches do. Or you can just walk away."

There would seem to be little doubt as to which of the choices has dominated his thinking thus far.

"I came here as an assistant coach," he says, "because I thought, well, I'd done a good job in New England. I liked it there. I had had some problems with my wife prior to going there. That was the year I came here first and then went back to Colorado. Most of those problems at home were my fault. I take the blame for that.

"But when I finally got here, Perkins was in his second year. Contrary to what everybody else thinks, I believe if Perkins didn't win in his third year (which he did at 9–7), he would have been fired. He was 6–10 and 4–12 and the two coaches before him had similar records. I also thought if I could come here [as defensive coordinator] I could maybe do something and be recognized for it. Then there was the thought that I was coming home. They gave me a two-year contract, which wasn't very much but it was enough so that I could do what I wanted plus paying the bills because I had a daughter in college and another getting ready to go. I needed the money.

"Well, the first year, we're in training camp and I made about four or five position changes. I put George Martin [defensive end, 1975–88] on the bench, I moved Brian Kelly [linebacker, 1973–83], and we got Taylor and traded for [Bill] Currier [safety,

1981–85] and made a couple of other moves. But I didn't have a nose tackle.

"We had drafted this kid from Pittsburgh named Bill Neil. He was a defensive end, had been one in college. So now the scouts are all there and at the end of their stay we have the scouts and the coaches all get together to go over the talent and they all give their opinions. This is my first one of those. We didn't have this in New England. Shit, we got together and talked about it, but this thing was like the fuckin' United Nations Security Council.

"So I'm sitting there and I just got there. You know I'm just one of sixty assistant coaches that these same guys have probably seen pass through. Now all I know is we have had knee operations and guys who can't do the job and we still don't have a nose tackle. So I say I'm gonna put Neil there.

"You'd think I just said I was gonna move the franchise back to New York. The first thing I got was six or seven scouts saying, 'He's never played there! He can't do it.' Then George [Young] says, 'He doesn't look like he's physically suited.' Now I'm looking over at Perkins and he isn't saying a word. What all of them are thinking is that here's a new coach and we just drafted this guy to be a player and he's gonna move him to nose and it won't work out and he's gonna cut him and our draft is gonna look like shit.

"So they talk some more and then they look at me to see if they've convinced me and still Perkins isn't saying anything. So I tell them I know I just got here and I don't want to be disrespectful but—and I looked at all of them, including Perkins, because I didn't know where he stood—and I said unless any of you fuckin' guys got a better idea, I'm gonna move the son of a bitch there tomorrow. And nobody said a word."

And you know who played nose tackle that year.

"Now I have to be the first to say that this franchise has been very good to me. But I've had to do a lot of things to get this team

winning the media doesn't know about. And not just me. George
has supported me and he's been a part of it, too.

"But I told them, look, you want to win. It costs money. You
better understand it. You don't want to lose players to the USFL
and I have to take my hat off to them. They did it. But it's a
vicious struggle.

"You can fight just so many fights and God takes it away
from you. Every guy that I know that's out of coaching—I
mean guys I respect, Vermeil, Madden—guys that have been
there and know what I'm talking about, they all say the same
thing. Bill Walsh said to me, 'Don't worry. You'll know.'
They all had different reasons for leaving but they all said
the exact same thing. Madden told me, 'You'll know. You
won't have the energy because you won't have the interest.
Suddenly, you don't care about the draft. You're not interested
in minicamp. You don't care who the best college linebacker
is. You don't care if they've signed any of your veteran players
to contracts. When you don't care, it's time to go . . . you're
history . . . you're done.'

"The thing I want to do at all costs is go on my own terms. I'm
in a position where I should be able to do that. They could've got
me seven or eight years ago but not now. I'm gonna get them.
That may be a competition within itself but I'm gonna win. Now
when I say "they' I don't mean the owners or the general manager. Not at all. They aren't the problem. It's a 'they' that's more
of a feeling . . . if you're a coach, you understand what I'm
saying.

"This is probably the worst time of year to talk about this.
You've gone through almost a whole season and your mind is
filled with so many things. But now I feel like it's a boring job
most of the time except on game day. What we've done in this
business is to take a nine-month-a-year job of ten or twelve
hours a day and turn it into a fifteen-month-a-year job of fifteen

hours a day—and that's what gets us. Sometimes it's not even a test of your intelligence. I could do this job right now with a fax machine on the beach in Florida and probably not fuck it up.

"If it wasn't for games like this, I wouldn't be here.

"You know what I'd want if I quit? I'd take a year off. The things I want to do center around places—not people—and the places aren't very far away. I'd want to go to New England and just travel around by myself. Maybe I'd get bored. I don't know. I love the Jersey shore. I was a kid and I spent my summers there. Five times during the football season I've driven down there at night and sat on the boardwalk and sat on that bench in Sea Girt and walked down to the water. Pitch dark. Go back and sit all night. Five o'clock in the morning I go to a 7–11 and get my coffee and then drive back up."

He's right. It is a difficult time of year to discuss this kind of thing. How much of it is fatigue, how much of it is wishful thinking, and how much of it is inevitable? Probably parts of all three.

"At some point you say, 'That's it. That's the end of the line.' I'm sure," he continues, "at some point you say that. You walk away from a lot of money and I'm not sure what I would do. I know I don't lack the confidence to try it.

"My wife said to me once, 'Explain to me why you continue to do this? The times that you enjoy it are so much fewer than the rest of the other stuff. What kind of ego do you have that you have to keep proving things to yourself? What else do you have to do? I don't understand. Is it that you have to prove you can get to the top of the profession, that you can sustain yourself at the top of the profession? Why do you do it? You're not happy, so why do you keep doing it?'

"That's a good question. I told her she didn't understand, which, of course, is the easy answer for me. I told her it's just about competition because my whole life, since I was seven years old, you went to the gym or you went to the playground. It was always, 'Who are we playing and where?' I'm still doing it. Nothing has changed. It's still, Who are we playing today?

"Well, now I have to take a long look at that.

"The way I feel is if I win another Super Bowl, I'm gone. No chance of coming back. No chance.

"I doubt very strongly we could do it this year. Of course, if we get in the tournament, anything can happen.

"I don't know who will win it—probably San Francisco again. The Rams have a chance, but I think you can forget Minnesota. If Green Bay wins the Central they'll be one of those teams that maybe could win a game, but they'll just be glad to be there. I don't think Philadelphia can. I think their structure with the kind of guys they got and how they do things can only take them so far.

"The team in the AFC that should win is Houston but they're very much like the Eagles—too volatile. The Colts can't cut it. Buffalo will be there, Miami doesn't have enough. Cincinnati is a shadow of what it once was. In the AFC West, Denver may win it all but I can't see them winning the Super Bowl. The Broncos just can't deal with power. In two Super Bowls they've proved that."

And then mention of the Super Bowl strikes a responsive chord in him that probably only a coach or player could really understand. When he talks about it, it is almost as though he is alone in the room. There is no television set, no tape recorder, no interviewer—nobody and nothing that hasn't been there.

"The thing about the Super Bowl is that it is so different. I can't tell you what it's like to run out of that tunnel. You're standing in there and you can see out and it's this beautiful sunny day and it looked like a million people out there waiting, waiting for you. I remember standing there and looking out there and then we started to run out and it was . . . it was . . . all I can say is that it was a great thing."

And in his mind's eye he is suddenly in this year's playoffs, where anything can happen on any Sunday—that slice of the season Parcells likes to call "the tournament." And the challenge of the Eagles begins to work inside him like an animate thing. It's name is Competition and it is saying in a voice only he can hear, "All right, you wanted this. 'Who are we playing today and where?' you said. Well, it's us and we're here and you damned well better be ready or we'll kick your ass."

"It's gonna be hungry dogs," he says. "You could play this game in the parking lot. I'd just as soon do it there with nobody watching at eight o'clock Sunday morning. If I tell Taylor or Carthon or Mowatt we're going to the parking lot at Bloomingdale's and we're playing on concrete tomorrow morning and nobody is going to be there but the Eagles, they'll all show up.

"They don't care. Because that's where the game is."

8:30 P.M., Hamilton Park Center Convention Wing

The corner next to the Hamilton Room looks like an all-night convenience store. Two large freezers containing ice cream pops, a counter set up with coffee, tea, and hot chocolate urns, and enough sodas to satisfy an army of bedouins line the wall. The Giants are fortifying themselves for their last set of meetings before it is time to go out and do the job.

Leonard Marshall steps out of the elevator and almost bumps into one of several security guards patrolling the floor. "My man, Leonard," the guard says, high-fiving him. "You feel mean?"

"Don't get me any meaner," Marshall replies, and then laughs.

"All right, Leonard, go out and kick some ass tomorrow."

On a pair of low couches across from the general meeting room, Ron Erhardt, Tommy Coughlin, and Fred Hoaglin are listening to Al Groh explain how Randolph Township High

School won the game of the year. But the clock is running on all of them and the talk naturally turns back to the task at hand.

"The weather report still the same?" Erhardt asks.

"It was cold out in those bleachers today," Groh replies. "Last I heard we're supposed to get snow tomorrow and a lot of wind."

"Well, either way, we're still going to have to handle those blitzes in the red zone this time. We'll see them again. He [Buddy Ryan] won't be coming in tomorrow with a lot of new fronts or coverages. He sells his people on what they do and doesn't deviate much. They'll be the same Eagles tomorrow that they always are."

"If we handle the blitz in that red zone," Coughlin interjects, "you're gonna see a complete reversal. You'll see touchdowns instead of field goals and that was the difference down there."

"Well, on the big red zone play in Philly," Hoaglin says, "we still should have hit it because the receiver got all tangled up by accident with the 'hot' blitzer [an unexpected extra rusher who gives the defense a numerical advantage over the offensive blockers] and they took each other out of the play. So there was still plenty of time for him [Simms] to hit the touchdown. But he did get a little pressure in his face and we blew it."

Most of the squad has now begun to file into the meeting room. In a masterpiece of living theater, Lawrence Taylor appears at the end of the corridor. As usual, he is dressed all in black. He walks with no visible sign of a limp. Whether this is due to rapid improvement or tremendous self-control is unclear. He knows every coach in the hall is watching him.

9:05 P.M., Hamilton Room, Hamilton Park Center

Parcells is facing the entire squad. Tonight he will speak to them for about ten minutes before they break off in offense and defense. He has come to the moment convinced that it is an exercise in redundancy to point out to them what's at stake other than to note that if they don't understand it by now there's no point in their being here.

"Now you know you have to stay alert for cheap shots and fighting," Parcells tells them, "because they are going to try to bait you. The officials have got to be watching this team after the bounty business last week. They're watching that and you're out there so they're watching you, too. I don't want anybody to cost forty-five guys a chance to win the division because he makes some macho deal.

"You all know the weather report. We've played games like this before. We know how to do this. We played a game here once on just the kind of day we're going to have tomorrow and their guy [the punt returner] let the ball hit the ground and roll for 119 yards in negative yardage. Our guy caught every punt. On kickoff returns, this guy [The Eagles' Roger Ruzek] can only kick to the 15-yard line anyway. Against a twenty-mile-an-hour wind, where do you think it's gonna go? It might not go to the 30. I can promise you a wind chill of minus-seven and a twenty-five-mile-an-hour wind.

"It's our kind of day."

10:40 P.M., Phil Simms's room, Hamilton Park Center

The meetings lasted almost until 10:00. Then there was a mass for the Catholic players and a Bible study group for a number of others. Phil Simms is back in his room, ordering a snack of strawberries and a glass of milk. The television set is tuned to a college football game.

He is thirty-three years old and he has been with the Giants for eleven years. Few, if any, professional quarterbacks have ever had to endure what he went through after a brilliant debut in midseason of his rookie year in 1979, when he quarterbacked a highly marginal football team to six wins in his eight starts.

And then it was nightmare time. In 1980 he was on his way to shattering a number of club records when he separated his shoulder. The next year, the same injury kept him out of five games and the playoffs. A year later, a knee injury cost him the entire season. And in 1983, Simms fractured his thumb against a player's helmet while throwing a pass and missed fourteen games. That was the year in which Parcells became head coach and immediately told him that he had made up his mind to make five-year veteran Scott Brunner the starting quarterback.

The impression grew that Phil Simms wasn't a quarterback at all. What he was was Job in shoulder pads. He worked harder than any other player on the team. His rehab program during times of injury would have made a Spartan blush. Everything about him—his work ethic, his determination, his unchallenged courage, his almost fanatical devotion to doing what Parcells calls "the right thing"—makes the strange up-and-down relationship between head coach and quarterback even more ironic.

The ankle he damaged against the Vikings and reinjured on Monday night against San Francisco is public knowledge. Maurice Carthon, who has developed into a kind of elder statesman on this team, says, "Phil is playing in unbelievable pain. He is unbelievably courageous." What is not common knowledge is the fact that he has been playing with a damaged pectoral muscle and a damaged thumb. Now he is sitting there, recalling the way it was and the way it suddenly is threatening to become again.

"I tried to go full out in practice yesterday. I didn't practice on Wednesday because of the ankle. It went pretty good on Thursday but I guess I was sore yesterday. So in my mind, I'm thinking it's the same old crap. That's what I'm thinking—the same old crap. So I bitch at the trainers, 'When is it going to get well?' I don't understand it, but I've been doing this four or five weeks now so I'm starting to accept it.

"During the week, Parcells and I aren't speaking a lot, just a few short conversations. Wednesday, he comes to me and he says, 'Now, if you're not 100 percent you ain't playing this week.' Stuff like that. And I looked at him and I didn't say it but I wanted to say it. I wanted to say, 'Well, then I guess I'm not playing. I'm not going to be 100 percent until March.'

"But I think I knew what he was doing. He knows it plays on my mind a little. Bill was letting on in his own way to push it out of my mind or not try to play.

"A lot of people think that's because of my early years and all the things that happened to me but they're wrong. What it is is that in the back of my mind I know I can't be as good as I want to be, so it changes my thinking. In the 49er game, instead of dropping back and feeling confident and throwing it 20 yards to the out, I knew in the back of my mind [because of the ankle] I couldn't do that and be safe. So I'd adjust and try to do something else. You don't say that, but your body makes you adjust. You can only do what it will let you do."

He has heard the boos and he no longer cares. He knows what he's had to contend with this season and they don't. He feels the pain, they do not. He knows that on a January day in Pasadena, California, when he played the greatest game any Super Bowl quarterback had played up until then, the cheers that followed him in the off-season came from the same people who are jeering him now.

They did not make him a better player when they were on his side any more than they make him a lesser one now. When you ask him about what qualities gave him the ability to overcome a set of freak breaks that cost him the better part of three straight seasons, he shrugs it off by saying, "What was I going to do? Quit? Where was I going to go?"

But there is more to it than that. It probably goes back to Parcells's fascination with "doing the right thing." As Simms talks it is clear that it did not come to him by accident. His parents same page. A player's down, he wants to pick him up. If he thinks the player's a little too up, he wants to bring him down. Whatever it is, he knows how to play us. Most of us are still out there looking for our daddy to pat us on the butt and say we're doing a good job. Once in a very great while he'll tell you that in private. But most of the time it's, 'Oh, you complete twenty passes and you think you're a fuckin' superstar?' And then he'll bluster but you get the message and deep down you want to get it.

"And then we go through those periods when he isn't talking to anybody—me against the world. I've seen him keep it up for a long time. The year of the strike he kept it for weeks and weeks. And it works because deep down the biggest thing in our game is emotion and I think he knows that."

In a very strange way it may be that the common obsession to "do the right thing" both Parcells and Simms share is what brought them together in spite of themselves. Logically, it should have exploded when Parcells passed over him in 1983.

"I was devastated," Simms says, "because I worked hard and put in all that effort. My first thought was, 'Bill, you and me are never gonna get along. I don't want to be a part of your program and you don't want me, so get rid of me.'

"Did I tell him? I don't speak out against people as a rule—especially people in authority over me. That's the way I was raised. But I broke the rules with him. I told him every chance I had, 'Get me out of here. I hate this.' I can't believe I did that today. I lost my mind. I was out of control. Then I thought maybe something will happen here. And when I did get a shot, after a couple of weeks I was playing and that's when I broke my finger and lost the rest of the year. I couldn't believe it could happen. I thought, 'Here we go again.'

"But the next year I was the quarterback and we went to the playoffs."

He has an incredible candor about him. He has moved

and the family of eight left the farm in rural Kentucky whe
was seven and came to Louisville so that both of them could w
in a factory there.

"I am a believer that most of your adult life is led because
your childhood. It stays with you. I grew up in a big family an
I always had to take care of myself. I mean if I wanted a new shir
for school, I had to make the money for it. I worked from the age
of eight—maybe before—every day of my life. Every single
morning until my junior year in high school, I delivered papers at
five o'clock in the morning. And when I wasn't in sports, I came
home and did the afternoon papers, too, because we had two
papers in Louisville.

"All my brothers had paper routes. We all woke up every
morning and took off to where the papers were delivered and
we'd run and we'd get 'em and make our deliveries. We all had
separate routes and when we'd get done we'd come home and
cook breakfast for everyone else. We did this every damned
day. It never broke. There wasn't a day off for ten years. I'll
never forget the day I quit that paper route. It was the greatest
day in my life.

"Back then, I didn't know anything else. That was life. I'd get
jealous every once in a while. I'd see the other kids doing what
they wanted to do.

"It's funny because my mom and dad got in that very discussion tonight at dinner. They're up with my aunt and two of
my brothers and some other relatives and I've got them in the
hotel near my house. It's the only game they'll be up for this
year."

Now, of course, the authority figure is the coach, and even at
thirty-three, the quarterback admits that his own nature and up-
bringing gives the authority figure an intangible hold on him.

"Parcells knows enough about the players and what goes on in
our heads that he knows he has to say things to keep us all on the

through a world that chews up athletes and spits them out at a frightening rate, a world where spoiled-brat superstars have been takers since they were twelve years old, where general managers and agents can't shake hands without having to count their fingers afterward.

In a large sense, for many of the quarterbacks who perform within it, it is a world of swagger and sham, where fear unacknowledged will simply disappear—they think.

Somehow, the paper boy grown older has remained untouched by that kind of thing. It is the reason that on this night, with a bum ankle, the memory of terrible injuries past, and the season's biggest moment of truth hurtling toward him less than fifteen hours away, he sits there and says what all of them know in their heart and refuse to admit.

"Your body betrays you. In the off-season, I work much harder than the average quarterback. I'm always scared that if I don't, then I won't be good enough to play. It comes from the fear that I have to do more than he does—whoever he is—because I want to make sure I'm better than him. Everybody is scared what will happen to their body.

"No matter how good this game is to you, generally before it's over, it shits on you. Look at some of us. There are so many players who had it so good and let it end so badly for them and you watched them and knew it was never gonna end good. It's like George Young said, 'Almost all of us go out kicking and screaming.' And you know that's right. That's how I'm gonna go out. I'll probably be bitching and screaming.

"I wonder if the athlete ever sees when the end is coming. I think about it. Every year I pull out films from two years back to see what's different now and then I say, 'Well, I'll remember and I'll stop what I'm doing now and do it like I used to do it.'

"I used to think this game would always make me happy. I don't know anymore.

"I don't know if there's ever complete satisfaction in this thing. You win the Super Bowl and, God, it's the greatest damned thing in the world. And then all of a sudden it's like you never did it and it doesn't mean shit if you don't win it again because then you've failed."

Outside the wind slams against the hotel. It is thirteen hours before game time.

6. SUNDAY, DECEMBER 3, 1989

5:30 A.M., River Edge, New Jersey

For a dozen years now, Ed Wagner, Jr., has beaten the dawn's early light to Giants Stadium before every home game. Now, as he dresses quietly, he can hear the sound of the wind outside and he thinks to himself, "Those guys are gonna have a bitch of a time with the tarp this morning. At least I'll have a lot of time to get warm before I go out there."

He is the team's equipment manager and he will not be alone among the early arrivals. By the time he gets there, his father, Ed, Sr., will have begun his tasks as locker-room manager, and perhaps a dozen supernumeraries will be moving around under their direction.

As he starts his car and heads toward the Meadowlands, he is already going over the order of his mental checklist. The first order of business will be to recheck each locker and make sure the uniforms are laid out. Then he will return to the equipment room and check each helmet, inserting the proper amount of air and tightening the face masks and chin straps.

Next comes the cold-weather gear—the gloves, the capes, and the players' thermals. Later this morning, he will supervise the private contractor who will set up the specially heated benches on both sidelines. The benches are fired up by kerosene heaters. "Sometimes you have to be careful," Wagner says, "that nobody lays a coat on them before the temperature is adjusted. Otherwise, it would catch fire in a matter of seconds."

There are equipment trunks to be moved onto the field, towels have to be schlepped down to the visitors' locker room. John Simaluca, Brian Finnerty, and Andy D'Andrea, his three regular Sunday helpers, will do the lugging. At the same time, the officials' dressing room will be stocked with coffee, hot chocolate, soft drinks, and sandwiches. As usual, the big washing machines will be running. Morning, noon, and well past 10:00 P.M. each night, the Ed Wagner, Jr., Wet Wash Service neither sleeps nor slumbers.

"I stand at the right end of the bench and never leave that spot so that the trainer can come to me for injury pads or the players can find me for equipment changes."

He will not leave the stadium until 8:00 P.M. When he goes, he will take the torn jerseys with him and drop them off on Monday morning at his mother's for repairs.

6:30 A.M., Hamilton Park Center lobby

The Sunday papers were still tied in neat unopened bundles in front of the gift-shop door. From the coffee shop next door, he could hear the early morning sounds of the kitchen staff and the waitresses setting up for Sunday brunch. There was a little more urgency to their task this morning. Normally Sunday brunch conjures up the image of late arrivals, leisurely dining, and a meal that is as social in content as it is caloric.

But this Sunday morning, the first wave of customers would be the Giants and they would get there early. Their meals would arrive quicker and, of necessity, so would their checks. The players would be long down the highway before the first brunch customers even stumbled toward the bathroom to brush their teeth.

Now he crossed toward the front desk and dropped his key on the counter. The night clerk was waiting for the change in shifts along with a security guard. They spotted him from the little office just beyond the counter and waved.

"Good luck, coach," one of them said.

"Kick some ass," the other one shouted.

"Thank you," he said and waved back, "we're going to try."

Then he walked out through the heavy double doors and into the lead-gray morning. The wind came at him from an angle and at first his body, still carrying the warmth of the lobby with it, did not feel the chill. He paused for a moment, his overnight bag in his left hand, and let it hit him full-face. Then he grunted.

He is a December man with a December team about to play a December game and he knows from hard experience that the winds of Madison, New Jersey, have nothing to do with the winds of the Jersey Meadowlands. He will have to wait and see and the sooner he gets there, the sooner he will know. Now he looks overhead at the angry gray sky and he feels just the hint of a few snowflakes against his face.

He walks down one level to the parking lot, the wind at his heels now. As he noses the bronze Lincoln down the winding exit and out onto the empty street, he is thinking to himself, "If we could get snow, real snow, then I'm going to blitz and blitz and blitz again. And if Taylor can do it, we might be able to . . ."

And then, like a kind of Tevye in a blue winter ski jacket, he must say to himself, "On the other hand . . ."

On the other hand, it may not snow at all. On the other hand, Taylor might not go at all. On the other hand, something just might happen on the first or second or third play of the game that rewrites any script he can possibly conjure up here and now.

As he sights his first target ahead, the car radio is tuned to

WNEW and the disc jockey is reminding his audience that the pregame show will, of course, be preceded by the "Bill Parcells Show." Every week, since that long-ago dot in time when his team first assembled at Fairleigh Dickinson's Madison campus for preseason training, he has done these daily taped reports along with the station's sports director, John Kennelly.

They open with the staccato sound of a quarterback's voice chanting, "Set, green right, twenty-one—hut, hut" and then music takes over with a driving beat. This one will open with Kennelly posing the question, "How much can the home field mean to a team which is hobbled at key positions? More about that with coach Bill Parcells after this."

Parcells gives little thought to the promo. The show was taped Saturday morning along with his weekly television show and it is hardly a guideline to his inner thoughts. Mostly he will talk about the game being for the divisional title and keeping his players focused and doing the best they can. Then they will talk about the ifs that could have beaten Philadelphia last time.

Parcells sees the small convenience store up ahead on his left. When the team trained here during the summer, it was a regular morning stop for him, as it has been before every home game since the season began. The coach is an early-morning, dawn's-early-light kind of creature. Convenience stores are the pit stops that punctuate his daily beginnings.

He buys his container of coffee and makes the clerk's day when he offers his hello first. Then he is back in the car, swinging past the fork in the road that leads to picturesque Drew University, a former seminary which grew into a full-fledged college, under the Erie-Lackawanna Railroad trestle that signals the immediate approach of Madison's little downtown center and the first traffic lights. The narrow thoroughfare will widen into State Highway 24 South and once he clears the town, the coach will be well on his way.

Now he is playing the guessing game he always likes to play on Sunday mornings: who will be first?

He can take you back to the Super Bowl team, close his eyes, and see the exact order in which they arrived each week.

"It's a one o'clock game and I'm gonna be there at 7:30 and I know that at a quarter to nine, [Brad] Benson [guard, 1977–87] is comin' through that door. And we have an old saying, 'Well, where the fuck you been?' And even though he's there four hours before the game, he'll start telling me he got stuck in traffic.

"So Benson will come in and he'll sit down and start to put his shit on and he'll sit on that stool and he'll be ready to play the game at ten o'clock. Then, the next three would be [Chris] Godfrey [guard, 1984–87], Karl Nelson [offensive tackle, 1984–88], and the rest of the offensive line. They got more to do. They got to tape their shoulder pads down and things like that. I mean, you could set your watch by those guys.

"Today, I know exactly who is gonna come when and how long it's gonna take every one of them to get ready. Maurice Carthon will be the first. He likes to drink coffee like I do. So he goes in and gets taped and gets his pants on and all that and everything from the waist down is ready by 9:30. Then he comes over and we drink some more coffee and bullshit.

"After him, it will usually be Zeke [Mowatt]. Now, Zeke's not very talkative [a fact of life that can be confirmed by reporters and teammates without fear of contradiction] but he's a great kid and I'll say, 'How you doing, Zeke?' and he'll mumble something back. George Adams and Zeke ride together, so he will be there, too. And then it will be Simms."

Parcells can just about take you right through the whole roster and then he starts to laugh and says, "Now, Taylor, you don't know if he's even gonna come to the game or not. He's one of those. He wants to come there, put his shit on, and go play. He's so late he's never dressed by the time he's supposed to go out."

And then he pauses.

"I don't know about today. You'd think he'd be in early but he's got things to do. He's going to some hideout. He's got things to do. I mean, he knows he can't get a shot here but he's got his own doctor so who knows what he's gonna do? That doctor doesn't work for us so I think, probably, Taylor is going to go over there and get some kind of shot. He knows I don't want him to do that, so he's not saying anything and he's going to hide as long as he can.

"See, when Dr. Warren told him it can't be damaged any more no matter what he does, Taylor just said, 'You mean the only thing I have to worry about is that it's gonna hurt?' Then he didn't say anything else and he avoided both of us.

"So I'm pretty sure he's gonna do something. He'll be in a mind-set today that if he's decided he's gonna play, he'll just intimidate the doctor. Where we got him is he's trying to figure out what he's gonna do at the half because he knows he isn't going to get injected in my locker room. I know what he's thinking. On Friday, he starts to double-talk me and I tell him, 'You know I can always tell when you're lying because your lips start to move funny.'

"So he just laughs and walks away and we haven't spoken since then."

The stadium comes into view like a large gray lump on the horizon. As he drives past the huge empty parking lots, the sight that grips him almost defies description. A sea of old newspapers and debris swirls in all directions above the blacktopped pavement. Battered by the wind, the trash alternately soars high above the expanse, crashes to the ground, skips along the surface, and then takes off again.

Against the chain-link fences, a brigade of yellow snow plows stand at emergency parade rest. He notes with some disappointment that the snow flurries that had blossomed into a light snow shower along Route 24 have dissipated. But as he rolls down the window to say hello to the gate guard, he is heartened by a strange repeated sound.

It is the clink-clink-clink of metal against metal. Every sign post and every loose gate is rocked and hammered by the wind. As he slowly noses down the ramp, he is thinking, "Super Bowl year. Washington kick returners tortured by the wind, unable to discern a predictable flight path of the ball, helpless as it hits and rolls," and the numbers that took him to the Super Bowl that day—Washington, minus 119 yards, negative punt-return field position.

And as he eases into his parking space, the last thing he thinks is, "Meggett can catch the ball. Meggett better catch the ball."

7:00 A.M., Elizabeth, New Jersey

Gordon McCarter and the rest of his officiating crew are entering the vestibule of St. Rocco's Roman Catholic Church on North Avenue. They are nomads in the largest 100-yard world and consequently no two Sundays are ever the same. But ever since they first assembled as a crew they have been coming here for early mass when the luck of the draw assigns them to the Meadowlands. It is only about a twenty-minute ride from their hotel and they will still have time for breakfast and yet one more meeting before they head out to the stadium. Unlike their Saturday discussions, this session will be devoted strictly and specifically to what they might expect from the Giants and the Eagles.

As they leave the church, an usher recognizes them from previous visits and says to McCarter, "Take care of my Giants today." McCarter laughs and a second usher calls after them as they head through the open door and back out onto the street, "It's a good thing you guys came to church this morning. You are going to need all the help you can get out there with those two teams.''

Later, at breakfast, they get down to specifics. They have far larger concerns than the animosity that exists between these teams. After all, they have been to that mountain before. The league has no shortage of macho armies. The Houston Oilers have even gone so far as to call their home field the House of Pain. Short of a full-scale riot, there is nothing in that department they are not equipped to handle.

What troubles them is something far less visible, but which carries within it the seeds for a massive officiating screw-up if it is not continually handled.

"We all know that this guy [Cunningham]," says McCarter, "is the master of the broken play. That means if we aren't very careful, somebody is going to wind up out of position. Let's say he takes off running to the side judge's side of the field. What do we do if a receiver has taken Dick [Creed, the side judge] deep? In that case, you know, Dave [Anderson, the head linesman], you have to go deeper and get into the coverage.

"Now with this guy moving around so much, I don't have to remind you that we have to keep an eye on that line of scrimmage because the line is so fine, he could be across it, not know it, and still throw.

"Another thing we have to make ourselves aware of is paying special attention to the illegal check rule and when it's in and when it's out. Cunningham leaves that pocket and he becomes a runner. That affects the rule. Once he moves, we've got to adjust."

Finally, he gets around to the one single peculiarity of the stadium that can embarrass an official as much as a player—the wind.

"I've had three coaches come to me this year to complain that the Giants are creating a wind advantage by leaving that great big corrugated metal stadium gate open. It's up the ramp in direct line with the field tunnel. I checked it out the first time and there's a municipal fire ordinance which says it has to be open at least seven feet at all times for emergencies. So that's the way it is.

"In that wind, you all know, there's an increased chance for a muff by the kick returner, so if anyone has any doubts about that rule, let's go over it right now. And the wind is so tricky that a ball could die as well as take off. If that happens and the guy has to come up 10 yards all of a sudden to catch it, then look out for the possibility that we may have some kind of interference with his right to catch it.

"One last thing," and here he pauses for emphasis, although he knows that what he is about to say is already very much on everyone's mind. "What we have here today is a burner and game control is going to be very important both with what's at stake and the way both of these teams feel about each other. If it comes up after a play, then move in and try to get them apart instead of throwing the flag. But if you have to throw it, then let it go. None of us can back away from it when it's necessary."

8:00 A.M., Hamilton Park Center

Ronnie Barnes is hurrying across the lobby. Moments earlier, Bart Oates, the center and aspiring lawyer, had checked out. Oates spent a lot of time on Saturday night thinking about Reggie White. He knows there will be times when he must fight that battle alone despite the Giants' intricate area blocking schemes. He also knows there will be nothing new today. He has both won the battle and lost the battle before. It is not the individual battles that will decide this thing from his standpoint. What it will be is the total individual war and that will run throughout the entire frostbitten sixty minutes.

Barnes, meanwhile, has a lot to occupy him this morning. The obvious is Lawrence Taylor and the scene from "General Hospital" that Lawrence will play later in the morning with Barnes and Dr. Warren. But there are other things on his mind as well. There is Jumbo Elliot's ankle for one. Elliot has played above and beyond the call ever since it was badly twisted. If there is a way, he will play today. How long he can play and what is to be done if he can't go any further is not Barnes's problem. Making sure Elliot has the best shot to go is.

And one other thought nags at him. Eric Moore's battle with the flu has made very slow progress. Barnes had thought that by now the prescription medicine would have done the job. He might be even more worried if he were aware that Moore had also begun to doctor himself.

8:30 A.M., Giants Stadium

There are nine of them, counting the teamster who drives the truck and the supervisor. They are coming out of the tunnel very close together, almost as though whatever body heat they can save under their heavy parkas will rub off on each other. As they shiver on the sidelines in the wind, they take on the look of an Eskimo clan in search of polar bear meat for the winter.

Slowly, almost as though they have discovered that movement of any kind is better than the alternative, they fall into formation and begin to uncover the field. Despite the magic of modern groundskeeping and the science to which tarp removal has been reduced, it is slow going in the teeth of the wind.

Before they can retreat back inside the tunnel and the warmth beyond, they will have put out the yard markers, attached the cords that control the football-catching nets behind each goal post, helped adjust the heated benches, and checked the goal posts. Because of the wind, the posts will be checked one more time before the game starts by the officiating crew. On more than one occasion since the Giants moved here from across the Hudson, the winds of the Meadowlands have forced some last-minute adjustments. Later this morning, two technicians from AT&T will reinstall and check the telephones that connect both overhead coaching booths to their respective benches.

In an hour, alone on the stadium floor, a tiny dot against a backdrop of more than seventy-six thousand empty seats, Bill Parcells will walk the field. It is not the field he is checking. It is the wind. "I know," he says, "that it won't quiet down until after five o'clock. If it's bad that early in the morning, it will be worse throughout the game."

9:30 A.M., Giants' locker room

Parcells has already changed into his blue-and-white coaching gear, and is sitting in the empty locker room with Barnes, sipping coffee from a Styrofoam container. Both are quiet for the moment. The blue game jerseys, hung neatly in each locker, seem to add a new and almost jarring dimension to the cavernous dressing area. There is an interesting bond between the two, which transcends more than the strong working relationship needed between coach and trainer. In some ways the coach may be closer to him than anyone else in the organization.

Now with just the two of them there, the coach turns and smiles and says, "I hope I don't have an anxiety attack today."

In the wake of the particular set of confusion and misunderstanding, which will follow within just a few hours, it may well be the most ironic statement of the day.

Now the coach looks toward the doorway and at the man who has just entered and laughs. "I was right," he says. "Maurice, where the fuck have you been? You're late." Just as he predicted, Maurice Carthon is the first one through the door. The others follow in the exact order he expected.

Back in the trainer's room, Barnes and Mike Ryan have already begun the taping for the early birds. An assortment of braces is spread out across the table—knee braces, ankle braces, plastic hip donuts—each inscribed in clear blue ink with the owner's name.

As usual, for reasons nobody has ever figured out, most of the offense has arrived before the defense. As the room begins to stir with the complex procedure football players must follow to deal with the heavy equipment they wear, Wellington Mara sits quietly in one of the imitation-leather chairs that form a rectangle in its center. He is reading the sports section. He offers conversation only when someone approaches him. He has been in far too many lockers over far too many years not to understand the intensity of the white-hot fire that has begun to burn inside most of them.

There is that—as there always is—but this Sunday, there are other things too. The players' lounge is empty. The television set, which normally blares nonstop all the way up to pregame warm-ups on most game days, is surprisingly stone-cold silent— a coal-black eye which will not blink once on this Sunday.

The defensive players have begun to trickle in. They tape in silence and, for the most part, they sit in silence. Myron Guyton is in front of his locker, head bowed, reading his playbook so intently you get the feeling that he is hoping that somewhere in that wind and cold this afternoon a familiar X will click deep in his brain and he will be in position to steal the ball away from what until then had simply been a hand-drawn O in the game plan.

Erik Howard is alone with his thoughts. His private ritual will take him about forty minutes, although he has already been taped. When he is fully dressed, he will continue to sit there, occasionally tapping his thighs or feeling the chest portion of his shoulder pads—like some knight-apparent carefully fingering his armor during the all-night vigil before he receives knighthood.

Simms is now here, later than he expected, wearing a brown

checked shirt and dark slacks and a dark leather jacket. He walks into the trainer's room, where Barnes will tape him. He takes his twin knee braces off the table and Barnes starts to go to work. There is some small talk and Barnes comes away with the impression that the ankle is, at least for now, quiet.

As Simms moves back toward his locker and Mike Ryan continues to tape the players, Barnes sticks his head out the training room door trying to figure out the sound he cannot identify. It is the sound of serious silence, seemingly a million decibels from the way it was in this very same room just twenty-four hours ago. "It's been a long time," he says, "since they were this quiet. I can't get a handle on what it means." Occasionally, a player will idly leave his locker, walk a few feet to another stool and ruffle the occupant's hair or rub his shoulder. The conversational response is uniformly low key.

Then, almost precisely at 11:00 A.M., Lawrence Taylor steps into the locker room.

11:00 A.M., Upper Saddle River, New Jersey

Judy Parcells has a pain in the neck. She has had it for years. Like clockwork, it starts every September and does not disappear until February. "I didn't figure it out until a couple of seasons ago," she says, "when my mother first pointed out to me that I sit through a whole game and wring my hands. I've been doing it for years. The further we get into the game, the more I tense up. My neck hurts all season."

She and her three daughters and the youngest daughter's boyfriend have arrived well ahead of the pregame traffic. They are having brunch in the crowded Stadium Club now. Economically, but not necessarily calorically, Giants fans are divided into two castes. Outside in the parking lots, tens of thousands of tailgaters are devouring everything from char-broiled hot dogs to elaborately rewarmed quiche in a ritualistic football version of the Last Supper. But inside the warmth of the Stadium Club, the hot-ticket people are no less absorbed. In both places the food and the alcohol are about what you would expect at a 100-yard bacchanal.

But the Stadium Club is a tougher seat to obtain than those in the ballpark. Tim Mara got the rights to its game-day operation as part of the deal that brought the Giants across the river. "It's the toughest ticket in town," he says with more than a little satisfaction. "In my office I still have thirty-five game tickets. But I only have two left for the club."

Judy Parcells and her group will eat leisurely. Mercifully, most of the dinners at the boisterous tables surrounding them do not even know who she is. They will kill time until a half hour before the kickoff and then take the elevator up to their seats. She and her family will sit next to Lee Pope, the wife of the Giants' receivers coach.

One thing she knows for sure. Rain, sleet, wind, or snow, Dan Paulino will be there. And his magic hat will not.

Paulino has had the same lower-stand 35-yard-line seat ever since Giants Stadium opened. It is directly behind the two rows where the coaches' wives sit. In 1986, a year remembered by Giants fans young and old simply as The Season, Paulino presented Judy Parcells with what in section 110 has become known simply as The Hat.

Mara Tech had won two of its first three games that season and at the fourth game of the year, at home against the Saints, he gave her a blue baseball cap emblazoned with "I Love the Giants" in white. "You wear it, we'll win," he said. "I guarantee it." A month later, the Giants took a 5–2 record into their home game against the Redskins, having lost to Seattle on the road the previous Sunday.

"Mrs. Parcells," Paulino said as she took her seat about an hour before the kickoff, "nothing personal about this, but did you wear the hat last week?"

"I didn't go. I watched the game on television."

"I know, but did you wear the hat?"

"In front of the television set?"

"Yes, you have to wear it no matter where you are when they play."

"So here I am," she says, "sitting in front of the television set in my own living room with this baseball cap on my head. And you know what? We didn't lose another game all year. I even wore it to the Super Bowl. One game, I got up to go to the rest room and left the hat on the seat. When I came back it was gone. The Giants were driving for a touchdown and nobody saw it. We had everybody in three rows crawling around the floor until they found it."

And where is the hat now?

"It's in my dresser drawer and it's not coming out. I started wearing it the next season. We lost the first five games."

11:00 A.M., officials' dressing room

They are sitting around in various stages of dress. The coffee pot is on a nearby table. Half an hour earlier, they had pulled the rental car up to the players' and officials' gate and before Mc-Carter could point to the credential card, the security guard was waving them through. The other guard on the passenger side was thinking to himself, "I hope it ain't the same guys who worked the game in Philly. Cunningham ain't scored yet."

Gordon McCarter looks like a sporting goods salesman on a busman's holiday. Clad only in his underwear, he is surrounded by twenty-four footballs. In his hand is a small air gauge bearing the official NFL logo. If it's good enough for everything from souvenir telephones to lamp shades then it's good enough for the official air gauge. Each ball must contain no less than $12\frac{1}{2}$ pounds of pressure and no more than $13\frac{1}{2}$. Each time the dial falls out of the approved margin, McCarter lets a little air in or a little air out.

Meanwhile the keepers of the forty-five-second clock and the official game clock are huddling with the field judge and the line judge. It is only the beginning.

One suspects that D-day was launched with fewer conferences. Before the pregame meetings are over, the umpire will visit both locker rooms to check the size, weight, and padding of any cast worn by a linesman. The side judge and the head linesman will make their way to the visitors' dressing room, and the back judge and the line judge will visit the home team for further consultation. Among the topics will be the pregame schedule, the names and numbers of all unit captains, and the kicking leg of the field-goal people.

"It helps in our positioning," McCarter explains, to know whether the kicker is left-footed or right-footed.

There will be further discussion among the officials and a TV representative about commercial breaks and the home team's p.r. man, who will deliver a written record of both teams' roster changes.

There is, however, one key conference. It is the brief huddle between the chain man and head linesman. The head linesman will go over all the procedures, but in his heart of hearts, the one thing he will stress with the most fervor is the attention paid to the down marker.

Every official who ever blew a whistle from the sandlots to the NFL has heard the legendary horror stories about the day some official—and not necessarily an obscure one—misplaced a down. "It is," says Gordon McCarter, "every referee's nightmare."

11:00 A.M., Giants' locker room

Lawrence Taylor is wearing his traditional black-on-black-on-black ensemble. One suspects that if you peeked into Lawrence's bedroom closet, you would find five hundred pairs of black pants and as many black shirts. He has arrived earlier than Parcells expected and right on time in Barnes's thoughts.

"He knows the doctor [Russ Warren] usually arrives at 12:30," Barnes says, "so he has it all figured. He doesn't want him involved during the taping. He is thinking, 'Get me taped and dressed before he gets here so I can do my thing with him before he decides I can't play.'

"So what happens?" Barnes says. "Russ is smarter than he is. Russ gets here at 11:30."

Taylor carefully hangs his jacket in his locker and strips down. He is smiling and his mood seems to trigger more conversation in the room. Then he walks the length of it to the trainer's room, disappearing around the corner that bears a sign reading, Good Players Inspire Themselves, Great Players Inspire Others.

It was enough to want to make you roll the screen credits.

"Listen, Ronnie," Taylor says before Barnes can make a move, "I thought the brace felt a little too heavy yesterday. I don't want to wear it." He is speaking, of course, of the only brace in the Western world to be air-expressed cross-country on an emergency priority basis along with its own living-color videotape and preceded by a series of lengthy telephone calls which would gladden the heart of an AT&T stockholders meeting.

"Here's what we should do," Dr. Taylor continues. "Remember how you put an air cast [a splint with an inflatable back] on me the other day? Try that, will you?"

Barnes fashions the cast and carefully tapes him. Now Lawrence puts his shoe on and runs around the training room. He does not try to leap the training tables with a single bound.

"No good," he says. "I don't like it. Cut it off."

Barnes cuts away the tape and the cast.

"Look, this is going to work," Lawrence says. "What we'll do is just tape me up the way we usually do, see, and then tape the shoe. I got a spot that's only about the size of a dime on my ankle that hurts. But that's all. Otherwise I feel fine.''

More running.

"Now take some off here and see if you can't get some more on over there.'' Carefully, Ronnie Barnes, who has just moved up to number two in the patience standings behind Mother Teresa, cuts and snips and tapes. Normally, it takes three minutes to tape a professional football player. Under Dr. Taylor's guidance, Barnes has finally managed to do the job in forty.

And with almost no time to spare Russ Warren is walking through the door.

"I want you to go out with the team for warm-ups (which are now just ten minutes away) so I can watch you,'' Warren says.

"I'd rather run in here,'' comes the reply.

"I don't want you to do that.''

"I can run in the hallway. It's carpeted. Look, I can get up on my toes and I can walk on my heels.''

It is a fundamental rule of anatomy that if you can't get up on your toes, you can't run. To everyone's amazement, Lawrence proves he can. It is a powerful argument.

"Medically,'' Warren tells Barnes, "I can't argue with what he's shown us. Let him try it if he's so determined. It isn't the damage that will get him because the X rays prove he can't do any more. It's the pain, and personally, I don't think he'll make it through the first quarter.''

There are no secrets in any locker room. You could seal yourself in the bathroom, turn on all the showers, and whisper to a guy six inches away from you, and before you leave the room, everyone on the ball club will know exactly what you said.

When Lawrence emerges they already know—even before they see his smile. They have been waiting and watching and hoping. But Barnes reads the restraint with which they view the news as a barometer explaining the earlier silence.

This is intensity at its highest level. It is clearly the most intense, purposeful pregame locker room of the year—perhaps even since the Super Bowl.

The silhouette of Leonard Marshall could be its logo. He is sitting on his stool in the far corner. He has not spoken for some time now. When the coach sends them out for warm-ups, he will come off the stool and out the door like a sprinter exploding out of the blocks.

The kickers have already taken their ten-minute head start onto the field. Parcells has said very little. A word here, a sentence there. He has judged this team to be about as ready as it can be. This is no time to alter its mood. He has no intention of playing Knute Rockne as he sends them out to loosen up.

Eric Moore rises slowly from his stool and crosses toward the trainer's room. Since Friday afternoon, he has diligently taken his antibiotics and his cough syrup. He has also taken anything else the drug store recommends. He sticks his head through the door and looks at Barnes. His helmet is in his hand. His face is ashen and huge beads of sweat stand out on his forehead.

"Ronnie, I feel awful," he says. He leans against the wall for a moment and then turns back toward the main locker-room door and heads for the field.

12:15 P.M., Giants Stadium field

The wind is all they thought it would be and worse. Kicking with it at his back, Sean Landeta, the Giants punter, feels as though he could kick the ball halfway to Atlantic City. When he turns around, he runs the severe risk of kicking it back into his own face mask.

Down at the other end, the Eagles in their white jerseys and their green helmets are thinking much the same thing. Their arrival was greeted with more cheers than expected. Somehow, perhaps because the teams live only the length of a turnpike apart, Philadelphia fans do manage to get more tickets for this game than you'd normally expect.

The stands are about half full now, with the kickoff only forty-five minutes away. This is not unusual in this park, what with the elaborate tailgate efforts going on out in the parking lots. The early afternoon is both a tailgater's nightmare and a tailgater's miracle.

While it is clearly too cold to stand on level ground in the face of the wind and bite into a hot dog, it is also the one day when Giants fans, never noted for decorum or imagination, will not have to think up new excuses to drink.

The wind chill is, indeed, minus-seven. The weather bureau is calling the wind steady at twenty-five miles an hour. But Parcells knows his park. Before the day is over, some of the gusts will hit forty. It is what he has hoped for all week long. It is the kind of day when his Giants own the park no matter who the other guys are.

Out on the stadium floor, the coaches are walking among their individual units. Despite the weather, both teams approach their routine repetitive warm-ups with an intensity which both coaching staffs feel they can almost reach out and touch.

Gordon McCarter and his zebras are on the field now. He stations himself at the 40-yard line and faces the press box, switches on his field mike, and tests it. Then he walks toward the end zone to check the breakaway markers and the goal posts themselves.

Shortly before the teams leave the field, Lionel Manuel breaks from a simulated line of scrimmage, runs a slant pattern toward the end zone, reaches up, and snuggles a pass to chest. As he returns to where the other receivers are waiting, he shouts into the wind, "I never been to the North Pole before, but you'll find it straight ahead."

12:40 P.M., Giants' locker room

There are perhaps a half-dozen players in the training room and Ronnie Barnes and Mike Ryan are tending to some last-minute adjustments among the troops. Down the hall in the coaches' locker room, Parcells and the defensive coaching staff have decided that if Taylor is going to try to play, then there's no point in trying to finesse the situation. "I'd rather just start him," says Belichick as Groh nods in agreement, "and let him go as far as he can."

"All right, then let's do that," Parcells says.

The door is closed. None of them, therefore, has even a clue that back in Ronnie Barnes's world, all hell has broken loose.

As Barnes and Ryan continue to touch up a couple of early taping jobs, Eric Moore is sitting on the edge of one of the training tables, face buried in a small garbage can. He is in full uniform. The others in the room can hear the sound of him gagging as he tries to vomit.

"It happens," Barnes says. "The moment, the tension, players react in different ways to nervous tension. He's not the first guy to throw up before a football game. And we knew Eric had the flu as well. Nobody thought much about it one way or the other."

Then Moore drops the waste can and lets out a half-choked scream.

The room turns dead silent except for his sobs and his gasps. From the look on his face, it is clear that something has happened but nobody knows what. He is fighting desperately for air. All three team physicians rush toward him along with Barnes. It is clear to them that he is hyperventilating.

"With all his pads on and restricting him so, there's no way he is going to catch his breath," Barnes says. "Sometimes, it's hard enough to breathe in all that equipment even when you just get winded."

Barnes rushes out and finds a plastic bag. "Calm down.

Breathe into this,'' he says and the doctors are saying the same thing. "When you hyperventilate the blood gas changes. The idea behind the plastic bag is that if you rebreathe that air, you'll get more CO_2 and the breathing returns to normal.''

The more the doctors and Barnes cajole, the more panic-stricken Moore becomes. You see a plastic bag and the first thing you recall is that all your life people have told you never to get your head stuck in one. Several players rush to the door to see what's happening.

Moore is worse. Barnes and Ryan clear the room while the doctors try to calm him down. Then Barnes gets a towel, wipes off the big guard's face and neck, and slides it around to his mouth to stop his breathing for five seconds, which is what the doctors have been trying to get him to do in the first place.

Outside, Parcells, totally unaware of the confusion, is starting to talk to the team. He reminds them of all the things he told them all week:

The weather . . . we win in this weather . . . the Eagles . . . nobody is going to do it for us. The rest of their schedule stinks . . . the Eagles . . . you know what they will try to do to you and the more they try it, then the more you're getting to them . . . the stakes . . . you win this and you win the division . . . you win this and you're in the tournament.

Then they bow their heads in a pregame prayer.

Back in the trainer's room, Russ Warren is talking softly to Eric Moore. The attack lasted fifteen minutes and Moore is totally washed out. "What you felt was normal. You didn't understand why you couldn't breathe,'' he reassures him. "And all of that made you anxious. You'll be all right.''

And out front, unaware of the scene being played out between Warren and Moore on the other side of the wall, Parcells finally turns them loose.

They are clapping and stamping their feet all the way up the tunnel. The Eagles are already on the field. Just before the introductions, Carl Banks starts to holler. Other voices shout back and echo off the concrete walls. LT is ready. Simms is ready. The emotions are boiling up and down that narrow strip of concrete ramp.

And then they are running out of the tunnel—into the wind and the cold and into the full-throated roar of the crowd, which is further magnified when the winds of the Meadowlands catch the sound in their tiger paws and mix it with their own eerie threnody.

It is a duet fit only to accompany wolves and Eagles and Giants.

It is time to play the game.

7. 12:59 P.M.,
Midfield, Giants Stadium

At the top of the stadium, the wind hurls itself at the circle of flags as though it is intent on tearing away their very fibers. Down below, the uprights on both sets of goal posts visibly sway back and forth in steady rhythm as though driven by some unseen metronome. In between, as far as the eye can see, seventy-six thousand potential frostbite cases, wearing everything from ski masks and stocking caps to thermal underwear and battery-powered socks, are watching, as through a single set of eyes, the two figures slowly moving toward the center of the field from the Giants' bench.

It is the sight of the big number 56 on Lawrence Taylor's back as he slowly walks alongside Carl Banks that triggers a shattering crescendo of noise. It is almost as though they are saying with a single frozen tongue: "Have no fear. Superman is here."

The sound is almost primeval and the sight of the twin lines of players strung out in helmets and cold weather capes (blue for the Giants, green for the Eagles) on opposite sidelines heightens the image. Moving toward Banks and Taylor are the Eagles' captains—Reggie White, Ron Heller, Izel Jenkins, Ricky Shaw, and Al Harris.

There is nobody in this concrete igloo who is not aware that whoever wins this coin toss will take the wind, concede the ball, and tell the other people to take their best shot if they dare.

Gordon McCarter tosses the coin. He is wearing five different layers of clothing. Incredibly, he wears no gloves. "I feel clumsy handling the ball when I do," he says, "and I have to touch it on every play."

The Eagles win the toss and Reggie White runs back to his own sideline, knowing that he gets first crack at them instead of the other way around. The night before the game somebody asked White about a series of aches and pains which had threatened to slow him down the past few weeks.

"I feel like this is the most important game of my life," he had said. "I am not going to miss it."

On the Giants' sidelines, Romeo Crennel is talking to the kickoff return team. He is looking at Ingram and Meggett. "We have to catch the ball," he says. "We have to catch it."

And then the blue jerseys and the white jerseys are on the field and as Roger Ruzek, the kicker, sets the tee down, he turns and asks for help. The wind is so violent, he does not even try to place the ball on it. Sammy Lilly will kneel down and hold it there.

Up in both coaches' booths, the tension is as great as if they were on the field. Every technical aid known to this business has carried the workload all week long. Now there will be no Xs, no Os. Now there will be human beings at the heart of each equation and whatever help they get from the booth above or the sidelines below will serve as little more than a detailed road map.

They are the ones who will have to make the journey.

Ruzek comes forward and as he approaches the ball, the circle of crowd noise seems to stretch the ballpark at the seams. If, as cynics in this state like to claim, part of the stadium was built on the bridge of Jimmy Hoffa's nose, he will be hard-pressed to sleep through this one.

Ruzek gets it high up in the wind and from the front line of defenders, Reyna Thompson has begun to peel back in search of his mark. But the maneuver is strictly academic. The ball has hit almost on its point at about the 20-yard line. It kangaroos back up off the artificial turf and shoots forward between Meggett and Ingram, who give chase and down it in the end zone.

Simms and Cunningham will begin this game with contrasting cold-weather philosophies. The Giant's quarterback will wear special gloves on both hands. His counterpart will wear no gloves at all but will grasp twin plastic handwarmers inside the slash pocket of his jersey before each play.

The Giants break the huddle for their first sequence and to nobody's surprise, including the Eagles', they send OJ at them— and nothing happens. Over on the sidelines, Handley is wearing an orange ski jacket and wigwagging out to Simms, relaying the next play from the booth.

If the Giants are going to move against this wind, they are going to have to prove that the infantry is ready, willing, and, most of all, able. The call goes to Anderson again.

This time Roberts, Oates, and Brian Williams (who is playing in Moore's place) are able to create a seam. But Roberts fails to hold his block and Jerome Brown eventually loops around him and nails OJ from behind after a 4-yard gain.

Up in the booth, down on the sidelines, and out on the field, everyone realizes that one way or another, Simms must now throw the ball and try to force something out of the wind. He is now in the shotgun with Meggett in the backfield to his left.

The Eagles are coming. They are blitzing and there is pressure in the middle, but Oates and Roberts and Williams have managed a standoff. But down at right tackle—Doug Riesenberg's end of the world—Reggie White is loose and coming. He had lined up outside Riesenberg and at the snap, he hammered his right arm into Riesenberg's side and shoved him hard to the inside. He has dead aim on Simms, who has made his own decision and is about to release the ball. Simms is looking to his left and White is coming from his right. At the moment of impact, White drives through Simms, slamming into the side of his chest just below his throwing arm.

The ball seems to roll up Simms's arm and then it is loose, dribbling free between the battered Simms and the wall of blockers struggling directly in front of him.

William Frizzell, the Eagles' safety, who was also charging, has had the ball in sight from the moment it squirted loose. Now he scoops it up and starts to his right at the Giants' 15. Meggett gives chase and hangs desperately to the back of Frizzell's waist at the 3. But there are three other white jerseys in the tableau. Frizzell pivots slightly to his left before he goes down, feathering the ball back to his strong safety, Andre Waters, who pounds into the end zone untouched.

The game is just a minute and thirty-five seconds old and the Eagles lead, 7–0.

Up in the booth, Erhardt and Coughlin are reasonably calm. They know that 7 points will not win this game—at least not these 7. And they still believe in the game plans—the crossing patterns, which they believe will work, the use of Meggett as either receiver or bait, and the passes underneath to the tight ends. They are convinced—and several teams will prove them correct later in the season—that when the Eagles' pass defenders get hooked up in either-or situations and have to make a choice, the Giants have the receivers to beat them.

Down on the sidelines, Hoaglin is burning despite the weather. Reggie White may be all-universe and difficult one-on-one, but Riesenberg was never in that contest. Hoaglin holds his temper and waits. He, too, knows that one first-quarter play isn't going to decide the football game.

Meanwhile, Simms and Hostetler are talking quietly on the sidelines with Parcells just a few feet away. Then Simms reaches for the phone to Erhardt as the kickoff return team runs out on the field again. "Catch the ball!" Crennel yells as they leave. "Help each other," he tells Ingram and Meggett. "Don't let the other man run it out of the end zone if you don't have the room."

The Giants are lined up to receive once again and the crowd, which sees itself as part of the contest, has begun yet another roar. Its focus remains on David Meggett.

This time, Ruzek, whose kickoffs are usually short, finds a powerful ally in the wind. The kick carries all the way to the 2. And this time David Meggett catches the ball. This time, the block Thompson throws has meaning. He is not alone. Meggett sees the return alley they have shaped to his left. He is moving now and for a fleeting instant, the crowd, which is focused only on him, thinks he is going to break one. They do not see Anthony Edwards, angling across at him from the right. Edwards and Meggett tumble to the turf on the Giants' 33. But the 29-yard return pumps new life into the offense as it heads for the field.

The wind is worse and it will continue to worsen for the team that is trying to drive west to east on this field as the game progresses. In its teeth—at least until field position improves—there will be only one way to move the ball with any kind of safety. OJ Anderson, the old gunfighter reincarnated, is going to have to get the Giants far enough away from their side of the field so that Simms can look for the crossing wide receivers and the shallow tight end to carve out what the coaches are convinced they can.

On the first play of the sequence, Anderson powers to his left, where Roberts and Jumbo Elliot have hammered against Jerome Brown and Clyde Simmons to create an opening. OJ picks up 7. As he gets to his feet, he grunts and adjusts his shoulder pads. This is the kind of assignment he thrives on.

The Giants have come out with two tight ends on the right side—Mowatt and Cross. At the snap, OJ is swinging right and the tight ends have powered down on Reggie and Mike Pitts, who is trying to loop toward the action. The linebacker, Jessie Small, comes up on a collision path with OJ as Anderson nears the line of scrimmage.

Suddenly, he is gone. Brian Williams, Mr. Donut, has pulled out from the right guard spot and he levels Small with a ferocious block.

Anderson is free and running and before the cornerback can cut him down, he has picked up 17 yards. And up in the stands, the faithful are on their feet, stamping and shouting. The Eagles have failed to take the crowd out of it and the inmates have once again taken over the asylum.

This has become that roll-around, hammer-and-slammer kind of game Fred Hoaglin said he so dearly loves—the kind of game he had promised his offensive line. Anderson will go up the middle or through the right side on three straight plays, making a total of five consecutive carries.

The offensive line is moving the Eagles off the ball. As the wind hammers the Giants, Buddy Ryan knows he must disrupt their running game and force Simms to throw before he is ready. Despite the field position, Ryan knows his people. He feels reasonably secure with a total commitment to stop the run on the first two downs of each sequence. Finally, it works. This time Brian Williams cannot handle Pitts, who steamrolls straight ahead and is into the backfield before OJ can even begin to make a read off the direction of lead blocker Maurice Carthon's move. He drops Anderson to the ground for a 3-yard loss.

Now, the Giants, with a third and 9 at the Philadelphia 30, are thinking pass, the Eagles are reading pass, and the crowd is demanding pass. With decent field position, the wind can be less of a factor if Simms can get somebody loose just 9 yards downfield.

The blitzer is Frizzell and he is coming too quick and too hard for anyone to pick him up. Ingram is wide open on the left side of the secondary but Frizzell is almost in Simms's face, leaving him no option but to throw before he is ready. Both arms raised toward the sky, Frizzell gets a hand on the ball and swats it away before it can go 5 yards. It falls harmlessly to the ground in the Giants' backfield.

On the sidelines, Parcells is calculating the variables. He desperately would like to take something away from this drive to prove he can score against the wind and to increase his offense's confidence when it gets the wind at its back. Bjorn Nittmo, the Swedish placekicker who earned a job after a groin pull cost the Giants Raul Allegre, the placekicker they really want, is not much on either range or height. But the coach figures he has to try.

The kick is far too short and far too wide to the left. Now, in this strange game, which has already eaten up six and a half minutes and sees the Giants trail, 7–0, Randall Cunningham finally gets into the game.

With the ball on its own 30, Philly determines to try to establish its own running game. Twice, they send Anthony Toney to the side away from Taylor, preferring not to test Lawrence's mobility at this point. Taylor does, in fact, combine to help make one of the stops.

It is third and 1 and this is the time when Cunningham will give the ball to Byars, his bread-and-butter back. And it is here that Leachman's down linemen reach back for a gospel he preaches which is devoid of Xs and Os. "You got to knock them on their asses. Knock them sons of bitches down," is its thrust. The Giants' coaching staff has never been thrilled with Johnny Washington's lateral movement. It is no secret that, as soon as Eric Dorsey returns from the disabled list, Washington will return to the bench. But on this play, the call is for straight-ahead power and Washington slams his 275-pound frame straight at Ron Heller, the Eagles' tackle. Meanwhile, Erik Howard refuses to be moved. He reads the play and hurls himself in the direction of the traffic, forcing two Eagles into the path of the ball to further complicate things for Byars.

They stand him straight up and then Gary Reasons and Terry Kinard come up to hit the pile and flatten him.

The Eagles must punt and, on the sidelines, Parcells is shaking his fist at the defense in triumph as it comes off. The Giants are still only down 7 and they have made the Eagles go three-and-out on their first crack. Now they are beginning to believe. There are more omens. Runager's punt rides the wind all the way to the end zone—and then is nullified by a delay of game. The snap on the second try sails in the wind, forcing him to run and he comes up inches short. The Giants get the ball at the Eagles' 39.

On the first play, Pitts stands OJ up at the line of scrimmage. No gain. Now Simms is peering in toward the sideline and Handley is signaling the play. Up in the booth, Erhardt feels that this is the first chance to take advantage of the confusion they hope their wide receivers can create in the Eagles' secondary.

It is second and 10. Simms will throw out of the shotgun. Anderson is set to his left as the lone back. With the snap of the ball, Odessa Turner runs straight ahead, posts, and cuts to his left for the open sideline area. He has outrun his coverage and nobody is near him. Further downfield there is double coverage. But all of these people are suddenly relegated to bit players with a single forward thrust of Simms's arm.

The middle has held and Simms has the time. But as he releases the ball, all hell breaks loose. Perhaps its trajectory has somehow been influenced by his gloved hand. Whatever the reason, he does not get the ball up. It whistles incredibly low on a direct line to Clyde Simmons, the big defensive end, who has been totally neutralized and is nowhere near the action.

Simmons grabs the ball at the level of his jersey numbers and takes off for the Giants' end zone, 60 yards away. Anderson slices over to his left in pursuit but a white jersey hits him and subtracts him from the equation. Simms makes a rolling dive which Simmons sidesteps. At the 30, Zeke Mowatt has the only shot. He does not try for the tackle. Instead he tries to knock Simmons off stride with his shoulder. Mowatt bounces off and Simmons steams into the end zone.

As Ruzek lines up his extra-point try, Barnes grabs Mike Ryan on the sidelines. "You better get back to the locker room and get Moore out here!" he shouts over the noise. "Tell him we're gonna need him."

Simms has started for the sidelines. He unbuckles his chin strap and turns for a brief word with Parcells. Then he walks several strides away and violently shakes his head. He stamps his foot three times and then shouts into the wind. The sound is indistinguishable but the lip movements need no translation.

The game is a little less than ten minutes old, the Eagles' offense has gained just nine yards, and the Giants are trailing, 14–0. Parcells slowly removes his headphones, turns his back to the field, and lifts his head toward the iron-gray sky. His face reveals none of his thoughts.

As the Giants await the kickoff, Moore has returned to the sidelines. He is pale and he is weak. He seeks out Barnes and says, "It's not that I don't want to play. It's just that I don't know if I can. I think it would better if Brian were in there."

There is no time for discussion. On the sidelines things happen so fast, there is precious little time for anything at all. Barnes locates Hoaglin and tells him, "Eric's out until you hear differently from me."

As he walks back to his position near the bench, Barnes is thinking, "He ought to try. Maybe he can't do it but he ought to try. We got a guy in there with a broken ankle. At least he [Moore] should try. There's no disgrace if he has to come out."

Ruzek's kick reaches the 12 and this time, the Eagles' special team is flying. Led by Frizzell and Robert Drummond, they drop Meggett on the 18.

The Giants are watching the clock as they fight the wind. Old newspapers and assorted garbage are beginning to blow in their faces. They must either hold the ball for five minutes or score. Already down by 14, they cannot give both the wind and the ball to number 12 with a two-touchdown lead in what is left of this quarter.

Almost without warning, they bring the game back within reach. A 24-yarder from Simms to Manuel is the touchstone which finally moves them to the Eagles' 41 with a third and 8. Throughout this drive, Simms is standing in there under heavy pressure.

But not this time. As the ball is snapped and the receivers come off the line of scrimmage, the secondary moves to double-cover Meggett to the outside. Now Ingram is one-and-one inside with Andre Waters. He cuts and outruns his coverage and Simms reads it perfectly. Waters's futile dive at Ingram's heels at the 5 is more obligatory than realistic.

The Giants have pulled themselves back into the ball game. The wind is only two minutes away from befriending them. And up in the booth the offensive coaches smile with very good reason.

They have begun to close in on their Great White Whale. And, just as they planned, David Meggett was the bait.

The rest of the quarter belongs to the defense. Twice it misfires and Cunningham completes passes of 31 and 29 yards. The cornerbacks have been jamming Keith Jackson at the line but he fights his way clear this time and beats Guyton by two steps with a sudden burst of speed. Guyton makes the hit from behind and shakes his head as Jackson says nothing and walks back toward the huddle.

But good things are happening. A lot of them flow from Erik Howard, the man who says his artistic world is confined to "six inches away from bad breath and leather." Because the Eagles have had little success moving him, they are hard-pressed to provide daylight for their ball carriers.

And then there is a moment when the coaching staff holds its breath. For the first time in this game, Randall Cunningham has found an unplugged escape route on a third and 20. Adrian White, Cunningham's mirror, is all that's left. White chases number 12 down and holds him to a 7-yard gain. The Giants' coaches are convinced it has begun to turn.

Shortly before that there was a moment which silenced everyone.

Lawrence Taylor is down and Barnes is sprinting toward him. "I thought," the trainer says, " 'uh-oh, there goes the ankle.' But no. Lawrence is spitting teeth." Technically—and fortunately—they are not his own.

Shortly before Taylor's one and only acting appearance (in HBO's *First and Ten*) he had his teeth bonded into a Hollywood smile. "They told me I was a natural out there," he had told Barnes after the taping. Now as he left the field he was telling Barnes, "Walk down there and get Dr. [Hugh] Gardy [the team dentist]. Ask him if he can do something about this."

On the final play of the quarter, from the Giants' 32, the rush is all over Cunningham. He has no choice but to throw the ball away. The roar that greets the zeroes on the clock is almost as penetrating as the wind.

Second Quarter

Now it will become a chess match with muscles. Landeta will punt early with the wind at his back for 53 yards, and up in the seats, the Abominable Frostbite Cases will take that as an omen as well. For four minutes the Giants and Eagles will play vicious, basic football. Jerome Brown will thunder over Roberts and lay highly ungentle hands on Simms, forcing him to unload the ball before Brown slams him down in the end zone.

Then Jackson will assert himself once more, grabbing a 23-yarder, hauled down from behind by a frustrated Guyton. It is impossible to handle Jackson time after time, but the rookie has done his share.

So has the wind, which captures Cunningham's next pass. Pepper Johnson is caught in a black hole in space with a receiver free both in front and behind him. But as the wind captures the ball, it hangs between both of them and Johnson steps up and picks it off. Simms, however, returns the favor when Eric Allen intercepts his pass on the next sequence to trigger a modest drive by the Eagles from the Giants' 30 to the 18.

Now, for the first time, the Giants' defense has been backed into the outer perimeter of its red zone. But with the Eagles unable to throw into the killer wind, they jam the running game with a violence that warms their frozen constituency.

In the middle of the war, Erik Howard is playing hell with the Eagles' offensive line. He has plugged it so well that he sets the stage for first John Washington and then Leonard Marshall to bring down Toney and Byars on the first two thrusts. On the third, Cunningham, in trouble, misplays his handoff and the Eagles must settle for a 35-yard field goal.

It is difficult for the home side faculty to be angry. The Giants' offense has done just about everything wrong but still the margin is only 10 points and the Giants have seven and a half minutes to use the wind. This is a typical Giants-Eagles game. The play up front is ferocious. What makes it atypical at this juncture is that Randall Cunningham has not hurt them. Taylor, back in the game, has slowed to a limp—so much so that the Eagles have even tried to run to his side.

Now it has become two body punchers in the center of the ring going toe to toe and somebody is going to have to back off. With 2:55 left, the Eagles have crossed into Giants territory, primarily off a 12-yard run by Toney on a play called 31 slant, which splits Washington to one side and Howard and Marshall to the other with superior blocking at the line.

By the nature of the ebb and flow of the contest, the Giants' defense must either win this battle or die. It wins it on a single play which even brings a smile to Belichick's face. Cunningham fires a short pass underneath for Jackson, who has running room. As he seeks to turn it up a notch, he shifts the ball into his right hand. Reasons cannot quite reach him for the tackle but as he slides by, he reaches out and knocks the ball loose. Pepper Johnson falls on it.

The Giants have the ball, the wind, and the time.

On first down, Simms stands up to the tremendous rush of Simmons and drops off a little delay to Tillman coming out of the backfield for 9. Two plays later, Tillman gets the first down.

And then in a single instant, all the Xs, all the Os, all the late-night planning jumps straight off the drawing board and stings the Eagles.

Simms is getting superb protection as Mowatt and Manuel are flooding the same side of the field. In that do-or-don't moment, which Parcells was talking about, the Eagles must make a hair-trigger decision. Manuel is one-on-one with Jenkins.

Frizzell looks where Mowatt is also single-covered and takes a hesitant step in that direction. In that instant, the battle is decided. Manuel is running flat out and now we have a desperate foot race that Jenkins cannot win without help. Up in the booth, Erhardt and Coughlin are pounding each other. On the sideline, Lee Pope, the receiver coach, throws a fist toward the sky. As the offensive coaches had predicted, they have made the Eagles guess—and guess wrong.

The play goes all the way to the Philly 12. But there is a yellow flag on the ground and Oates and Simms are racing toward the official in a panic. Gordon McCarter backs away and calls in a clutch of zebras. Yet another official positions himself between the two Giants and his boss. On the other side of the conference a covey of white shirts is trying to get in on a piece of the discussion. Then the two Giants are throwing their fists in the air and running back to their huddle with a bonus.

Jerome Brown has been nailed for head-slapping Oates and the penalty, which becomes half the distance to the goal line, is tacked on to the play. The ball is down on the 6. The clock hits 1:55 and they get the two-minute warning. All over the ballpark, they are standing and stamping their feet. On the sidelines, Simms is huddled with Parcells and Handley. And out on the field, the Giants' offense is thinking they were told that Manuel was going to catch big passes today, they were told they could confuse the Eagles' secondary, they were told they could count on the wind.

And they were told they could win.

The Giants' offense is in the red zone for the first time today. This is where the Eagles had buckled up their chin straps earlier this year down in Philly and stuck it to them. This is where they had been forced to accept field goals for touchdowns. And every man on this offensive unit had heard the same refrain all week long: "You have to win the red zone. Taking a field goal isn't winning."

Deep in their hearts, the Giants believed something even more strongly. A touchdown here would devastate the Eagles.

Meggett is in the backfield and as they break the huddle, the Eagles are shouting at each other. And on the sidelines and up in the booth, the coaches are hoping that the Eagles are thinking: "Meggett . . . pass . . . watch it."

But there isn't going to be any pass. The Giants have loaded up with three tight ends. At the snap, Meggett is swinging to his right. Cross hits Jessie Small, driving him out of the play. Reggie White is handled. The hole is open. Riesenberg is leading the charge and for a frozen instant he seems to have locked away Mike Pitts.

And up in the booth they almost dare to say, "He's got it, he's got it." But Pitts claws free at the 4 and as Meggett comes within his reach Pitts gets his left hand on the ball just as Andre Waters makes the hit. The ball pops free and bounces backwards behind Meggett and to his right. At the 5, Byron Evans of the Eagles falls on it.

Parcells balls both fists and grits his teeth. Meggett walks slowly toward the sidelines, slams his helmet down, and slumps onto the bench next to Odessa Turner. Further down the line, the face of OJ Anderson, the good soldier, betrays nothing. He would have been called upon had Meggett held the ball. Later, he will pretend he does not hear the question when he is asked whether he was surprised he was not sent in to run the sweep.

The defense is back on the field, convinced that if it doesn't steal the ball, the Giants may never score. But the obvious intensity catches up with them before the Eagles can complete a play. Lawrence Taylor has lined up in the neutral zone and the yellow flag permits Cunningham to acquire five critical yards of additional breathing room.

The Giants will not see the ball again until the third quarter. The wind cannot dissipate the boos that follow them off the field.

Halftime, Giants' locker room

They file into the room in dead silence, walking beneath the sign that proclaims, Individuals Win Games, Teams Win Championships.

The silence is punctuated only by the occasional slam of a helmet against the floor. Back in the trainer's room, Barnes is surprised that Taylor is his only customer.

"I can play some in the second half," Taylor tells Barnes, "but I don't think I can do the team much good. Johnie [Cooks] will get the job done. You better tell Bill."

"I can give you something to ease the pain some," Barnes says. "Do you want an Anaprox [a powerful aspirin without codeine]?"

Taylor just shakes his head.

Among the coaches there is some brief talk about Moore and "stage fright." Later, Moore will actually play briefly. His situation will be compounded when he tells a reporter that he had suffered an anxiety attack. Apparently he was confused by Dr. Warren's reference to "being anxious when you couldn't breathe."

"I really didn't think about it too much," Howard says. "The offensive guys? I don't know. I wondered a little why he [Moore] wasn't out there, but I had my own war to deal with."

The coaches have begun to make adjustments—ahead by 30 or down by 20, halftime has never passed through any locker room without this ritual. But what adjustments to make when the game plan is sound and two freak plays have created the trauma? They have gained more yards, have more first downs, and, even with Taylor virtually useless, Cunningham has scrambled for only 10 yards.

Hoaglin is closeted with the offensive line, talking intensely with his group. The big messages are designed for Roberts and Riesenberg. Meanwhile, Erhardt is telling the quarterbacks, "We know we can move the ball on these guys. There's no mystery to what's happened. Hell, all we have to do is hold on to the ball." He speaks calmly and he is not accusatory.

As the halftime begins to run its course, Barnes can hear the voices clearly all the way back to his cubicle. Each is emotional and each is identifiable.

"We're beating ourselves," Carthon is shouting at his offensive teammates. "They aren't doing it to us—we are." The offense is depressed because it knows he is right. Carthon stays on them all the way up the tunnel. The loudest voice belongs to Banks. He says it is ridiculous to lose this game this way. He says, "We have done everything wrong and we're still only 10 points behind. This is for the championship. We damned well better get it together right now." He is part cheerleader and part accusing finger.

Just before they leave, Parcells tells them that they will have every opportunity to win this game but "We need everybody to show up for the second half."

He is not speaking about Eric Moore. What he is talking about is the offense and as they head for the door, they know it.

And over the babble of voices and anger as they start up the tunnel, the sound of one voice rises above the rest. It is Lamar Leachman and he repeats his Southern-drawled battle cry over and over: "Hang in there. We can win. We will win. Just keep knocking them sons of bitches on their asses."

Third Quarter

As they emerge from the tunnel and into the wind, the first thought that strikes them is that it has gotten colder. They do not know it but the weather bureau has revised its late-afternoon forecast, indicating there is a possibility that the wind chill can fall from minus seven to as low as minus ten. The wind, which continues to blow ferociously toward the east end zone from which the teams have emerged, carries with it a mass of debris.

The Giants must make a major decision. The second half option is theirs. They have moved the ball and Parcells does not think the Eagles have done very much on offense. He feels the gap on the scoreboard must be immediately narrowed. It would be terrific to have the wind in the fourth quarter but he cannot afford to wait.

The Giants elect to defend the west end zone.

As the kickoff return team breaks from its huddle on the sidelines, Carthon is shaking his fist in encouragement. The wind has increased so much that Meggett and Ingram move up to the 20-yard line to deploy themselves. Ruzek's kick is immediately caught up in the gale and wobbles sideways in midflight like a herniated duck. Meggett circles under it and makes the catch on the 18.

He is rolling. For an instant, it appears as though he is going to break this kickoff and the Eagles' hearts all in one fluid motion.

Again the return is left. At the Giants' 40, David Little dives at him and gets a piece of his ankle. Meggett stumbles just long enough for Britt Hager to finish off the plane.

The Giants will start from their own 43. On the sidelines, Ray Handley has his arm around Simms, discussing the sequence ahead. He slaps him on the back and sends him out. As the Giants break the huddle, William Roberts can still hear Hoaglin's message: "Do not let him [Jerome Brown] discourage you. You have to keep coming back. You have to be aggressive, William, you have to make him work."

Simms barks out the snap count. In his eagerness, Williams moves before the ball. It costs the Giants five yards. They start again with three receivers on the right side. Lionel Manuel, who is one of them, comes in motion to the left. At the snap, he heads straight up the middle. The blocking is superb. So is the pass Simms throws, which is laid out there for the plucking by Manuel, who is wide open on a mismatch with linebacker Byron Evans. Manuel is finally hauled down on the Eagle 23. The play covers 39 yards.

The crowd is into it with a passion that is almost frightening. If there are demons in what until now has been an ill wind for them, they surely emerge in the next few plays. What happens is enough to send Buddy Ryan in search of a silver bullet.

On the very first play, the Giants go for the tight end pass that they have said all week would produce a touchdown. The pass is a shade high but Mowatt is wide open in the end zone. In the confusion, which the Giants sought to create from the crossing patterns, he has beaten two defenders.

He drops the ball. It is the only break the Eagles will get on this sequence.

On second down, Simms is rushed and his arm is hit as he tries to unload to Mowatt. Downfield on the 21-yard line, Izel Jenkins has done his own unloading on Mowatt. The yellow flag negates the incompletion and moves the Giants to the 18. They are in the red zone for the second time today.

On the next play, the Eagles are coming from all directions and the blocking has collapsed. In desperation, Simms unloads before he is hit. The ball is tipped away by a defensive lineman and falls harmlessly to the ground. Then Simms throws again. This time Odessa Turner is hooked up with Eric Allen. Allen reaches in and steals the ball. Nobody is going to catch him. He is gone 86 yards to yet another Eagles defensive score—he thinks.

But back at the line of scrimmage there is another flag. The Eagles' coaches on the sidelines are raging but they are not going to win this argument. Clyde Simmons had jumped offside before the snap. The interception is nullified. The Giants get 5 yards and now they are down on the 13-yard line.

Again they are haunted by the refrain they have heard all week long from every offensive coach: "Field goals aren't winning. You have got to stick it in there and get the 6."

Here come the Giants. They are four wide and out on the end, Andre Waters is up in Meggett's face, set to take him on the instant the ball is snapped. It looks pass but it's a draw, with OJ getting the ball. The hole opens for the barest fraction of time and just as Anderson gets there, Byron Evans throws his body into his path and takes him on, one on one. Through sheer determination, Evans shuts OJ down for no gain.

Second down from the 12. Cross is in motion to the right, more to block than catch. Simms takes the snap. He is scanning the end zone. Odessa Turner is running a crossing pattern and he is going to get there uncovered. It appears to be the ultimate translation of the blackboard wish to the end zone deed. But Turner stops. His knee has twisted and he goes down. With nobody to throw to, Simms unloads the ball over the end line.

Third down and the battle of the red zone is slipping away from them. They send Simms into the shotgun. At the snap, Wes Hopkins comes up to cover Meggett. But Meggett is not the primary receiver. He is looking to hook Hopkins and take him out of the coverage. He misses and Hopkins, who has a clear vision of Simms, decides to come across the line of scrimmage. With nobody left to block him, Hopkins becomes the "hot" and he drills Simms to the ground for a 7-yard loss.

The Eagles are mobbing Hopkins. On the other sideline, Parcells calls for the field-goal team. Somewhere in this game he will need the three to draw even in any event. Moreover, he will still have the killer wind at his offense's back for almost thirteen minutes more. He is a realist. You do what you have to do.

Nittmo's kick is yet another adventure. It covers 38 yards and it is life-and-death up to and including the instant it hits the left upright. It kicks inside for the three and the Giants have cut the spread to 17–10.

They go back into the trenches again, determined to keep the Eagles pinned down, make them kick into the wind, and turn this game around. Twice, Philly sends Toney at them on slant 31. The first time, Howard fights off the block and drives him into the arms of Johnie Cooks, who is now at Taylor's spot, and they hold the gain to 2 yards. Then it's Toney up the middle and again the guard and the center cannot handle Howard. He drives them toward the ball carrier and Carl Banks lays on a tremendous hit.

Third and 5. Cunningham is rolling to his right with Banks closing in. With no time to spare, Cunningham looks downfield and fires into the wind for Cris Carter, who has curled back toward his quarterback. But Sheldon White has him covered and times the hit perfectly. The ball bounces high in the air off Carter. If it goes to his right, it will fall out of bounds. If it pops to the left, Keith Jackson will not have to move for it. The ball blows left and the Eagles have moved 33 yards to the Giants' 27. There will be no punt into the wind.

For the first time in this game, Cunningham has room to operate. He passes to Byars, coming out of the backfield for 10. Then he sends Toney up the middle on a draw and this time the Eagles have blown Howard away from the hole. By the time Guyton plugs it, the white shirts have gained 11 more.

The Giants are not only in their defensive red zone, they are running out of yards to defend. It is first down on the 6. Just before the snap, Cunningham audibles and Byars is running 31 slant. The Giants have no trouble locating him because he is running right over them. Legs churning, body twisting, he has fought his way past the initial charge and Mark Collins and Guyton hurl themselves at the moving mass to halt its progress at the 1.

Now the goal-line unit is on the field for the Giants and the margin of error is less than three feet. At the snap of the ball, Cunningham lays it into Toney's stomach. Howard has fought the world off his back and Reasons leaps over the stack and hits hard. Guyton has come in from the side. Marshall has knifed in under the stack and Greg Jackson has added a punctuation mark to battle.

No gain.

Suddenly, the crowd is into it as it has not been since Nittmo's field goal. This is Giants football to them. This is the Meadowlands in December and deep down in their macho voyeurism, this is what they have come to see.

Third down and the ball is on the 1. Well before the snap, Banks is hurdling the left side of the line. Whistles blow, flags fall and the Giants are penalized 18 inches.

The Eagles are back again, the sound of their breathing all along the line is like a bomb in search of a fuse. Again it is Toney, coming straight ahead. Again Reasons leaps across the stack. Howard and Marshall are there at ankle level. At the same time Rob White gets a piece of the runner and drives him back. Nobody has to tell the Eagles they didn't make it. Nobody has to tell the crowd.

It is fourth down and 18 inches. At the line of scrimmage, you can almost feel the fire burning on both sides of the line. It is as though in this moment, the final score, and the team standings, mean nothing. It has become personal. The red zone is only a foot and a half deep. The nasty side of professional football, which Fred Hoaglin had described so well, envelops all twenty-two players. This is cinema verité and it needs no director.

Cunningham is wedged in tightly against his center. Again the call is Toney. The two lines lock together in violent embrace. The issue hangs there within both sides' grasp. And then Steve De Ossie, a veteran in the league, but a first-year man with the Giants and a player who this very morning has been reactivated after a foot injury, is coming from the left side, rocketing out of his linebacker's spot. He lowers his shoulder directly into Toney's gut.

The Eagles do not score.

So the Giants stand there in their finest moment with the wind slamming into their backs and their fists in the air and the crowd above them stamping against the concrete flooring so hard it is a wonder a thousand frozen feet do not shatter.

Surely, this must be yet another omen. The Giants are down by a single touchdown and they will have the wind for yet another seven minutes. There is not one among them who does not think they will win this game.

Now the problem is room for Landeta to milk the most out of the wind when he kicks. The Giants do not get him much. Anderson gets only a yard. Two Simms passes fall incomplete. The Eagles are coming after Landeta to pressure the punt. Ricky Shaw, an ex-Giant, comes through unblocked straight up the middle and gets a hand on the ball. It is rolling loose and Andre Waters scoops it up and powers his way down to the 2. Another whistle. Another flag. Now we know why Waters got to the ball so quickly. He was offside.

With 5 extra yards in which to operate, Landeta gets the punt away, but a poor snap forces him to hurry. It is an ordinary effort for Landeta, but Gizmo Williams, the Eagles' safety, is having trouble following it in the wind. The ball falls untouched at the 41 and it rolls and it rolls and it rolls as Gizmo backs up, tracking its path. It finally stops at the Eagles' 22.

The roll has given Landeta a 71-yard punt. The crowd rocks. The Giants' bench is alive. Parcells had told them this would happen. Now it is just a matter of time.

The Eagles are stunned. On the first play Cunningham tries to run the ball but his left tackle beats the snap count and it costs them 5 yards. Pushed back to their 17 and with just a 7-point lead, they dare not throw into the wind this close to their goal. Their answer is Toney, Toney, and Toney. He is dropped first by Johnson and Guyton, next by Guyton and Howard, and finally by Cooks and Marshall.

It is fourth and 4 and the Eagles' worst fears are realized when Runager must punt into the wind. The ball travels only 21 yards. The Giants have it at the Philadelphia 49.

Simms is on the sideline with Parcells and Handley. He has now taken off both gloves. They are talking about what is next. The game plan, so badly mangled almost before the ink was dry, now seems to be falling into place.

On first down, they get Mowatt one-on-one with a linebacker. It is the same play where the ball had sailed through his hands in the end zone earlier. This time he makes a dandy catch 29 yards downfield. The Giants are on the Eagles' 20 and they will still have the wind at their back for the next three minutes.

This time Simms is looking deep, but up front Simmons has broken free of Jumbo Elliot and Simms senses the problem. He throws the ball away an instant before Simmons catches him waist high and slams him down. On second down, with two tight ends in the lineup, Simms is looking for a receiver when Reggie White, who has been handled reasonably well since his early spree, overpowers Riesenberg and comes straight at him. As Simms releases the ball, it bounces against White's outstretched arms and falls to the ground.

Third and 10. The blocking is superb. Simms takes his time. Frizzell is desperately trying to cover Ingram, who makes an acrobatic catch, fights him yard for yard, and is finally pulled down on the 6.

Once again, the ghosts of red zones past are sitting on the Giants' shoulders.

On first down, Oates is pulling back almost as he snaps the ball and it sails. Simms recovers it and manages to throw it away over the end line. Second down. Odessa Turner runs a slant and heads for the corner of the end zone. Eric Allen is beaten. He turns and faces Turner, playing the man instead of the ball. The pass bounces off Allen's back and the flag hits the ground along with it. Pass interference. The Giants get a first down on the one.

The wind has increased to the point where any second you expect the flags above the stadium to tear loose and sail away. The stadium lights have begun to cast odd patterns on the corners of the end zones.

When Simms looks to the sideline, he sees exactly what he expects. Ottis Anderson, the old gunfighter, is headed for the corral.

The first carry is straight ahead and Mike Golic, the tackle, and Mike Reichenbach, the linebacker, come up to meet him and drop him for a yard loss.

Handley turns to look at Parcells, who nods in agreement. Handley is wigwagging furiously to Simms, who peers in and then walks back to the huddle. As Simms begins the cadence, Carthon moves in motion to his left. At the snap, Anderson is coming behind him and reads off his lead block. Oates, Williams, and Riesenberg provide the hole and Anderson dives. As he crosses the goal, a leg whips out of the pile and catches his helmet.

He is face down in the end zone and in midcelebration, they see him. Oates has kneeled down and put his arms around him. Barnes is racing toward them. Slowly, OJ rises and walks off. The ovation is awesome.

They have tied the score and when Mark Higgs butchers the kickoff return in the wind and finally fights his way back to the 13, the defense comes onto the field determined to deliver a knockout right here. They do not miss by much. On the first play they are all over number 12, chasing him, hounding him, and finally he recovers his own fumble and fights his way back to the line of scrimmage. Washington and Reasons sandwich Toney after a 1-yard gain and Perry Williams gets a hand on the ball to bat away Cunningham's pass intended for Ron Johnson.

After Runager's punt against the wind is returned 10 yards by Meggett to the Eagles' 39, the officials are mysteriously huddled along the sideline. Dick Creed, the side judge, is talking to Gordon McCarter.

"Gordon, I can't walk. It's my foot—it's my foot—I can't move. I don't know what's wrong," he is saying. The wind is swirling garbage all around them and Creed is very pale.

"Just hold on a minute," McCarter says. "Here, go to the end of the bench and sit down." Two other officials help him to the sidelines and McCarter runs over for Barnes.

"I don't know what's wrong. I'm going to have to take him inside and let the doctor look at it," Barnes says.

As if things weren't complicated enough and if this thing wasn't going to come down to hammers and axes in the trenches before it ended, the officiating crew is suddenly in a reshuffled, emergency six-man mold. Inside the dressing room they will discover that because of the extreme cold, Creed has dislocated a small bone in his foot. They will tape it and he will return on the fifth play of the final quarter.

There is time for just one more play in the period and Simms hits Meggett for 7 yards to the Eagles' 32. Then the quarter runs out. The crowd is on its feet. If there were a moon, they surely would be baying at it.

A great weight seems to have been lifted. The Giants have cleaned up their mess, mopped up the blood, and they are finally all even.

What could possibly go wrong?

Fourth Quarter

So this is the what everyone thought it would be. The Eagles and the Giants never do it simply. They never do it gracefully. This series has become shot-and-a-beer football played by two teams and two coaching staffs that would spit in your eye if you told them they bore any resemblance to each other.

And it may be that of times they do not. But put them on the same field and the result is always the same. Somebody will make a terrible mistake and spend the rest of the game trying to mitigate it—and they generally do.

Then, invariably, it will come down to the fourth quarter and what wins it will be as unexpected as it is dramatic. Both sides had that thought with which to conjure when the clock started running in the fourth and the Philadelphia Eagles took possession of the wind.

It began with the Eagles' defense suddenly falling upon the Giants' offensive line as if they had turned the pages of this particular book back to the game's opening minutes.

The message is delivered to the Giants immediately. On second and 3, Anderson hammers his way for four yards but Jumbo is caught tripping and they are set back 5 yards. The Eagles are coming with all they have and if Simms didn't know better, you couldn't blame him for thinking that it wasn't weather-induced vapor streaming from their mouths—it was pure fire.

Simms rolls to his right, sets up to throw and then sees the Eye of the Dragon. Untouched by human hands, Mike Pitts is barreling through an alley of flesh and headed straight for him. There is no time to throw and nowhere to go. Pitts levels him and the Giants lose another 9 yards.

On third down, Simms must throw after moving forward to avoid a forest of white jerseys and he has no chance to complete his pass to Turner. Now Sean Landeta must come off the bench and kick into the maw of the wind from the Giants' 49.

Once the ball gains altitude it seems to freeze and fall straight down. It rolls dead on the Eagles' 26.

Cunningham goes straight into the wind for Byars, but this

time the wind is friend to no quarterback. The ball sails beyond everyone's reach. On second down, he sends Sherman bulling straight ahead for 2, but Ron Solt, the right guard, is detected putting a stranglehold on Howard's waist and it costs the Eagles 10.

After what follows next you cannot find a frostbite case in the stands or a man on the Giants' bench who does not think they are about to win this game.

On second and 20 Cunningham tosses short to Byars, coming out of the backfield. But Adrian White has read the play perfectly. He slants from left to right and slams Byars to the ground 3 yards behind the line of scrimmage. It is now third down and 23 to go at the Eagles' 12.

This is where number 12 kills you—and the Giants know it. This is where he slides and glides and scrambles and ambles and suddenly you have to go all the way down to the other end of the field for the next snap.

But not this time. Cunningham drops back . . . and back . . . and back. But the lanes are plugged and Erik Howard fights through a wall of blockers, pushing them toward the quarterback. Marshall comes in from the side. Howard strips away David Alexander in the final instant and nails Cunningham to the artificial turf.

Much of the quarterback's body falls across the goal line. Marshall is leaping in the air with his closed palms pressed flat against each other and held over his head, signaling a safety.

But the refs spot the ball at the Philadelphia 2.

As the defense leaves the field, they are met by the Giants' entire team. The crowd is standing and screaming. The wind is rattling toward the Giants' goal line. With such a set, "The Twilight Zone" could tape thirty episodes.

Now the Giants' punt return team is on the field, remembering all the film and all the planning centering around Runager's lack of distance. Unnoticed in the confusion, Cunningham has walked to the sidelines and he is talking to Buddy Ryan.

They know something that nobody on the other side of the field does. Back on Thursday, with the wind howling down in South Philly, Randall Cunningham sought out Gizmo Williams and told him: "Don't make any plans after practice today. You and me got a date."

Alone in Veterans Stadium, there was Randall Cunningham with a bag of balls and Gizmo was down the field. Cunningham was working on his punting.

"I can kick," Cunningham would later say. "I kicked in college. I know all about that wind up in the Meadowlands. I thought there just might come a time when I could fool everybody." At the University of Nevada at Las Vegas, number 12 had been the team's regular punter and had led the nation one season. Just a year earlier he had set the Giants back on their heels with a surprise 55-yard quick kick in Philadelphia. But that was gimmick stuff.

He kicked and kicked on Thursday until his leg began to hurt.

"Now," Randall Cunningham said. "Buddy, I'd like to do it now."

"Well, go ahead, if you think you can get it done."

So, suddenly, Randall Cunningham was running back onto the field, waving Runager off to the sidelines.

Years from now, the Giants who played in this football game and the men who sat up night after night with nothing but number 12 on their minds will be able to tell you that they had stopped Randall Cunningham from beating them with his right arm—he would complete just nine passes for 130 yards.

And they had stopped Randall Cunningham from beating them with both his legs—he would run for just 10 yards, 7 of them on one play.

What they could not do was stop him from beating them with his right foot.

Parcells is watching Meggett standing all alone in the face of the wind, thinking "He'll catch it. They're doing the right thing. Cunningham can outkick Runager. But this is our park. We win these games. Meggett will catch it and will stick it in the end zone."

Cunningham is standing straight up at the point where the blue-and-white artwork meets in the end zone. At six-foot-four, he is a solitary figure outlined against the glare of the stadium lights.

And the wind is breathing on the back of his helmet like a living thing.

Just down the road in the state's largest inner cities, places like Newark and Jersey City and Paterson, they call this kind of wind the Hawk. They know all about the Hawk. It rattles down empty streets and slams into deserted doorways and only a fool would stand in its path. When the Hawk visits the Meadowlands, it grows teeth. All week long the Giants had prayed for it. The Hawk won a lot of games for them in this park. In the Year of the Super Bowl, it even won a conference championship for them, blowing the Washington Redskins into submission.

In thirty seconds the Giants would learn something they had never even once considered. The Hawk belongs to no man.

With the Giants' kick return linemen breathing fire in front of him and the Hawk blowing pure ice at his back, Randall Cunningham took the snap and put his foot into the ball.

Back at the Giants' 38-yard line, David Meggett watched the ball, which seemed to take forever to drop. It was angled off to his left and he was sliding over trying to get a fix on it. At the last possible instant he decided to field it on the bounce.

The ball had traveled 60 yards in the air. When it hit, the Hawk pursed his lips and started to blow. The ball skipped. It slithered. It rolled. By the time Meggett picked it up, he was on his own 7-yard line. Desperately, he tried to turn it upfield. He managed just nine yards before Sammy Lilly and Dave Rimington sandwiched him and sprawled him on the ground.

And for an instant there was a hint of the stone, cold, cemetery silence of which Parcells had spoken when he was recalling the opener down in Washington. The only noise you could hear was coming from underneath green capes on the Eagles' sideline.

As Meggett came to the sidelines, Parcells walked over to him. "Come on," he said, "you've got to play with your head." And then, as the enormity of the moment seemed to set in and as though it had suddenly reaffirmed what every coach knows—that all the hours of talking and planning mean nothing if your people can't translate them into the deed on Sunday—he said in a much louder voice: "This is the championship. Don't you understand what we're doing here? This is the championship game!"

Randall Cunningham had punted the ball 91 yards—a third of which had accrued when the ball was permitted to drop untouched.

The Giants were 84 yards from the Eagles' goal and they had to move the ball into the bite of the Hawk.

And then there were the teeth of the Eagle defense.

On the first play, Simms fails to connect with Mowatt on a bad pass and it costs even more when the Giants are penalized for an illegal formation.

Second and 15, the ball on the 11.

Simms is not in the shotgun. At the snap of the ball, Reggie White breaks free of Riesenberg and is headed toward Simms. At the other side of the line, Mike Golic is hooked with William Roberts. But now Golic forces him back, spins off his block, and is running free. Simms sees White and takes two steps forward to avoid him. In that instant, Golic has circled in from behind the quarterback and wraps him up. The ball squirts free and Pitts recovers it on the 7.

In the stands, they are chanting for one more miracle: "defense . . . defense . . . defense." As for the Eagles, they have dumped old slant 31 in the garbage can for this one. Now they will go with the red zone plays that got them here.

On first down, Cunningham lofts the fade to the corner Belichick had worried over during the week. Pepper Johnson is out there just as they practiced it, but the receiver, Robert Drummond, has a step on him. Both men go up. Drummond juggles the ball and it squirts away, falling for an incompletion.

Again the chant: "defense . . . defense . . . defense." And again, Cunningham goes to an old formula. He lays the ball in Byars's stomach and the big back hits the right side of the line. The Eagles' line gets off the ball quickly. Byars's legs are churning. Banks hurls himself into the hole just as Reasons angles in from the side. The ball is spotted at the 2.

Over on the sidelines, Cunningham is talking with two coaches, shaking his head, and gesturing. He knows what he wants to call now and apparently they are going to let him. As he trots back out, the Giants are shouting at each other and shaking their fists. They have been here before in this very game. Now they are telling each other it can be done again.

Cunningham is over center, calling the cadence. Behind him, Byars is the lone set back. At the snap, Keith Jackson, lined up on the right side, throws his body into John Washington and drives him back. Byars reads off a block by his right guard, Ron Solt, who moves Pepper Johnson in the other direction and he powers through the hole and into the end zone.

There are ten minutes left in this game, but as far as the Giants are concerned it might as well be ten seconds.

The Giants will never again get closer than the Eagles' 30-yard line.

Postgame locker room

Phil Simms is slumped in an upright position on one of the training tables. Ronnie Barnes is trying to clean up Simms's left hand, which is covered with blood and has been bleeding ever since it was hit full force by someone's helmet. As Barnes works, Simms is motionless, his chin on his chest. The trainer crouches to cut the tape off his ankles. Both Tim and Wellington Mara have paused to pass some kind of encouragement to him but he stares straight ahead. Now George Young is talking to him. He draws no response.

Out in the big locker room there is more silence. Odessa Turner sits motionless on the stool before his locker. The sprained knee, with which he had continued to play, throbs bitterly. But he is as angry with himself and with the offense's failure as the rest of them. He does not limp off to Barnes for treatment.

David Meggett is away from his locker. In a moment, they will open the doors and let the press inside. When they arrive, Meggett will not be there.

Down the hall, in the big classroom, Bill Parcells faces the worst moment of the afternoon. Meeting the press in New York is like nowhere else. The television people and the still cameras, the largest number of beat writers and columnists and sidebar writers in the league make movement almost impossible. Today their ranks are swelled by a large Philadelphia contingent and a variety of writers from around the country who are here because of the game's overall significance.

He is totally surrounded by them. Because professional football is a business, he does not have the luxury to mourn or curse or smack the wall in private. The league rules say the locker room must be open twenty minutes after each game and the coach must meet the press.

"You couldn't say that this was one of Phil Simms's better

days," he starts. "I told them [the Giants] before you came in that you cannot make mistakes like that and win. I think you'll try to win but that's up to you. It looks like Philadelphia will win the division. There isn't much we can do about that now. Yes, I think Meggett should have caught the ball and, yes, he's fumbling too much."

Within the hour, he would leave the building. Judy Parcells had already said good-bye to her children and was headed home to wait. There would be no steak dinner at Manny's tonight.

Back in the dressing room, Phil Simms had returned to his locker. He knew what was coming but he had to do the right thing.

"It's hard to go out there and screw it up but I did it," he said. "I can't blame the protection. I had enough time to dig myself out of the hole I put us in. My ankle wasn't the reason. I could move well enough to buy the time I needed. And it wasn't the gloves. I've played long enough not to make those mistakes."

And then he limped away.

Johnie Cooks is exhausted. "We might see them again in the playoffs," he says. "Who knows? But what we're gonna find out these next few weeks is who wants to win around here and who wants to pay the price."

In the row of lockers across from Cooks, Erik Howard is shaking his head. His hand is swollen again. There is blood on his pants. "We [the defense] hold 'em to 3 points until the last quarter and they win—ridiculous. We gave it away. We [the defense] don't get out there until we're down 14–0, we fight our way back in. We even stop 'em on the goal. Shit, Merry Christmas, Philadelphia. We should have gift-wrapped the damned thing, mailed it to them, and not even bothered to show up."

7:30 P.M., Upper Saddle River, New Jersey

He is sitting in the brown chair in the family roon, the half-eaten sandwich by his side. On the television screen, the Chicago Bears and the Minnesota Vikings have become a blur. Now he sighs, rises from the chair, and walks slowly up the stairs to bed.

At 4:00 A.M., his private demons will hammer him awake. He does not go back to sleep.

At 6 A.M., he is on his way back to the office.

8. MONDAY, DECEMBER 4, 1989

7:00 A.M., coaches' wing, Giants Stadium

The doors to the offensive and defensive meeting rooms are closed. From behind them you can hear the harsh grinding noise of the videotape machines as the controls are clicked toward the next sequences. Belichick, Groh, and Leachman are back at the big table in the defensive coaches' room and Lamar is saying, "We gotta get them juiced up today. Let 'em know what's ahead. We gotta get them thinking Denver."

"Juice 'em up tomorrow," Belichick says. "Today's not the time. The worst thing about this is that they [the Eagles] scored twice and we hadn't even been on the field. All we could do is sit there and there wasn't a damned thing we could do about it."

"Last time," Groh says, "we had a chance to stop 'em down there [in the first Eagles-Giants game] so we could say, 'Look, fellas, we played our asses off for three and a half quarters but we didn't stop 'em when it counted.' But we can't even tell 'em that today. Maybe we could point out that last year the situation was reversed. Last year they were in our position and we were in theirs—and we lost the last game and they made the playoffs, so if we . . ."

"All right," Belichick says and sighs. "Let's not confront

anybody down there today. Let's just make the damned correc-
tions and move on. What hurts so much is that the preparation for
the game was good and our guys played good. Shit, I don't think
the Eagles are all that great," Belichick says. "Maybe they'll
lose to somebody."

Next door in the offensive coaches' conference room, Erhardt,
Hoaglin, and Coughlin are waiting for the rest of the staff to
assemble.

"It was awful," Hoaglin says. "On the very first pass both
tackles broke down and Simms never had a chance. Awful."

"When you get back in the game," Erhardt says, "and then
you go on and give it away again, that's discouraging. The defense was out there and they make that great goal-line stand and
then—nothing. I thought we had 'em going in at the half but
Meggett lays the ball down and we don't get anything. And then
Simms . . ."

"They didn't have to work for it," Coughlin says, "the Eagles
didn't have to work for a damned thing."

8:00 A.M., Bill Parcells's office

He is wearing a white Giants sweater with the words in red
with blue piping. The coffee cup and the cigarettes are on the
desk in front of him. He has been there since 6:30.

"I looked at the films by myself early this morning," he says.

"Offensive turnovers. We gave them three touchdowns and
fumbled away one ourself. That's a 28-point swing right there
and that's the game. And Simms, that ball he threw right at
Simmons was the worst pass I've seen him throw since I've been
here. He did some terrible things out there. But still, he stood in
there and threw some good ones. We had one play there near the
end where it could have been pass interference but they're never
gonna make that call.

"The defense forced two turnovers and they got a goal-line stand. I felt like they [the defense] played good enough to win. But . . .

"Meggett hurt us. He let them get away with that punt. He didn't catch the ball—a 91-yard punt. It's a fuckin' shame. I told them about it all week. I told them about it again on Saturday night. It's devastation, that's what it is. I look at the schedule and I don't see how we can get it back. I know it's possible but I don't see it."

He pauses to take a sip of coffee.

"See, I don't think we're very good but I don't think Philadelphia is, either. They could fuck it up. I mean, we did last year and they're in the same position we were. They have to go down to New Orleans to play. It could happen, but I doubt it. It looks like New Orleans will be down the tubes by then."

But part of his mind is still frozen in yesterday.

"To come back there like we did and then lose it. Shit, we should get that one [Meggett's fumble] at the half. Mowatt doesn't get that touchdown pass and then he doesn't get Simmons on the interception. He tries to block-tackle him when he could have had him easy. Instead of 17–7, we should be at least 17–14. Then when we get 10 in the third quarter, the pressure would be reversed."

He pauses to light a cigarette. He glances at the game tapes on his desk and shoves them to one side. "I don't want to spend any more time with them. I'm not going to watch them again. That's over, dead, finished.

"You come to camp, you work all those weeks. You go through the preseason games. You plan, you worry, you get off fast. And then on one Sunday in just three hours . . ."

He grinds the cigarette out in the ashtray and he looks up.

"I feel like a failure. That's what I feel like today. I feel like a fuckin' failure."

9:00 A.M., utility room, coaches' wing, Giants Stadium

Al Groh is pouring coffee into a Styrofoam cup. He is explaining that he knows the defense is angry at the offense and how this afternoon, he will take the seven linebackers he coaches aside. He will try to make them understand that the only way a player or a coach can survive in this business is to understand that necessity dictates you win as a complete team and you lose as a complete team. "My job is easy," he says. "This morning I really feel for him.

"Everybody is always talking about team leadership," Al Groh says. "You know, you gotta have leaders on the team and all that stuff. The best leaders on the team have gotta be your coaches. The most difficult thing on any team that went through what we did yesterday is that you gotta overcome human nature. We're people, too. At one o'clock today when the players show up, we can't act like we feel.

"When I was a head coach in college I went through this. Maybe that's why I have an insight into what Bill is feeling today. Unless you've ever been a head coach, you can't understand that. We can suffer and all of that, but there's only one person the players gotta take their reading off and it's him.

"No matter what Bill [Belichick] or Lamar or I tell our defensive people today, he's the one. I haven't had many games where I felt like I felt yesterday. What I'm feeling can't even begin to match what he's going through."

9:30 A.M., Bill Parcells's office

The door is ajar. He is sitting in the big brown easy chair off to the side of his desk. The venetian blinds behind him are closed and the lights are off.

He is a coach who would have won and should have won and

so he could no more avoid what he is doing now than a compulsive gambler can walk away from a crooked craps table when it happens to be the only game in town. He is staring at the television set.

On the screen in front of him, Phil Simms is dropping back to pass, the blocking is breaking down, and Reggie White is coming . . . coming . . . coming.

EPILOGUE

Bill Belichick was right. The Giants went out to Denver the following Sunday and kicked ass in the snow. The next week, they walloped Dallas at home and finished the season by handling the Raiders with ease.

On Monday night, December 18, the New Orleans Saints rose up from the dead and beat the Eagles in the Super Dome. The Giants were champions of the Eastern Division. Then the Rams pushed the Eagles all over Veterans Stadium and knocked them out of the playoffs in the wild-card game.

That brought the Rams to the Meadowlands on January 8. There was no wind. There was no cold. The game might as well have been played in California.

The Giants totally dominated the first half but they couldn't get into the end zone. Twice they had to settle for field goals instead of touchdowns. Ahead, 6–0, with 30 seconds left before intermission and the ball on their own 35, they tried for one more score. Simms's pass for Lionel Manuel over the middle was tipped by Jerry Gray and intercepted by Michael Stewart, who ran it back to the 20. On the next play, Los Angeles took the lead on a pass from Jim Everett to Flipper Anderson.

At the end of regulation play it was 13–13. The Rams won the coin toss and the Giants never got the ball again. It took Everett just 66 seconds of the overtime to beat them, 19–16, on a 30-yard pass to Anderson.

After the game, in the Giants' locker room, a reporter asked Erik Howard about the Los Angeles interception just before the half.

His answer was not without irony.

"It hurt to give up those points," Howard said, "but I can't fault the offense for trying.

"Trying is what this game is all about."

Without medals, the Giants' 1989 season was over.

INDEX